Study Guide to Accompany

THIRD EDITION

Financial Accounting

Lanny M. Solomon
The University of Texas at Arlington

Larry M. Walther
The University of Texas at Arlington

Richard J. Vargo
University of the Pacific

Prepared by
Larry M. Walther
The University of Texas at Arlington

West Publishing Company
Saint Paul ■ New York ■ Los Angeles ■ San Francisco

COPYRIGHT © 1992 by   WEST PUBLISHING CO.
50 W. Kellogg Boulevard
P.O. Box 64526
St. Paul, MN 55164-1003

All rights reserved
Printed in the United States of America
99 98 97 96 95 94 93 92   8 7 6 5 4 3 2 1 0

ISBN 0–314–00023–2

TABLE OF CONTENTS

CHAPTER **PAGE**

Chapter	1	An Introduction to Accounting	1
Chapter	2	Processing Accounting Information	23
Chapter	3	Income Measurement and Adjusting Entries	43
Chapter	4	Completion of the Accounting Cycle	65
Chapter	5	Accounting/Reporting for Merchandising Operations	89
Chapter	6	Accounting Systems and Internal Control	115
Chapter	7	Cash and Short-Term Investments	133
Chapter	8	Receivables	155
Chapter	9	Inventory	175
Chapter	10	Property, Plant, and Equipment/Natural Resources/Intangibles	197
Chapter	11	Current and Long-Term Liabilities	223
Chapter	12	Bonds Payable and the Time Value of Money	247
Chapter	13	Entity Alternatives and Owners' Equity	271
Chapter	14	Corporations: Additional Equity Issues and Income Reporting	295
Chapter	15	Long-Term Investments	319
Chapter	16	Statement of Cash Flows	343
Chapter	17	The Foundation of Financial Accounting and Reporting	367
Chapter	18	Financial Statements: Analysis and Further Disclosures	391
Appendix	A	Reading A Corporate Annual Report	415
Appendix	B	Special Journal Systems	429
Appendix	C	Corporate Income Taxes	441
Tutorial		The Electronic Tutorial	A-1

PREFACE

This study guide is designed to accompany **FINANCIAL ACCOUNTING**, third edition, by Solomon, Walther, and Vargo. The study guide was designed and written to be totally interactive with the text - to facilitate and expedite the learning process. In reviewing the organization of the study guide, notice that each chapter consists of the following:

Learning Objectives - identify the key points which are critical to your understanding the material covered in the chapter.

Chapter Highlights - a summary of the chapter, organized in outline form. The outline exactly follows the organization of the text, with key heading areas (from the text) noted in bold (in the study guide). This structure provides for a rapid and well organized review of the chapter, and provides for easy cross-reference to the text when more detail is needed.

Class Notes - blank pages are provided for you to augment your study guide with additional class notes.

Self Tests: Fulfillment of Learning Objectives - provides a series of two-response (i.e., true/false, etc.) type questions which are useful in measuring the degree of understanding of key elements identified by the learning objectives.

Self Tests: Fill in the Blanks - provides a series of questions which help identify important terminology and concepts. The correct answers are provided.

Self Tests: Multiple Choice Questions - provides ten multiple choice questions covering a variety of issues and techniques. This section is best used as a self-test (after thoroughly studying a chapter) to judge your depth of understanding and provide a gauge to assess whether more time should be devoted to the chapter. The correct answers are accompanied by complete explanations.

Self Tests: Demonstration Problems - provides a series of exercises which require fairly detailed written solutions. In addition to providing drill material, the problems (and their related solutions) should prove useful in helping you understand how to formulate correct solutions to the exercises and problems in the text.

Electronic Tutorial - In addition to the above features included in each chapter, also note that the appendix includes complete instructions for the electronic tutorial which accompanies this study guide.

With this study guide also comes my personal wish for your academic success, and a hope and belief that the effort you expend today will yield handsome returns for the rest of your life.

Very truly,

Larry M. Walther

CHAPTER 1

AN INTRODUCTION TO ACCOUNTING

LEARNING OBJECTIVES

After studying this chapter, you should be able to:

1. List the users, uses, and limitations of accounting information.

2. Describe the accounting profession and its related career paths.

3. Explain the use of generally accepted accounting principles (e.g., the entity assumption) in financial reporting.

4. Define assets, liabilities, and owners' equity, and state the relationship of these components in the accounting equation.

5. Explain the historical-cost principle, objectivity, and the going-concern assumption.

6. Identify the four items that cause owners' equity to change: investments by the owners, distributions of assets to the owners, net income, and net loss.

7. Recognize the basic accounting issues that relate to corporate equity.

8. Analyze the impact of transactions on the accounting equation.

9. Understand the content of a company's financial statements.

CHAPTER HIGHLIGHTS

I. Accounting is a set of concepts and techniques that collectively measure, summarize, and report financial information about an economic unit.

    A. The **USERS AND USES OF ACCOUNTING INFORMATION** are diverse. Typical users include owners, creditors, managers, government agencies, financial analysts, employees, labor unions, and numerous other interested parties. These users are concerned about such things as the security of their investment, the furtherance of their career, or fulfillment of regulatory responsibilities. Accounting information about specific entities helps satisfy the needs of these interested parties.

    B. Accounting is multi-faceted; the two primary thrusts can be described as the **FINANCIAL AND MANAGERIAL ORIENTATION**s. Financial accounting is concerned with external reporting (i.e., reporting the results of activities to parties outside the firm). In contrast, managerial accounting is primarily concerned with internal reporting (i.e., providing information for planning, control, and decision making). Financial accounting is highly structured. Managerial accounting is less structured and typified by an "anything goes" philosophy.

    C. Although financial statements are widely distributed and appear very concrete in nature, one must understand the **LIMITATIONS OF ACCOUNTING INFORMATION**. Accounting measurement necessarily involves estimation, utilization of assumptions, and subjective judgment. Additionally, accountants are bound to express events in dollars or monetary units. These monetary measures are generally based on cost rather than current worth. For example, land is reported on financial statements at historical cost (rather than current value or some nonmonetary measure such as acres). Understanding such limitations is essential for proper utilization of accounting information.

II. **THE ACCOUNTING PROFESSION** has evolved and matured to a position of respect and credibility, and offers a variety of challenging and rewarding careers.

    A. Many accountants engage in **PUBLIC ACCOUNTING** -- that is, providing auditing, income tax, and advisory services to the general public. These individuals are typically licensed as CPAs (Certified Public Accountants).

        1. **AUDITING** involves the investigation and examination of transactions that underlay an organization's financial reports, with the ultimate goal of providing an independent report on the appropriateness of financial statements.

        2. **INCOME TAX** services relate to the providing of help in the preparation and filing of tax returns and the rendering of advice on the tax consequences of alternative actions.

        3. **MANAGEMENT ADVISORY SERVICES** are broad in scope and pertain to helping others better run their business (e.g., installation of computer systems, review of manufacturing techniques, and so on).

    B. Another major branch of the accounting profession is **PRIVATE ACCOUNTING**. Many accountants are employed directly by small and large businesses. Specific job descriptions vary from routine transaction processing to high level financial planning functions. Professional designations in this field include the CMA (Certified Management Accountant) and the CIA (Certified Internal Auditor).

        1. One area of private accounting is **COST ACCOUNTING**. Cost accountants perform important tasks related to product costing and pricing, budgeting, and the examination of investment alternatives.

        2. Another area of private accounting is that of **INTERNAL AUDITING**. Internal auditors focus mainly on controls and procedures in use by their employers. Objectives of these reviews are to safeguard company resources and assess the reliability and accuracy of accounting information and accounting systems.

        3. Larger companies employ accountants for numerous **OTHER ACTIVITIES**, such as systems development, planning, and tax related matters.

C. **GOVERNMENTAL/NOT-FOR-PROFIT ACCOUNTING** is a rapidly growing professional area. Accountants are employed at local, state, and federal levels. Some of the more visible government career paths are with the Internal Revenue Service and General Accounting Office. Not-for-profit enterprises that hire numerous accounting professionals include hospitals, universities, and charitable organizations.

III. **GENERALLY ACCEPTED ACCOUNTING PRINCIPLES** (GAAP) are comprised of the concepts, assumptions, standards, and practices that define accepted accounting practice. This foundation serves to instill public confidence in the reporting process and assist users in their evaluation of a firm's informational output. Two bodies that oversee external reporting are the Financial Accounting Standards Board (FASB) and the Securities and Exchange Commission (SEC). The FASB is a private sector body, and issues pronouncements known as <u>Statements of Financial Accounting Standards</u>. The SEC is a government organization, and has specific authority over companies that issue securities to the public.

    A. One important accounting assumption is that an organization is viewed as a unit separate and apart from its owners and other firms; that is, accounting information is prepared for specific units. Application of this **ENTITY ASSUMPTION** means that separate accounting records are maintained for each sole proprietorship, partnership, and corporation. This occurs even though the business transactions of a sole proprietorship may at times be mixed with the owner's day-to-day personal financial activities. Likewise, the financial affairs of two separate corporations may be separately reported even if the corporations are owned by the same individuals.

IV. **FINANCIAL POSITION AND THE ENTITY**: determination of financial position involves the identification of resources owned by a firm (assets) and claims against those resources. Claims against resources are attributed to either creditors (liabilities) or the owners (owners' equity). The financial position of a firm can be described by the accounting equation: Assets = Liabilities + Owners' Equity.

    A. **ASSETS** are economic resources owned by a company, such as cash, accounts receivable (amounts owed to a firm by its customers), inventories, land, buildings, equipment, and even intangible assets like patents and other legal rights and claims.

    B. Amounts owed to creditors and other similar economic obligations of an entity are known as **LIABILITIES**.

    C. **OWNERS' EQUITY** represents the owners' net worth or "interest" in the assets of a business. Owners' equity can be defined as the residual interest in the net assets (assets minus liabilities) of a particular business.

    D. **THE IMPACT OF GAAP ON FINANCIAL POSITION** is significant. Different principles and practices will produce widely varying results. The following provides an introduction to three important concepts.

        1. One important accounting principle is the **HISTORICAL-COST PRINCIPLE**. Historical cost means that assets and liabilities are entered in the accounting records at acquisition costs. This principle, though objective, is often criticized because inflation may cause asset values to differ from their historical cost.

2. Accountants adhere to the **OBJECTIVITY PRINCIPLE**, which holds that accounting valuations should be definite and verifiable.

3. In the absence of evidence to the contrary, accountants assume that a business will continue to operate indefinitely into the future. **THE GOING-CONCERN ASSUMPTION** means, among other things, that asset values are based on historical cost rather than liquidation value.

V. Owners' equity is equal to assets minus liabilities. Numerous factors can cause owners' equity to change. **A CLOSER LOOK AT OWNERS' EQUITY** reveals that owners' equity changes because of investments by the owners, distributions of assets to the owners, net income, and net loss. Investments and income cause increases in owners' equity; distributions and losses cause decreases.

   A. **INVESTMENTS BY THE OWNERS** occur when personal assets of the owners are put into the business. In such cases, equity increases by the value of the asset.

   B. When business assets are dispensed to the owners for personal use, such **DISTRIBUTIONS OF ASSETS TO THE OWNERS** cause a decrease in owners' equity.

   C. When business revenues exceed expenses or vice-versa, the result is a **NET INCOME/NET LOSS**. Net income enhances the financial position and equity of a particular entity. Losses naturally result in decreases in equity.

      1. Amounts charged to customers for goods sold or services rendered are **REVENUES, AND EXPENSES** are the costs incurred in producing revenue. A typical business will encounter a variety of expenses, such as salaries and wages, utility costs, interest costs, advertising, taxes, and so forth.

   D. The ownership of a corporation is divided into transferable units called shares of stock. Accordingly, **CORPORATE EQUITY** consists of a category ("capital stock") representing the amount received from investors for the shares issued.

      1. **RETAINED EARNINGS AND DIVIDENDS** are also unique to corporations. Retained earnings reflect the firm's lifetime earnings (net of losses) less distributions to shareholders. Corporate distributions are called dividends. Retained earnings is included along with capital stock to comprise owners' (stockholders') equity.

VI. **THE ACCOUNTING EQUATION: AN EXTENDED ILLUSTRATION** is provided in the text. You should become very familiar with this illustration, and understand the impact on the accounting equation of transactions like investment by the owners, purchase of assets for cash, generation of revenue on account, recognition of expense on account, collection of accounts receivable, payment of accounts payable, payment of expenses, sale of an asset, and distribution of dividends. This basic model provides the foundation for an understanding of most accounting transactions.

VII. Accounting information is conveyed to owners, managers, lenders, and others through a standardized set of reports referred to as **FINANCIAL STATEMENTS**. The four fundamental financial statements are the income statement, statement of retained earnings, balance sheet, and statement of cash flows.

A. A summary of an entity's results of operation for a specified period of time is revealed in the **INCOME STATEMENT**. The income statement provides information about revenues generated and expenses incurred. The difference between revenues and expenses is reported as the net income (or loss).

B. The beginning retained earnings balance, plus income (or less losses), minus dividends, results in ending retained earnings. The **STATEMENT OF RETAINED EARNINGS** provides amounts for each of these components, with the objective of reporting ending retained earnings (and how it was derived).

C. The **BALANCE SHEET** focuses on the accounting equation by revealing the economic resources owned by an entity and the claims against those resources (liabilities and stockholders' equity). The balance sheet is prepared as of a specific date, whereas the income statement and statement of retained earnings are for a period of time. The statement of cash flows is discussed in later chapters.

D. Please refer to the exhibit in the text to observe the **STATEMENT INTERRELATIONSHIPS**. Specifically, note that the computed net income from the income statement is an important component in the statement of retained earnings. Likewise, the ending retained earnings amount is an important component in the balance sheet.

E. In addition to exercising professional care and competency, accounting professionals are also expected to demonstrate ethical behavior. **ETHICS AND REPORTING** is the subject of an appendix to this chapter.

VIII. **APPENDIX: ETHICS** are the broad set of moral principles that groups adopt as behavior standards, **AND THE ACCOUNTANT** is no stranger to ethical concerns.

A. **A CASE STUDY** of the ethics policies of a major corporation reveals three goals: to support individual employees in their daily business conduct, to enhance the administrative performance of the company in basic business relationships, and to build the bond of trust between the company and the parties with which it interacts.

B. Specific **ETHICAL CHALLENGES FOR THE ACCOUNTANT** include such things as maintaining independence from a client that "pays the bills," and dealing with the disclosure of information that is potentially damaging to an employing company.

C. **A CONCLUDING COMMENT** is to observe that there are unethical people, and that ethics is ultimately a matter of personal choice. Hopefully, most individuals will recognize the wisdom of moral and dignified behavior.

CLASS NOTES

CLASS NOTES

CLASS NOTES

CLASS NOTES

CLASS NOTES

SELF TESTS

FULFILLMENT OF LEARNING OBJECTIVES

Circle the appropriate response.

L.O. 1(a)   Accounting information is useful only to the owners of a business.

           true   or   **false** (circled)

L.O. 1(b)   Which of the following branches of accounting is concerned primarily with external reporting or communicating the results of economic activities to parties outside the firm?

           managerial accounting   or   **financial accounting** (circled)

L.O. 2(a)   Management advisory services are frequently associated with the practice of public accounting.

           true (circled)   or   false

L.O. 2(b)   Which of the following areas of the accounting profession is sometimes referred to as industrial accounting?

           public accounting   or   **private accounting** (circled)

L.O. 3(a)   The private sector organization that oversees the development of accounting standards is known as the:

           Financial Accounting Standards Board (circled)
           or
           Securities and Exchange Commission

L.O. 3(b)   The entity assumption holds that an organization's financial reporting should correspond to the strict legal structure of that organization (i.e., the affairs of a sole proprietorship should be reported together with all other transactions and events of the individual that owns the business).

           true   or   **false** (circled)

L.O. 4(a)   The economic resources owned by a company that are expected to benefit future periods are:

           assets (circled)   or   liabilities

L.O. 4(b)   The residual ownership share of a particular entity may be referred to as:

           assets   or   **owners' equity** (circled)

L.O. 5(a)   The objectivity principle and the going-concern assumption relate to the historical-cost principle in a manner that is:

consistent or inconsistent

L.O. 5(b)   Accounting measurements are based on the historical-cost principle, which holds that assets and liabilities are initially entered into the accounting records at acquisition cost, but subsequently change as market values change.

true or **false**

L.O. 6(a)   Distributions of assets to the owners causes owners' equity to:

increase or **decrease**

L.O. 6(b)   The term "revenues" means net income.

correct or **incorrect**

L.O. 6(c)   A company can experience a net loss and have distributions of assets to the owners during the same accounting period.

true or false

L.O. 7(a)   Corporate ownership is divided into transferable elements called:

units or **shares of stock**

L.O. 7(b)   Retained earnings is equal to the net income of a corporation less dividends. Retained earnings excludes stockholder investments.

true or false

L.O. 8(a)   Purchase of assets for cash cause total assets to:

change or **remain the same**

L.O. 8(b)   Payment of accounts payable with cash cause stockholders' equity to:

change or **remain the same**

L.O. 9(a)   The income statement is a statement:

for a period of time or at a point in time

L.O. 9(b)   Which financial statement most closely corresponds to the accounting equation?

income statement or **balance sheet**

FILL IN THE BLANKS

1. _Accounting_ is a set of concepts and techniques that collectively measure, summarize, and report financial information about an economic unit.

2. _Managerial_ accounting involves reporting results of operating activity to administrators within an organization.

3. The private sector agency that currently oversees external financial reporting is the _Financial Accounting Standards Board_.

4. Public accounting firms perform numerous services including _Auditing_, _income tax_, and _many advisory services_.

5. Not-for-profit enterprises that employ numerous accounting professionals include _Hospitals_ and _Universities_.

6. The _Entity Assumption_ holds that an organization must be viewed as a unit that is separate and apart from its owners and other firms.

7. The shortened form of the accounting equation is _Assets_ equals _Liabilities_ plus _Owners Equity_.

8. The objectivity principle holds that accounting valuations be _____ and _____.

9. _Net Income_ is the excess of a company's revenues over expenses for a given time period.

10. The four primary financial statements are the _Income Statement_, _Statement of Earnings_, _Balance Sheet_, and _____ _____.

11. _Net Income_ appears in both the income statement and the statement of retained earnings.

MULTIPLE CHOICE QUESTIONS

Circle the appropriate response:

1. The accounting profession can be divided into three major categories; specifically, the practice of public accounting, private accounting, and governmental accounting. An important service of public accountants is:

    a. Financial accounting.
    b. Managerial accounting.
    c. **Auditing.**
    d. Cost accounting.

Chapter 1

2. The primary private sector agency that oversees external financial reporting standards is the:

   a. Financial Accounting Standards Board.
   b. Securities and Exchange Commission.
   c. General Accounting Office.
   d. Internal Revenue Service.

3. Which of the following equations properly represents the fundamental accounting equation?

   a. Assets + liabilities = owners' equity.
   b. Assets = owners' equity.
   c. Cash = assets.
   d. Assets - liabilities = owners' equity.

4. Wilson Company owns land which cost $100,000. If a "quick sale" of the land was necessary to generate cash, the company feels it would receive only $80,000. The company continues to report the asset on the balance sheet at $100,000. This is justified under which of the following concepts?

   a. The historical-cost principle.
   b. The objectivity principle.
   c. Neither of the above.
   d. Both "a" and "b".

5. Owners' equity will change over time because of several factors. Which of the following factors would explain an increase in owners' equity?

   a. Net loss and investments by the owners.
   b. Investments by the owners and net income.
   c. Distributions of assets to the owners and net loss.
   d. Distributions of assets to the owners and net income.

6. Which of these items would be accounted for as an expense?

   a. Repayment of a bank loan.
   b. Distributions of assets to the owners.
   c. The purchase of land.
   d. Payment of the current period's rent.

7. Which of the following transactions would have no impact on owners' equity?

   a. Purchase of land with the proceeds of a bank loan.
   b. Distributions to the owners.
   c. Net loss.
   d. Investments of cash by the owners.

8. Which of the following would not be included on a balance sheet?

    a. Accounts receivable.
    b. Accounts payable.
    c. Sales.
    d. Cash.

9. Remington provided the following information about its balance sheet:

Bank loans	$1,000
Accounts receivable	500
Capital stock	300
Retained earnings	400
Accounts payable	200
Cash	100

    Based on the information provided, how much are Remington's liabilities?

    a. $200.
    b. $900.
    c. $1,200.
    d. $1,700.

10. Gerald had beginning stockholders' equity of $160,000. During the year, total assets increased by $240,000 and total liabilities increased by $120,000. Gerald's net income was $180,000. No additional investments were made by stockholders; however, dividends did occur during the year. How much were the dividends?

    a. $20,000.
    b. $60,000.
    c. $140,000.
    d. $220,000.

DEMONSTRATION PROBLEMS

DP-1   Jensen Publishing Company operates newspapers in a number of small communities. Determine whether each of the following is an asset, a liability, a revenue, or an expense from Jensen's viewpoint.

   a.   A loan that is owed to the bank
   b.   The cost of paper used in printing
   c.   Amounts collected from customers who advertise in the newspaper
   d.   Monthly rental charges paid to a landlord
   e.   Receipts collected from subscribers
   f.   Machinery owned by the company and used in the business
   g.   Amounts owed to suppliers of ink

DP-2 Write the accounting equation in the space below. By using plus and minus signs, indicate the impact of each of the following transactions on total assets, liabilities, and stockholders' equity.

   a. Recorded receipt of a utility bill to be paid the following month.
   b. Paid the utility bill that was recorded in part (a).
   c. Paid wages of employees.
   d. Purchased a building for $20,000, paid $5,000 down and agreed to pay the remainder at a later date.
   e. Rendered services on account to customers.
   f. Recorded receipt of payment for services rendered in part (e).

DP-3 Prepare an income statement, statement of retained earnings, and balance sheet for Victoria Mills Corporation. Necessary information in the following listing is for the year ending December 31, 19X1.

Capital stock	$1,700
Dividends	500
Rent expense	2,000
Revenue	3,500
Miscellaneous expense	500
Equipment	2,000
Accounts receivable	900
Cash	300
Accounts payable	1,000

Income

Revenue	3500
Less Expenses	2500
Net Income	1000

Statement Retained Earnings

Beg Balance	
Plus Net Income	$1000
Less Dividends	500
Ending Balance	500

Assets	
Cash	300
Equip	2000
A/R	900
	3200
Liabilities	
A/P	1,000
O/E	
C.S.	1700
RE	500
	3200

SOLUTIONS TO SELF TESTS

FULFILLMENT OF LEARNING OBJECTIVES

1(a)   False
1(b)   Financial accounting
2(a)   True
2(b)   Private accounting
3(a)   Financial Accounting Standards Board
3(b)   False
4(a)   Assets
4(b)   Owners' equity
5(a)   Consistent
5(b)   False
6(a)   Decrease
6(b)   Incorrect
6(c)   True
7(a)   Shares of stock
7(b)   True
8(a)   Remain the same
8(b)   Remain the same
9(a)   For a period of time
9(b)   Balance sheet

FILL IN THE BLANKS

1. Accounting
2. Managerial
3. Financial Accounting Standards Board
4. Auditing, income tax, management advisory services
5. Hospitals, universities
6. Entity assumption
7. Assets, liabilities, owners' equity
8. Definite, verifiable
9. Net income
10. Income statement, statement of retained earnings, balance sheet, statement of cash flows
11. Net income

MULTIPLE CHOICE QUESTIONS

1.   c.   Auditing, along with income tax and management advisory activities, are the major services offered by public accountants. Managerial and cost accounting are generally regarded as private accounting functions. Public accountants deal with financial accounting issues, but "financial accounting" is more of a concept than a "service."

2. a. The Financial Accounting Standards Board is the private sector oversight group for accounting standards. The Securities and Exchange Commission is a government organization with the ability to influence accounting rules. The General Accounting Office and Internal Revenue Service are also government agencies.

3. d. The normal expression of the accounting equation is: assets = liabilities + owners' equity. The only choice which is a correct mathematical expression is "d." In "d," liabilities are subtracted from both sides of the "normal" accounting equation.

4. d. Both of these concepts justify the continued reporting at $100,000, as this amount is an objective and verifiable historical-cost measurement.

5. b. Additional investments and income both cause increases in equity. In contrast, losses and distributions are factors which will cause decreases in equity.

6. d. Payment of rent for the current period would be accounted for as rent expense. The repayment of a bank loan is the reduction of a liability, distributions of assets to the owners cause direct reductions of equity, and the purchase of land establishes an asset.

7. a. The purchase of land with the proceeds of a bank loan would cause assets and liabilities to increase. Distributions of assets to the owners and net losses cause reductions in total equity, while investments cause increases.

8. c. Sales is a revenue item for the income statement. Accounts receivable and cash are assets and accounts payable is a liability.

9. c. $1,200. The only liabilities listed are accounts payable ($200) and bank loans ($1,000).

10. b. $60,000. Because total assets increased $240,000 and liabilities increased $120,000, the increase in equity must have been $120,000 ($240,000 - $120,000). Net income increases equity ($180,000) and dividends decrease equity. The increase in stockholders' equity of $120,000 is therefore comprised of $180,000 in income (add) and $60,000 of dividends (subtract).

DEMONSTRATION PROBLEMS

DP-1

(a) Liability

(b) Expense

(c) Revenue

(d) Expense

(e) Revenue

(f) Asset

(g) Liability

DP-2

	Assets	=	Liabilities	+	Owners' Equity
(a)			+		-
(b)	-		-		
(c)	-				-
(d)	+$20,000 and -$5,000		+$15,000		
(e)	+				+
(f)	+ and -				

DP-3

VICTORIA MILLS CORPORATION
INCOME STATEMENT
FOR THE YEAR ENDED DECEMBER 31, 19X1

Revenue		$3,500
Less expenses		
Rent	$2,000	
Miscellaneous	500	
Total expenses		2,500
Net income		$1,000

VICTORIA MILLS CORPORATION
STATEMENT OF RETAINED EARNINGS
FOR THE YEAR ENDED DECEMBER 31, 19X1

Beginning balance, Jan. 1, 19X1	$ -
Add: Net income	1,000
	$1,000
Deduct: Dividends	500
Ending balance, Dec. 31, 19X1	$ 500

VICTORIA MILLS CORPORATION
BALANCE SHEET
DECEMBER 31, 19X1

Assets		
Cash		$ 300
Accounts receivable		900
Equipment		2,000
Total assets		$3,200
Liabilities		
Accounts payable		$1,000
Stockholders' equity		
Capital stock	$1,700	
Retained earnings	500	2,200
Total liabilities & stockholders' equity		$3,200

CHAPTER 2

PROCESSING ACCOUNTING INFORMATION

LEARNING OBJECTIVES

After studying this chapter you should be able to:

1. Explain the nature of transactions and events as input to an accounting system.

2. Identify accounts, debits and credits, journals, and their interrelationships.

3. Journalize transactions and post entries to the general ledger.

4. Describe and prepare a trial balance.

5. Determine the impact of errors on the trial balance and apply the various steps necessary to locate an error.

CHAPTER HIGHLIGHTS

I. **THE ACCOUNTING SYSTEM** is necessary to produce financial statements, generate information for management, and satisfy governmental reporting requirements. **A CONCEPTUAL OVERVIEW** of an accounting system reveals that such a system allows transactions and events to be reliably processed into useful financial statements and reports. Reliability of the resulting information means that it represents what it claims to represent, and that it is free from error or bias.

II. The basic tools found in most **ACCOUNTING SYSTEMS** are accounts, debits and credits, journals, and the chart of accounts. From **A PRACTICAL PERSPECTIVE**, one would expect to encounter these basic elements, without regard to the degree of complexity of the system.

   A. The records that are kept for the individual asset, liability, and stockholders' equity components are known as **ACCOUNTS**. All accounts collectively comprise a firm's general ledger. Accounts may be represented in the T-account form or in the running balance form. The running balance form offers the advantage of an up-to-date balance with the recording of each transaction.

   B. **DEBITS AND CREDITS** are unique accounting tools to reflect the necessary change in a particular account. Mastering the debit and credit rules is essential to progress in your study of accounting. Please memorize the following table:

Account Type	Normal Balance	To Increase	To Decrease
Assets	Debit	Debit	Credit
Liabilities	Credit	Credit	Debit
Stockholders' equity	Credit	Credit	Debit
Revenues	Credit	Credit	Debit
Expenses	Debit	Debit	Credit

1. As transactions or events occur, **APPLICATION OF THE RULES** require that appropriate debits and credits be applied to the accounts affected. The balance of a specific account can be determined by netting or offsetting the debits and credits in that account. For example, the sum total of debits to an asset account, minus the sum total of credits to that account, would reveal the account's balance (which would "normally" be a debit balance for an asset).

2. There are two common **MISCONCEPTIONS ABOUT DEBITS AND CREDITS**. First, credits do not always reduce an account balance; second, credits are not always good and debits always bad. The nature of a particular debit or credit depends on the account to which it is applied.

C. The **JOURNALS** serve as the entry or starting point for transaction recording.

1. **THE RECORDING PROCESS** begins with an analysis of transactions to assess which accounts are affected. Next, the appropriate debits and credits to these accounts must be determined and entered into the journal. For example, a stockholder investment of $10,000 in cash involves both the Capital Stock and Cash accounts. Cash (an asset account) is increased, and should therefore be debited. Capital Stock (a stockholders' equity account) is also increased, and should therefore be credited. This "entry" (i.e., debit Cash and credit Capital Stock for $10,000) would be recorded into the journal in a manner similar to the following:

    Cash   10,000
       Capital Stock   10,000
    To record the issue of capital stock for cash

    Notice that for every transaction recorded, debits equal credits. Simply stated, journalizing is the process of translating transactions into the accounting language of debits and credits. As you will soon see, this mechanism enables ready measurement and determination of financial condition.

D. A listing of accounts in use by a particular company is called the **CHART OF ACCOUNTS**. A chart of accounts is useful in assessing which accounts are available. Individual accounts are often given a specific reference number. The numbering scheme helps keep up with the accounts in use, and helps in the classification of accounts. For example, all assets may begin with "1" (e.g., 101 for Cash, 102 for Accounts Receivable, etc.), liabilities with "2," and so forth.

III. The journalization process just discussed is a necessary first step in the accounting process. However, additional procedures must occur -- **POSTING: INTERACTION OF THE BASIC TOOLS**. Consider that the journalization process produces a chronological listing of transactions in debit and credit form. It does not, however, reveal the balance of specific accounts. To determine the balance of specific accounts necessitates posting; that is, accumulating ("transferring") debits and credits by specific accounts (then netting to determine the balance). The information for posting general ledger accounts is drawn from the journal. A graphic example may be found in the text.

IV. **AN EXTENDED ILLUSTRATION** of the important interrelationships between debits and credits, journals, and ledger accounts can be observed in the text. Becoming familiar with this illustration is a good investment of time.

V. A **TRIAL BALANCE** is a listing of ledger accounts along with their respective debit or credit balances. The trial balance is not a formal financial statement, but rather a self-check to determine that debits equal credits.

    A. If debits equal credits in a trial balance, a certain degree of comfort is achieved. However, **EQUALITY DOES NOT ENSURE ACCURACY**. For example, some transactions may not have been recorded, or may have been posted to the wrong accounts.

    B. Other errors may cause **UNEQUAL TOTALS**. This condition is not acceptable, and the errors must be located. Steps that may prove useful in locating the errors include re-adding the trial balance, evaluating the difference between total debits and credits (for transpositions, slides, etc.), and examining individual accounts and journal entries. It should be obvious that care in initial recording is more efficient than seeking to locate errors.

VI. For **A BRIEF OVERVIEW**, consider the basic sequence in the accounting process. The initial input consists of evaluating transactions and source documents. These inputs are converted and summarized via journal entries and postings to ledger accounts. The output of this process is the trial balance.

CLASS NOTES

CLASS NOTES

CLASS NOTES

CLASS NOTES

CLASS NOTES

SELF TESTS

FULFILLMENT OF LEARNING OBJECTIVES

Circle the appropriate response.

L.O. 1(a)   Transactions and events are happenings that have economic consequences for a business enterprise.

true or false

L.O. 1(b)   For transactions and events to serve as input to an accounting system, they must be measurable in dollars and the measurements must be of a:

subjective nature or **reliable nature**

L.O. 2(a)   The records that are kept for the individual asset, liability, and stockholders' equity components are known as accounts.

true or false

L.O. 2(b)   All the accounts taken together comprise a firm's:

general ledger or journal

L.O. 2(c)   Which form of account is more popular in practice?

T-account form or **running balance form**

L.O. 2(d)   Assets and expenses may be increased with a:

debit or credit

L.O. 2(e)   Liabilities, stockholders' equity, and revenue accounts are decreased with:

debits or credits

L.O. 2(f)   Accounts are increased with credits and decreased with debits.

correct or **incorrect**

L.O. 2(g)   Which accounting record is sometimes known as the book of original entry?

journal or ledger

L.O. 2(h)   The chart of accounts is a:

financial statement
or
listing of a company's accounts

L.O. 3(a) The transactions in the journal and the accounts in the ledger are linked together by a transfer process called:

posting or audit trail

L.O. 3(b) The ledger can be thought of as a:

chronological listing of transactions
or
a book with separate pages for each account

L.O. 3(c) Posting references for a specific journal entry would involve how many accounts in the general ledger?

one or more or **two or more**

L.O. 3(d) The journal entry to record the billing of clients for services rendered would involve:

a debit to Accounts Receivable and a credit to Revenue
or
cash

L.O. 3(e) Which account would be debited to reflect receipt of a $500 utility bill?

utilities expense or accounts payable

L.O. 4(a) The trial balance is prepared to determine whether accounting records are in balance.

true or false

L.O. 4(b) A trial balance is compiled from the account balance information contained in the ledger.

correct or incorrect

L.O. 5(a) A trial balance with equal debit and credit totals means that the accounting process is free of error.

true or **false**

L.O. 5(b) Errors like transaction omission, transaction duplication, and posting to the wrong accounts would cause trial balance totals to be:

equal or unequal

L.O. 5(c) Steps that may prove helpful in locating errors in a trial balance with unequal totals would include:

dividing the difference by 9
or
multiplying the difference by 2

32 Processing Accounting Information

FILL IN THE BLANKS

1. The _____ assumption effectively limits the input to a firm's accounting system by establishing a reporting boundary.

2. To qualify for recording into an accounting system, transactions and events should be _____ in dollars, and the measurements must be of a _____ nature.

3. The general ledger is comprised of numerous individual asset, liability, stockholders' equity, revenue, and expense _____.

4. A liability account should be increased with a _____ and decreased with a _____.

5. The normal balance of an expense account is a _____ balance.

6. The normal balances of accounts correspond to the fundamental _____ _____.

7. Evidence of transactions is often provided by the receipt or issuance of accounting forms known as _____ _____.

8. In any transaction, total debits must _____ _____ _____.

9. The individual accounts in a general ledger are frequently assigned a number based on the _____ _____ _____.

10. To record the payment of a previously established account payable requires a _____ to the Accounts Payable account.

11. Rather than debit Retained Earnings for distributions to stockholders', many businesses use a separate _____ account.

12. A _____ _____ is a listing of the general ledger accounts along with the dollar balances contained therein.

13. A _____ means that two digits of a given number have been accidentally reversed.

MULTIPLE CHOICE QUESTIONS

Circle the appropriate response:

1. Of the following account types, which would be increased by a debit?

    a. Liabilities and expenses.
    b. Assets and stockholders' equity.
    c. Assets and expenses.
    d. Stockholders' equity and revenues.

2. The following comments all relate to the recording process. Which of these statements is correct?

   a. The general ledger is a chronological record of transactions.
   b. The general ledger is posted from transactions recorded in the general journal.
   c. The trial balance provides the primary source document for recording transactions into the general journal.
   d. Transposition is the transfer of information from the general journal to the general ledger.

3. The following comments each relate to the recording of journal entries. Which statement is true?

   a. For any given journal entry, debits must exceed credits.
   b. It is customary to record credits on the left and debits on the right.
   c. The chart of accounts reveals the amount to debit and credit to the affected accounts.
   d. Journalization is the process of converting transactions and events into debit/credit format.

4. Failure to record the receipt of a utility bill for services already received will result in:

   a. An overstatement of assets.
   b. An overstatement of liabilities.
   c. An overstatement of stockholders' equity.
   d. An understatement of assets.

5. The proper journal entry to record Ransom Company's billing of clients for $500 of services rendered is:

   a. Cash   500
          Accounts Receivable   500
   b. Accounts Receivable   500
          Stockholders' Equity   500
   c. Accounts Receivable   500
          Service Revenue   500
   d. Cash   500
          Service Revenue   500

6. The proper journal entry to record the payment of $1,000 of dividends is:

   a. Dividends   1,000
          Cash   1,000
   b. Accounts Payable   1,000
          Cash   1,000
   c. Dividend Expense   1,000
          Cash   1,000
   d. Dividend Expense   1,000
          Service Revenue   1,000

Processing Accounting Information

7. Issuing capital stock in exchange for land valued at $5,000 would be recorded by:

   a. Cash   5,000
           Capital Stock   5,000
   b. Land   5,000
           Capital Stock   5,000
   c. Land   5,000
           Service Revenue   5,000
   d. Capital Stock   5,000
           Land   5,000

8. The trial balance:

   a. Is a formal financial statement.
   b. Is used to prove that there are no errors in the journal or ledger.
   c. Provides a listing of every account in the chart of accounts.
   d. Provides a listing of the balance of each account in active use.

9. Which of the following errors will be disclosed in the preparation of a trial balance?

   a. Recording transactions in the wrong account.
   b. Duplication of a transaction in the accounting records.
   c. Posting only the debit portion of a particular journal entry.
   d. Recording the wrong amount for a transaction to both the account debited and the account credited.

10. The basic sequence in the accounting process can best be described as:

    a. Transaction, journal entry, source document, ledger account, trial balance.
    b. Source document, transaction, ledger account, journal entry, trial balance.
    c. Transaction, source document, journal entry, trial balance, ledger account.
    d. Transaction, source document, journal entry, ledger account, trial balance.

DEMONSTRATION PROBLEMS

DP-1 Classify each of the following as an asset, liability, revenue, or expense and indicate the normal balance of each item.

    a. Equipment used in the business.
    b. Amounts due from clients for services previously rendered.
    c. Gasoline cost for a bus company.
    d. Food sales for a restaurant.
    e. Amounts owed to the bank.
    f. Cash on hand.
    g. Utility costs incurred in the operation of the business.
    h. Rent owed to the landlord.
    i. Rent costs incurred and paid to the landlord.
    j. Automobiles used in the business.

DP-2   Record the following transactions in general journal form, including explanations, as appropriate.

  a. Issued capital stock for $5,000 cash.
  b. Purchased tools and equipment on account for $2,500.
  c. Received $1,000 from customers for services rendered.
  d. Provided $300 of additional services on account.
  e. Paid half the amount due on the transaction recorded in part (b).
  f. Collected half the amount due on the transaction recorded in part (d).
  g. Received a $100 utility bill to be paid next month.
  h. Paid a $200 dividend to investors.

DP-3 Mirage Corporation has misplaced a page from its general ledger. Mirage began operations on January 1 of the current year and has provided information about all account balances other than the missing item.

Accounts receivable	$13,200
Loan payable	10,000
Equipment	3,000
Service revenues	4,700
Rent expense	800
Cash	12,500
Utilities expense	1,700
Accounts payable	12,100
Wage expense	1,000
Land	5,700

a. Prepare a trial balance for Mirage Corporation and determine the amount of the missing account. All accounts have "normal" balances.
b. What is the most probable title of the missing account of Mirage Corporation?
c. Determine Mirage's net income for the period in question.

SOLUTIONS TO SELF TESTS

FULFILLMENT OF LEARNING OBJECTIVES

1(a)	True
1(b)	Reliable nature
2(a)	True
2(b)	General ledger
2(c)	Running balance form
2(d)	Debit
2(e)	Debits
2(f)	Incorrect
2(g)	Journal
2(h)	Listing of a company's accounts
3(a)	Posting
3(b)	A book with separate pages for each account
3(c)	Two or more
3(d)	A debit to Accounts Receivable and a credit to Revenue
3(e)	Utilities expense
4(a)	True
4(b)	Correct
5(a)	False
5(b)	Equal
5(c)	Dividing the difference by 9

FILL IN THE BLANKS

1. Entity
2. Measurable, reliable
3. Accounts
4. Credit, debit
5. Debit
6. Accounting equation
7. Source documents
8. Equal total credits
9. Chart of accounts
10. Debit
11. Dividends
12. Trial balance
13. Transposition

MULTIPLE CHOICE QUESTIONS

1. c. Assets and expenses are increased with debits. Liabilities, stockholders' equity, and revenues are increased with credits.

2. b. The general ledger is posted from transactions recorded in the general journal. The general journal is a chronological record of transactions. Invoices, checks, receipts, shipping reports, and numerous other items provide the source documents for recording transactions into the general journal; the trial balance is a listing of account balances. Transposition is the accidental reversing of two digits in a number.

3. d. Journalization is the process of converting transactions to their debit/credit form and recording them in the general journal. Of course, debits equal credits, debits are customarily recorded on the left, and the chart of accounts is a listing of accounts in use (and their corresponding reference number).

4. c. The journal entry would involve a debit to expense and a credit to a liability. Failure to record this entry causes expenses and liabilities to be understated. As a result of understating expenses, income and stockholders' equity are overstated. Notice that assets are correct.

5. c. Both Accounts Receivable (an asset which is increased with a debit) and Service Revenue (increased with a credit) increase by the rendering of services on account. Cash is not impacted and should not be debited or credited. The increase in revenue will ultimately cause an increase in stockholders' equity -- but this occurs through financial statement preparation, not a direct credit to Stockholders' Equity.

6. a. Dividends are increased with a debit and Cash is decreased with a credit. Accounts Payable and Service Revenue are not involved at all. Also, never record dividends as an expense.

7. b. Land, an asset, is increased and should be debited. Capital Stock is also increased and should be credited.

8. d. The trial balance provides a listing of the balance of each active account. The trial balance is not a formal financial statement, there are errors (such as transpositions and posting to the wrong account) that will not result in an out-of-balance condition in the trial balance, and there may be accounts in the chart of accounts that are not in actual use and will not appear in the trial balance.

9. c. Posting only the debit portion of a particular entry will cause debits to exceed credits -- an error that will be revealed by a trial balance. The other errors do not cause out-of-balance conditions.

10. d. Transactions occur, are documented (source document), reduced to debit/credit form (journal entry), and posted to the ledger. From the ledger, a trial balance can be prepared.

DEMONSTRATION PROBLEMS

DP-1

(a) Asset, debit

(b) Asset, debit

(c) Expense, debit

(d) Revenue, credit

(e) Liability, credit

(f) Asset, debit

(g) Expense, debit

(h) Liability, credit

(i) Expense, debit

(j) Asset, debit

DP-2

(a)	Cash	5,000	
	Capital Stock		5,000
	Issued shares of stock		
(b)	Tools & Equipment	2,500	
	Accounts Payable		2,500
	Purchased tools and equipment on account		
(c)	Cash	1,000	
	Service Revenue		1,000
	Received cash from customers for services rendered		
(d)	Accounts Receivable	300	
	Service Revenue		300
	Rendered services to customers on account		
(e)	Accounts Payable	1,250	
	Cash		1,250
	Partial payment for tools and equipment purchased on account		
(f)	Cash	150	
	Accounts Receivable		150
	Collected partial payment on accounts receivable		
(g)	Utilities Expense	100	
	Accounts Payable		100
	Received utilities bill to be paid next month		

(h) Dividends 200
 Cash 200
 Paid dividends to stockholders

DP-3

(a)
Cash	$12,500	
Accounts receivable	13,200	
Equipment	3,000	
Land	5,700	
Accounts payable		$12,100
Loan payable		10,000
Service revenues		4,700
Rent expense	800	
Utilities expense	1,700	
Wage expense	1,000	
	$37,900	$26,800
Missing amount		11,100
	$37,900	$37,900

(b) The missing amount is a credit amount, probably Capital Stock, given the absence of an equity component.

(c) Net income is $1,200 ($4,700 - $800 - $1,700 - $1,000).

CHAPTER 3

INCOME MEASUREMENT AND ADJUSTING ENTRIES

LEARNING OBJECTIVES

After studying this chapter, you should be able to:

1. Explain the impact of the periodicity assumption on accounting and income measurement.

2. Apply the principle of revenue recognition.

3. Apply the matching principle and record expenses in the proper accounting period.

4. Calculate net income under both the accrual basis and the cash basis of accounting.

5. Explain why the adjusting process is needed and recognize which items typically require adjustment.

6. Prepare adjusting entries and show their impact on the financial statements.

7. Prepare an adjusted trial balance.

8. (Appendix) Describe and use the "income statement approach" of accounting for prepaid expenses and unearned revenues.

CHAPTER HIGHLIGHTS

I. One of the most complex and significant objectives of accounting is **INCOME MEASUREMENT**.

   A. What is **THE MEANING OF INCOME**? Economists refer to income as a measure of "better-offness." Accountants, however, use a transactions approach to compute net income. That is, transactions and events which produce revenues and expenses are measured and reported, with the net amount representing income.

   B. Accounting divides a continuous process into specific measurement intervals, such as months, quarters, or years (sometimes called the periodicity assumption). When the year is used as the reporting period, the specific interval is not required to run from January 1 through December 31 (a calendar year); other reporting years could be used (such as fiscal years or natural business years). Selection of **THE ACCOUNTING PERIOD** is the first step to establish the interval of time for which revenues and expenses will be measured.

C. **REVENUE RECOGNITION** (i.e., recording revenue in the accounting records) normally occurs at the time services are rendered or when goods are sold and delivered to a customer. That is to say, revenues should be recorded as they are "earned."

D. It follows that business expenses which are incurred to produce revenue should be recognized in the same period as the revenue. **EXPENSE RECOGNITION** generally follows **THE MATCHING PRINCIPLE**. For example, sales commission expense is recognized in the same period as the related sales revenue. Other expenses are not so directly related to revenue production. For example, a machine may last many years; determining how much cost is attributable to a particular year is difficult. In such cases, accountants may use a systematic and rational allocation scheme to spread a portion of the total cost to each period of use (through a process known as depreciation).

E. Preferably, a business should use **ACCRUAL-BASIS ACCOUNTING**. With this approach, revenues and expenses are recognized as earned or incurred (i.e., utilizing the concepts just presented). An example of the accrual basis is presented in the text.

F. An alternative measurement approach is **CASH-BASIS ACCOUNTING**. This technique recognizes revenue when cash is received and expense when cash is paid. An example of the cash basis is presented in the text.

1. The **CASH AND ACCRUAL METHODS IN PRACTICE** are sometimes merged together to form a modified cash basis system. The modified cash basis results in revenue and expense recognition as cash is received and disbursed, with the exception of large cash outflows for long-lived assets (which are recorded as assets and depreciated over time). Importantly, proper income measurement and strict compliance with generally accepted accounting principles dictates use of the accrual basis; virtually all large companies use the accrual basis.

II. **ADJUSTING ENTRIES** are a necessary step in the accrual basis accounting cycle. The adjusting process is needed to split multiperiod costs and revenues among two or more accounting periods, and to recognize revenues and expenses that have been earned or incurred in a given period but not entered into the accounts.

A. Focusing on **MULTIPERIOD COSTS AND REVENUES**, consider that certain costs and revenues pertain to more than a single accounting period.

1. Specifically, **PREPAID EXPENSES** are goods and services purchased for future consumption and paid for in advance. Examples include insurance, supplies, and rent.

a. If a three-year insurance policy was purchased on January 1, 19X1, the **PREPAID INSURANCE** account would be debited and Cash would be credited. If the policy cost $600, by December 31, 19X1, $200 of insurance coverage would have expired. Therefore, an adjusting entry to record expense and reduce prepaid insurance would be needed (debit Insurance Expense and credit Prepaid Insurance for $200). The income statement for 19X1 would report insurance expense of $200, and the balance sheet at the end of 19X1 would report prepaid insurance of $400. The remaining $400 amount would be transferred to expense over the next two years.

b. **SUPPLIES** purchases are recorded by debiting Supplies and crediting Cash. As supplies are used, Supplies Expense should be debited and Supplies should be credited. This results in supplies expense on the income statement being equal to the amount of supplies used. The remaining balance of supplies on hand is reported as an asset on the balance sheet.

2. **DEPRECIATION** is the allocation of the cost of a long-term asset. Under the straight-line method of depreciation, an equal amount of asset cost is assigned to each year of service life. In other words, the cost of the asset is divided by the years of useful life, resulting in annual depreciation expense. Recording depreciation involves a debit to Depreciation Expense and a credit to Accumulated Depreciation (rather than crediting the asset account). Accumulated depreciation is reported on the balance sheet as a contra asset (a subtract from the specific asset being depreciated):

   Assets

Equipment	$50,000
Less: Accumulated depreciation	10,000
	$40,000

   The asset cost minus accumulated depreciation is the book value of the asset. By way of example, if a $50,000 asset with a 10-year life was purchased on January 1 of Year 1, depreciation expense would be $5,000 per year. This expense amount would be reported on the income statement each year. On the balance sheet at the end of Year 1, the asset would be reported at $50,000, less accumulated depreciation of $5,000, for a book value of $45,000. The following year the asset would continue to be reported at $50,000, but accumulated depreciation would have increased to $10,000. This reporting would continue in a like manner until the end of Year 10.

3. **UNEARNED REVENUES** represent future revenues that have been collected but not earned. For example, magazine subscription payments received in advance by a publisher would initially be recorded as a debit to Cash and a credit to Unearned Subscription Revenue (a liability). As the magazines are delivered, Unearned Subscription Revenue is reduced (debited) and Subscription Revenue is increased (credited). To the extent magazines have not been issued by the end of an accounting period, unearned subscription revenue would be reflected in the liability section of the balance sheet.

B. Another type of adjusting journal entry pertains to **UNRECORDED EXPENSES AND REVENUES**. **ACCRUALS** are expenses and revenues that gradually accumulate throughout an accounting period.

   1. Examples of **ACCRUED EXPENSES** are interest accumulated on loans, and wages owed to employees at the end of an accounting period.

      a. To further illustrate **ACCRUED SALARIES**; imagine that employees earn, as a group, $1,000 a day. If the last payday occurred three working days before the end of an accounting period, then the adjusting entry at the end of the period is a debit to Wage Expense and a credit to Wages Payable for $3,000. This entry would reflect work performed by employees during that accounting period, but not yet paid.

2. **ACCRUED REVENUES** represent amounts earned but not recorded. Therefore, the adjusting entry involves a debit to Accounts Receivable and a credit to Service Revenue.

C. Keep in mind that the trial balance introduced in the previous chapter was prepared before considering adjusting entries. Subsequent to the adjustment process, another trial balance can be prepared: the **ADJUSTED TRIAL BALANCE**. The adjusted trial balance demonstrates the equality of debits and credits after recording adjusting entries. A work sheet, such as the one illustrated in the text, can be used to assist in the preparation of the adjusted trial balance.

D. **ADJUSTMENT ERRORS** can have a far-reaching impact. For example, failure to record accrued revenue results in an understatement of revenue and income. When income is understated, ending retained earnings is understated. Accounts receivable is also understated.

III. **APPENDIX: AN ALTERNATIVE ACCOUNTING TREATMENT FOR PREPAID EXPENSES AND UNEARNED REVENUES.** The mechanics of accounting for prepaid expenses and unearned revenues can be carried out in several ways. No matter which method is employed, the resulting financial statements should be identical.

A. In our earlier presentation of **ACCOUNTING FOR PREPAID EXPENSES**, recall that the Prepaid Expense account was debited and Cash was credited at the time of purchase (called the balance sheet approach). However, an alternative (the income statement approach) is to debit the Expense account at the time of purchase. When this approach is followed, the appropriate end-of-period adjusting entry "establishes" the Prepaid Expense account with a debit (for the amount relating to future periods). The offsetting credit is to the related Expense account (which was originally debited for the total amount of the payment, but is reduced by this credit to an amount equal to the amount consumed during the period).

B. **ACCOUNTING FOR UNEARNED REVENUES** can also follow a balance sheet or income statement approach. The earlier presentation demonstrated the balance sheet approach. The income statement approach results in the initial receipt being recorded entirely to a Revenue account. Subsequent end-of-period adjusting entries should reduce Revenue by the amount not yet earned (via a debit) and increase Unearned Revenue (via a credit).

C. **A COMPARISON OF THE TWO APPROACHES** reveals that the balance sheet and income statement methods result in identical financial statements. Notice that the income statement approach does have an advantage if the entire prepaid item or unearned revenue is fully consumed or earned by the end of an accounting period. No adjusting entry is needed because the expense or revenue was fully recorded at the date of the original transaction.

CLASS NOTES

CLASS NOTES

CLASS NOTES

CLASS NOTES

SELF TESTS

FULFILLMENT OF LEARNING OBJECTIVES

Circle the appropriate response.

L.O. 1(a) Which concept holds that an organization's life can be divided into discrete accounting periods (months, quarters, years)?

transactions approach   or   periodicity assumption

L.O. 1(b) The periodicity assumption seems practical and logical; however, it introduces allocation problems when dividing the life of a company into specific units of time.

true   or   false

L.O. 2 Under the accrual basis of accounting, revenue should be recognized at the time services are rendered or when goods are sold and delivered to a customer.

correct   or   incorrect

L.O. 3 Business expenses should be recognized in the same period as the revenues they helped to produce. This concept is known as the:

matching principle   or   cash basis of accounting

L.O. 4(a) Under the cash basis of accounting, revenues and expenses are recognized as receipts and payments occur.

true   or   false

L.O. 4(b) Which method of accounting is theoretically preferred and used by virtually all large companies?

accrual basis   or   cash basis

L.O. 5(a) Adjusting entries are necessary to fulfill the goals of proper income measurement and are consistent with the cash basis of accounting.

true   or   false

L.O. 5(b) The recording and accounting for prepaid expenses, depreciation, and similar items is consistent with the adjusting process for:

multiperiod costs and revenues that must be split
among two or more accounting periods
or
revenues and expenses that have been earned or incurred
in a given period but not recorded in the accounts

L.O. 5(c) Revenues and expenses that gradually accumulate throughout an accounting period are known as:

accruals   or   deferrals

L.O. 6(a) An appropriate journal entry to record accrued interest would involve a debit to Interest Expense and a credit to:

Interest Payable
or
Unearned Interest

L.O. 6(b) Adjusting entries should be determined:

subsequent to preparing financial statements
or
prior to preparing financial statements

L.O. 7(a) An adjusted trial balance is prepared by changing specific account balances in the trial balance by the amount of the adjustments from the adjusting entries.

true   or   false

L.O. 7(b) An adjustment error will never impact more than one financial statement.

correct   or   incorrect

L.O. 8(a) Prepaid expenses would initially be recorded in an expense account under which adjusting entry approach.

balance sheet approach
or
income statement approach

L.O. 8(b) If the income statement approach is used to record revenues received in advance of being earned, then an adjusting entry will always be necessary at the end of the accounting period.

true   or   false

FILL IN THE BLANKS

1. Accountants downplay the economic concept of profit and employ a more objective _____ _____ in computing net income.

2. The _____ _____ is paramount to income measurement, and holds that an organization's life can be divided into discrete measurement intervals.

3. An accounting year that covers a period of time other than January 1 through December 31 is typically referred to as a _____ year.

4. Accrual-basis revenue is generally recognized at the time services are _____ or when goods are _____ and _____ to a customer.

5. The _____ _____ holds that expenses should be recorded in the same time period as the revenues they helped to produce.

6. Under the _____ basis of accounting, revenues are recorded in the period of receipt and expenses in the period of payment. This method is generally regarded as being inferior to the _____ basis of accounting.

7. _____ _____ are goods and services purchased for future consumption and paid for in advance.

8. The Accumulated Depreciation account is termed a _____ asset.

9. The reported amount for an asset, less its accumulated depreciation, is frequently referred to as _____ _____.

10. _____ revenue represents future revenue that has been collected but not yet earned, whereas _____ revenues have been earned but not yet received.

11. An adjusting journal entry to record an accrued expense would necessarily involve a _____ to an expense account.

12. Financial statements may be prepared directly from the _____ _____ _____.

13. The method wherein prepaid expenses are initially recorded into the expense account is called the _____ _____ approach.

MULTIPLE CHOICE QUESTIONS

Circle the appropriate response.

1. For purposes of measuring business income, the life of a business is:

    a. divided into specific points in time.
    b. divided into irregular cycles.
    c. divided into discrete accounting periods.
    d. considered to be a continuous cycle.

2. Adjusting entries at the end of an accounting period would not be required for which of the following?

    a. Multiperiod costs that must be split among two or more accounting periods.
    b. Multiperiod revenues that must be split among two or more accounting periods.
    c. Expenses that have been incurred in a given period but not as yet recorded in the accounts.
    d. Revenue that has been earned and recorded in the accounting records.

3. Blankenship Company pays its employees every Friday for work rendered that week. The payroll is typically $10,000 per week. Which of the following journal entries would Blankenship ordinarily record on the Friday payday?

    a. Salary Expense   10,000
            Salary Payable   10,000
    b. Salary Expense   10,000
            Cash   10,000
    c. Salary Payable   10,000
            Cash   10,000
    d. Salary Payable   10,000
            Salary Expense   10,000

4. Blankenship Company pays its employees every Friday for work rendered that week. The payroll is typically $10,000 per week. What journal entry would be recorded (on Wednesday) if the end of the accounting period occurred on a Wednesday?

    a. Salary Expense   6,000
            Salary Payable   6,000
    b. Salary Expense   6,000
            Cash   6,000
    c. Salary Payable   6,000
            Cash   6,000
    d. Salary Payable   6,000
            Salary Expense   6,000

5. Blankenship Company pays its employees every Friday for work rendered that week. The payroll is typically $10,000 per week. Blankenship's year-end occurred on Wednesday, at which time a correct adjusting entry was recorded. On the following Friday, which of the following payroll journal entries should be recorded?

    a. Salary Expense   10,000
            Cash   10,000
    b. Salary Expense   4,000
        Salary Payable   6,000
            Cash   10,000
    c. Salary Expense   6,000
        Salary Payable   4,000
            Cash   10,000
    d. Salary Payable   10,000
            Cash   10,000

6. The appropriate journal entry to record equipment depreciation expense would consist of a debit to Depreciation Expense and a credit to which of the following accounts?

    a. Equipment
    b. Accumulated Depreciation: Equipment
    c. Retained Earnings
    d. Cash

7. At the end of the current accounting period, Johnson Company failed to record utilities consumed during the period. Johnson will be billed for the utilities during the next accounting period. As a result, current period assets, liabilities, stockholders' equity, and income, respectively, are:

    a. Overstated, overstated, correct, correct
    b. Correct, understated, overstated, overstated
    c. Overstated, understated, overstated, overstated
    d. Overstated, understated, correct, correct

8. On November 1, 19X1, Limit Company purchased a one-year insurance policy for $12,000. Limit Company debited Cash and credited Prepaid Insurance for $12,000. At the end of December, 19X1, $2,000 of insurance had expired. The journal entry to properly state all accounts involved on December 31, 19X1, would be:

    a. Insurance Expense   2,000
       Prepaid Insurance   22,000
           Cash   24,000
    b. Insurance Expense   2,000
           Prepaid Insurance   2,000
    c. Insurance Expense   2,000
           Cash   2,000
    d. Prepaid Insurance   2,000
           Insurance Expense   2,000

9. Under the the income statement approach to adjusting entries, the receipt of $5,000 of unearned revenue would be recorded by debiting Cash. What account should be credited?

    a. Cash
    b. Revenue
    c. Unearned Revenue
    d. Prepaid Revenue

10. Simmons Company received and recorded a $5,000 payment for services to be rendered in the future. If the income statement approach to adjusting entries is used, the appropriate adjusting entry at the end of the accounting period for $3,000 of revenue not yet earned would be:

    a. Service Revenue   3,000
           Unearned Service Revenue   3,000
    b. Service Revenue   2,000
           Unearned Service Revenue   2,000
    c. Accounts Receivable   3,000
           Unearned Service Revenue   3,000
    d. No entry would be needed.

DEMONSTRATION PROBLEMS

DP-1   Linblad Company provides the following information about its first year of operation:

Linblad provides flyfishing lessons. During the year, 6,000 hours of instruction at $8.00 per hour were offered to clients. Half of the amounts had been collected by the end of the period; the remaining balance is still outstanding.

Linblad provides clients with a packet of fishing supplies. During the year, 800 packets were purchased at $10.00 per packet. All of the packets have been distributed, and payment has been made for 90% of the packets. The remaining unpaid amounts are to be paid in the following year.

Linblad paid employees, advertising, and other similar operating costs of $17,000 during the year. In addition, another $2,000 of operating costs were incurred but not yet paid.

    a.   Compute Linblad's accrual-basis net income for the year.
    b.   Compute Linblad's cash-basis net income for the year.

DP-2   Winding Trail Race Car Company purchased a new automobile on January 1, 19X1. The automobile cost $420,000 and had a three-year life. Winding Trail uses straight-line depreciation. Calculate depreciation expense for each of the three years, demonstrate the proper adjusting entry for each year, and show how the automobile would appear on the firm's balance sheet at the end of each of the three years.

DP-3 Carter Publication Company operates a newspaper. On May 1, Carter received a $2,500 advance payment for a series of 25 advertisements. By the end of the month, 10 advertisements in this series had already run. On May 10, Carter ran a $1,500 advertisement for a customer; by the end of May, Carter had yet to collect the amount due from the customer. Finally, on May 20, a customer purchased a $200 advertisement to be run in June. Carter collected the full amount on May 20. Carter uses the accrual basis of accounting.

    a.   Record the proper entries for May 1, 10, and 20.
    b.   Record the necessary adjusting entries on May 31.
    c.   Calculate total advertising revenue for May.
    d.   Repeats parts (a), (b), and (c), assuming Carter uses the income statement approach for recording unearned revenues.

SOLUTIONS TO SELF TESTS

FULFILLMENT OF LEARNING OBJECTIVES

1(a)	Periodicity assumption
1(b)	True
2	Correct
3	Matching principle
4(a)	True
4(b)	Accrual basis
5(a)	False
5(b)	Multiperiod costs and revenues that must be split among two or more accounting periods
5(c)	Accruals
6(a)	Interest Payable
6(b)	Prior to preparing financial statements
7(a)	True
7(b)	Incorrect
8(a)	Income statement approach
8(b)	False

FILL IN THE BLANKS

1. Transactions approach
2. Periodicity assumption
3. Fiscal
4. Rendered, sold, delivered
5. Matching principle
6. Cash, accrual
7. Prepaid expenses
8. Contra
9. Book value
10. Unearned, accrued
11. Debit
12. Adjusted trial balance
13. Income statement

MULTIPLE CHOICE QUESTIONS

1. c. Accountants divide time into specific intervals for measurement purposes. These periods may be a month, quarter, or year. This concept is highlighted by noting the date on an income statement: "For the Year Ending December 31, 19XX."

2. d. The accounting for revenue that has been earned and recorded is complete; no adjustment is needed. Multiperiod costs and revenues must be adjusted to reflect the amount consumed or generated in a given period, and the amount prepaid or unearned at the end of the period. Expenses incurred but not recorded (accrued) must be recorded via adjusting entries.

3. b. The amount paid on a normal payday should also be expensed. The expense and related payable would not have been previously recorded.

4. a. The $6,000 amount ($2,000 per day times 3 days) needs to be expensed for the work rendered. This amount should be recorded as a liability -- it will be paid on Friday. No cash is disbursed on Wednesday.

5. b. This entry reflects that the $10,000 cash disbursement is recorded as $4,000 of expense (for Thursday and Friday) and a $6,000 payment of the payable that was established on Wednesday.

6. b. The Accumulated Depreciation account is for exactly this purpose. Note that the Equipment account is not directly credited.

7. b. The correct entry to record utilities consumed is to debit Utilities Expense and credit Utilities Payable. Because this was not done, liabilities and expenses are understated. The understatement of expense causes income and equity to be overstated. Assets are not impacted.

8. a. Notice that the original entry is backwards. That is, Cash was debited and Prepaid Expense credited. To correct and adjust the accounts first requires a debit to Insurance Expense for $2,000 (to reflect the expired amount). Next, Prepaid Insurance is debited for $22,000; to establish the correct ending debit balance of $10,000, one must record a $22,000 debit (the existing balance is a $12,000 credit). Finally, Cash is credited for $24,000 (to correct the error which showed cash increasing by $12,000 when it really decreased by $12,000).

9. b. With the income statement approach, prepaid expenses and unearned revenues are initially recorded to expense and revenue; subsequent year-end adjustments update balance sheet accounts and reduce expense and revenue accounts as needed.

10. a. The $3,000 must be removed from the Revenue account (debited) because it has not yet been earned. This amount needs to be recorded into the Unearned Revenue account (credited).

DEMONSTRATION PROBLEMS

DP-1

(a) Accrual-basis income:

    Revenues earned: 6,000 hours of instruction X $8 per hour = $48,000

    Expenses incurred: 800 fishing packets used X $10 each = $8,000

                                    Operating expenses incurred = $19,000

$48,000 - $8,000 - $19,000 = $21,000 net income

(b) Cash-basis income:

    Revenues collected: 6,000 hours X $8 per hour x 50% collected = $24,000

    Expenses paid: 800 fishing packets X $10 each X 90% = $7,200

                                    Operating expenses paid = $17,000

$24,000 - $7,200 - $17,000 = $200 net loss

DP-2

Depreciation expense:

$420,000/3 years = $140,000 per year

Adjusting entry needed for each of the 3 years:

Depreciation Expense	140,000	
Accumulated Depreciation: Machinery		140,000
Adjusting entry		

Balance sheet presentation, end of 19X1:

Assets		
Machinery	$420,000	
Less: Accumulated depreciation	140,000	$280,000

Balance sheet presentation, end of 19X2:

Assets		
Machinery	$420,000	
Less: Accumulated depreciation	280,000	$140,000

Balance sheet presentation, end of 19X3:

Assets		
Machinery	$420,000	
Less: Accumulated depreciation	420,000	$ 0

Note: At the end of 19X3, the asset would be fully depreciated, and would probably be disposed of and removed from the accounting records.

DP-3

(a)
	May	1	Cash	2,500	
			Unearned Advertising Revenue		2,500
			Received payment for ten advertisements		
		10	Accounts Receivable	1,500	
			Advertising Revenue		1,500
			Ran an advertisement for a customer who will pay later		
		20	Cash	200	
			Unearned Advertising Revenue		200
			Received advance payment for June advertising		

(b)
	May	31	Unearned Advertising Revenue	1,000	
			Advertising Revenue		1,000
			Adjusting entry (($2,500/25) X 10)		

(c)
	May	10	$1,500
		31	1,000
			$2,500

(d)
	May	1	Cash	2,500	
			Advertising Revenue		2,500
			Received payment for for ten advertisements		
		10	Accounts Receivable	1,500	
			Advertising Revenue		1,500
			Ran an advertisement for a customer who will pay later		
		20	Cash	200	
			Advertising Revenue		200
			Received advance payment for June advertising		
	May	31	Advertising Revenue	1,700	
			Unearned Advertising Revenue		1,700
			Adjusting entry (($2,500/25) X 15) + $200		

	May	1	$2,500
		10	1,500
		20	200
		31	(1,700)
			$2,500

CHAPTER 4

COMPLETION OF THE ACCOUNTING CYCLE

LEARNING OBJECTIVES

After studying this chapter, you should be able to:

1   Prepare a work sheet and the accompanying financial statements.

2   Close a set of books and prepare a post-closing trial balance.

3   Name and describe the various steps in the accounting cycle.

4   Understand the concept of an operating cycle and construct a classified balance sheet.

5   Demonstrate a general knowledge of the notes to the financial statements and other disclosures found in a corporate annual report.

6   (Appendix) Explain the concept and mechanics of reversing entries.

CHAPTER HIGHLIGHTS

I. The **WORK SHEET** is a columnar form useful in the preparation of a company's financial statements. Think of the work sheet as a giant scratch pad for the accountant.

   A. **WORK SHEET CONSTRUCTION** begins by listing the various account titles in the first column. The next pair of columns is for the balance of each account (debits in the left column and credits in the right column). The following pair of columns is for end-of-period adjustments (again debits to the left and credits to the right). Combining the first two pairs of columns yields the adjusted trial balance, which is revealed in the third pair of columns. This portion of the work sheet should look very familiar, as it corresponds to the format introduced in the prior chapter (refer to the text and review Exhibit 3-5, "Preparation of adjusted trial balance," and Exhibit 4-1, "Work sheet . . .").

      1. In examining the work sheet, notice the last two pairs of columns -- **INCOME STATEMENT AND BALANCE SHEET**. Amounts from the adjusted trial balance columns of the work sheet are extended to either the income statement or balance sheet columns. For example, Cash is an asset account with a debit balance, and is extended to the debit column of the balance sheet pair of columns. Likewise, Service Revenue is an income statement account with a credit balance; notice that it is extended to the income statement credit column. This extension of accounts should occur for every item in the adjusted trial balance.
      One item that requires special mention is the Dividends account. On formal

financial statements, dividends are reported on the statement of retained earnings (not the income statement or balance sheet); nevertheless, in preparing the work sheet, extend dividends to the balance sheet debit column (because dividends reduce equity).

2. After all adjusted trial balance amounts have been extended, **FINANCIAL STATEMENT TOTALS** can be developed. In the income statement columns, if credits exceed debits, the company has more revenues than expenses (net income). On the other hand, an excess of debits over credits represents a net loss. To complete the work sheet, the amount of net income or loss is entered in the lower portion of the income statement columns, in a manner which causes total debits to equal total credits. For example, if the company had a net income (indicated by credits exceeding debits in the income statement columns), then a debit is needed to balance the income statement pair. An offsetting credit is entered in the lower portion of the balance sheet columns. This credit should result in equality between total debits and credits in the balance sheet pair of columns (in much the same manner that income for the year must be added to retained earnings to complete the preparation of a formal balance sheet). If the company incurred a net loss, then a credit would be needed to balance the income statement columns and a debit would be needed to complete the balance sheet columns.

B. **USES OF THE WORK SHEET** are numerous and varied. The work sheet lays the groundwork for preparing financial statements, completing the adjusting process, and assists in closing out the accounting records at the end of an accounting period.

1. The most obvious use of the work sheet is preparation of **FINANCIAL STATEMENTS**. It is apparent that the income statement can be prepared directly from information in the income statement columns of the work sheet. Also notice that balance sheet columns include dividends and income (and any beginning retained earnings amount); these are elements in the statement of retained earnings. Finally, the balance sheet can be prepared from the balance sheet columns of the work sheet (except that ending retained earnings is taken from the statement of retained earnings).

2. **ADJUSTING ENTRIES** may also be prepared from the work sheet. Notice that the adjustment columns provide information about needed adjusting entries. These adjustments must be formally recorded in the journal and posted to the ledger.

3. At the end of an accounting period special "closing" procedures must be followed. **THE CLOSING PROCESS** is facilitated by reference to the work sheet.

   a. The **PURPOSE** of the closing process is two-fold: First, closing is a mechanism to update the Retained Earnings account to equal the end-of-period balance. Second, revenue, expense, and dividend accounts represent amounts for a period of time; one must "zero out" these accounts at the end of each period (as a result, revenue, expense, and dividend accounts are called temporary or nominal accounts). In contrast, asset, liability, and equity accounts are called real accounts, as their balances are carried forward from period to period. For example, one does not "start over" each period accumulating assets like cash and so on -- their balances carry forward.

   b. Closing entries are typically prepared once each year. The closing **TECHNIQUE** is a four step process: (1) close revenue accounts, (2) close expense accounts,

(3) close the Income Summary account, and (4) close the Dividends account.

    c. **CLOSING REVENUE ACCOUNTS** means to prepare a journal entry to debit Revenue for the account's balance and credit Income Summary.

    d. **CLOSING EXPENSE ACCOUNTS** means to credit each expense account for its balance and debit Income Summary for the total of all expense accounts. Notice that closing revenue and expenses causes a zero balance in each of those accounts.

    e. **CLOSING THE INCOME SUMMARY ACCOUNT** is simple. One need merely determine the balance of the account (after closing revenue and expenses to Income Summary). If the balance is a credit, then debit Income Summary (to zero it out) and credit Retained Earnings. Vice versa, a debit balance in Income Summary would be closed by crediting Income Summary and debiting Retained Earnings. Note that a credit balance in Income Summary represents the net income (credits exceeded debits -- that is revenues exceeded expenses), or vice versa for a net loss.

    f. **CLOSING THE DIVIDENDS ACCOUNT** is carried out by crediting the Dividends account for the account's balance and debiting Retained Earnings. This has the effect of zeroing out the Dividends account and reducing Retained Earnings for the amount of the dividends.

    g. **AN OVERVIEW** of the closing process reveals that revenues and expenses are closed to Income Summary, and Income Summary and Dividends are closed to Retained Earnings. The Retained Earnings account is thereby adjusted from its beginning-of-period balance to its ending balance.

    h. Accountants sometimes prepare a **POST-CLOSING TRIAL BALANCE**. The post-closing trial balance reveals the balance of accounts after the closing process, and consists of balance sheet accounts only. The post-closing trial balance is a tool to demonstrate that accounts are in balance; it is not a formal financial statement.

II. **A LOOK BACK: THE ACCOUNTING CYCLE** reveals the following steps: (1) transactions are recorded in the journal and then (2) posted to appropriate ledger accounts. To determine whether the ledger accounts are in balance, (3) a trial balance is constructed. The trial balance is updated by certain adjustments in the process of (4) preparing a work sheet. From the work sheet (5) formal financial statements are produced, and (6) adjusting entries are recorded in the journal and posted to the ledger. Finally, (7) temporary accounts are closed and (8) a post-closing trial balance is prepared.

III. **THE BALANCE SHEET** provides information about a company's assets, liabilities, and stockholders' equity. A detailed balance sheet reveals not only total assets, but also the level and nature of debt and equity used to finance assets. The balance sheet suffers from weaknesses of historical cost (rather than value) and omission of certain assets not subject to measurement in dollars (such as good management).

    A. The balance sheet is divided into a special **STATEMENT CLASSIFICATION** scheme so that important groups of accounts can be identified and subtotaled.

1. **ASSETS** may be divided into five key classifications:

   a. **CURRENT ASSETS** are those assets that will be converted into cash or consumed in a relatively short period of time; specifically, those assets that will be converted into cash or consumed within one year or the operating cycle, whichever is longer. The operating cycle for a particular company is the period of time it takes to convert cash back into cash (i.e., purchase inventory, sell the inventory on account, and collect the receivable). In listing assets within the current section, the most liquid assets should be listed first (i.e., cash, short-term investments, and receivables). These are followed with inventories and prepaid expenses.

   b. Land purchased for speculation, funds set aside for a plant expansion program, investments in other entities, and so forth should be classified in the next category on the balance sheet, known as the **LONG-TERM INVESTMENTS** section.

   c. The **PROPERTY, PLANT, AND EQUIPMENT** classification consists of assets that are used in the operations of the business, such as land, buildings, and equipment.

   d. **INTANGIBLE ASSETS** lack physical existence. They represent rights like patents and copyrights, and should follow property, plant, and equipment on the balance sheet.

   e. The final major classification on a detailed balance sheet is the **OTHER ASSETS** section. An example of an item which would be listed here is a long-term receivable.

2. Special classifications also exist in the **LIABILITIES** section of the balance sheet.

   a. **CURRENT LIABILITIES** are those obligations that will be liquidated within one year or the operating cycle, whichever is longer. Normally, current liabilities are paid with current assets. An important measure related to current liabilities (and current assets) is the current ratio. This ratio is calculated by dividing current assets by current liabilities. Another measure is working capital; current assets minus current liabilities. Both of these measures provide clues about a company's ability to meet short-term obligations as they come due.

   b. Obligations expected to be paid after one year or the operating cycle are classified as **LONG-TERM LIABILITIES**. Examples include bank loans, mortgage notes, and the like. Importantly, some long-term notes may be classified partially as a current liability and partially as a long-term liability. The portion classified as current would be the principal amount to be repaid within the next year (or operating cycle, if longer). Any amounts due after that period of time would be shown as a long-term liability.

3. The appropriate financial statement presentation for **STOCKHOLDERS' EQUITY** was introduced in earlier chapters and consists of capital stock and retained earnings.

B. While a classified balance sheet is very revealing, additional **NOTES TO THE FINANCIAL STATEMENTS** should be presented to achieve a **FULL** and fair **DISCLOSURE**. Recognize that many important details about a company cannot be described in dollars on the balance sheet. Notes are used to describe accounting policies, major business events, pending lawsuits, and other facets of operation. The principle of full disclosure means that financial statements result in a fair presentation and that all facts which would influence investors' and creditors' judgments about the company are disclosed in the financial statements or related notes.

1. **ANNUAL REPORTS** reveal a firm's financial statements and notes. In addition, annual reports provide stockholders with various other information, such as the firm's audit report and management's analysis of operations and financial position. Appendixes A and D at the end of the text provide more information about annual reports.

IV. **APPENDIX: REVERSING ENTRIES** are an optional accounting procedure which may prove useful in simplifying the bookkeeping process. A reversing entry is a journal entry to "undo" an adjusting entry.

A. The examples presented earlier in the text assumed **NO REVERSING ENTRIES**. For example, if an adjusting entry was made to record accrued salaries at the end of 19X1, then the journal entry to record the first payroll of 19X2 involved debits to Salaries Payable (for the amount accrued at the end of 19X1) and Salaries Expense (for the amount earned by employees during 19X2).

B. In the alternative, **USING REVERSING ENTRIES** means that the first journal entries of a new accounting period are to reverse selected adjusting entries. For example, if an adjusting entry was made to record accrued salaries at the end of 19X1, then the reversing entry at the beginning of 19X2 is to debit Salaries Payable and credit Salaries Expense (i.e., "undo" the adjustment which was made at the end of 19X1). The journal entry to record the first payroll of 19X2 will be recorded in the ordinary fashion (debit Salaries Expense and credit Cash for the total amount disbursed). The net impact of these procedures is to record the correct amount of expense for 19X2 (the credit to Salaries Expense from the reversing entry and the debit to Salaries Expense for the full payroll result in a net debit equal to the amount of salary related to 19X2).

C. **AN OVERVIEW** reveals that utilizing reversing entries simplifies the accounting process. For example, on the first payday following the reversing entry, a "normal" journal entry can be made to record the full amount of salaries paid -- without having to give special consideration to any adjusting entry which might have been recorded at the end of the prior period. Reversing entries would ordinarily be appropriate for those adjusting entries which involve the recording of accrued revenues and expenses; specifically, those that involve future cash flows.

CLASS NOTES

CLASS NOTES

CLASS NOTES

CLASS NOTES

CLASS NOTES

SELF TESTS

FULFILLMENT OF LEARNING OBJECTIVES

Circle the appropriate response.

L.O. 1(a)   If the subtotal amounts in the income statement columns of the work sheet reveal debits in excess of credits, then which is indicated?

net income   or   net loss

L.O. 1(b)   The amount of ending retained earnings appears as a specific line item in the balance sheet columns of the work sheet.

true   or   false

L.O. 2(a)   Which account types are closed at the end of an accounting period?

nominal accounts   or   real accounts

L.O. 2(b)   The post-closing trial balance would consist of which account types?

income statement accounts
or
balance sheet accounts

L.O. 3(a)   Which of the following comes before the other in the normal accounting cycle?

posting   or   closing

L.O. 3(b)   A post-closing trial balance is prepared:

before closing   or   after closing

L.O 4(a)   The relevant time period related to the definition of current assets is one year or the operating cycle, whichever is:

longer   or   shorter

L.O. 4(b)   Which should precede the other on a classified balance sheet?

long-term investments
or
property, plant, & equipment

L.O. 5(a)   If a company has a 2:1 current ratio, and then pays half of its current liabilities, the current ratio would be:

3:1   or   4:1

L.O. 5(b) Current assets minus current liabilities is defined as:

working capital   or   current ratio

L.O. 6(a) Whether or not a company utilizes reversing entries, identical financial statements should be achieved.

correct   or   incorrect

L.O. 6(b) The possibility that errors will occur in the accounting records is reduced through the utilization of reversing entries.

true   or   false

FILL IN THE BLANKS

1. The _____ _____ is a large columnar form that assists in the preparation of an entity's financial statements.

2. Amounts in the adjusted trial balance columns of the work sheet are extended to either the _____ _____ or _____ _____ columns of the work sheet.

3. Revenue, expense, and dividend accounts must be closed or reduced to zero so amounts are not carried over from one period to the next. These accounts are appropriately known as _____ or _____ accounts.

4. Accounts whose balances are carried forward from period to period are commonly called _____ accounts.

5. The _____ _____ account is used only in closing, and summarizes the net income or net loss of a business.

6. The _____ account is closed directly to Retained Earnings.

7. To determine whether the accounts are still in balance after closing entries have been journalized and posted, accountants often prepare a _____-_____ _____ _____.

8. The _____ _____ is the length of time it takes a company to turn cash back into cash via investing in inventory and accepting accounts receivable.

9. Current assets should be listed on a balance sheet in order of _____.

10. _____ assets usually follow property, plant, and equipment on a classified balance sheet.

11. Working capital is computed by subtracting _____ _____ from _____ _____.

12. A _____ _____ is the exact opposite of an adjusting entry.

MULTIPLE CHOICE QUESTIONS

Circle the appropriate response.

1. The accountant's work sheet:

    a. lays the groundwork for formal financial statement preparation.
    b. is a fundamental financial statement.
    c. provides details necessary for full disclosure and the preparation of notes to the financial statements.
    d. is prepared at the end of each operating cycle.

2. In preparing a work sheet, a net loss would be computed and entered in the:

    a. debit column of the income statement columns of the work sheet.
    b. credit column of the income statement columns of the work sheet.
    c. in the debit column of the adjusted trial balance.
    d. in the credit column of the balance sheet columns of the work sheet.

3. Which of the following accounts would not be closed at the end of an accounting period?

    a. Income Summary
    b. Dividends
    c. Revenue
    d. Retained Earnings

4. After closing all revenue and expense accounts, Norris Company had a debit balance in its Income Summary account of $10,000. The proper entry to record the closing of the Income Summary account would be:

    a. Revenue   10,000
         Income Summary   10,000
    b. Retained Earnings   10,000
         Income Summary   10,000
    c. Income Summary   10,000
         Retained Earnings   10,000
    d. Income Summary   10,000
         Expenses   10,000

5. The following statements all pertain to the accounting cycle. Which of these statements is incorrect?

    a. A post-closing trial balance is prepared prior to closing temporary accounts.
    b. Formal financial statements may be produced from the work sheet.
    c. Adjusting entries are recorded in the journal and posted to the ledger.
    d. The post-closing trial balance is prepared by examining ledger balances subsequent to the closing of accounts.

6. Current assets are those assets which management intends to convert into cash or consume within:

   a. The operating cycle
   b. One year
   c. The longer of (a) or (b)
   d. The shorter of (a) or (b)

7. On a classified balance sheet, the appropriate ordering of specific classifications is:

   a. Current assets; long-term investments; property, plant, and equipment; intangible assets; other assets.
   b. Current assets; property, plant, and equipment; long-term investments; intangible assets; other assets.
   c. Current assets; intangible assets; property, plant, and equipment; long-term investments; other assets.
   d. Current assets; other assets; long-term investments; intangible assets; property, plant, and equipment.

8. If a company had a current ratio of 0.5:1, then which of the following statements regarding that company's working capital would be true?

   a. The company's working capital would be positive.
   b. The company's working capital would be zero.
   c. The company's working capital would be negative.
   d. The company's working capital would be 2:1.

9. Which of the following statements about reversing entries is true?

   a. Identical account balances are achieved in the subsequent accounting period whether reversing entries are utilized or not.
   b. Reversing entries may not be used with accrued revenues.
   c. Reversals are generally applied to those adjusting items that do not involve future cash flow.
   d. Reversing entries would not be prepared if a company also utilized closing entries.

10. Shipman Company had accrued salaries of $300 on December 31. The company recorded reversing entries on the following January 1. On the next payday, January 7, the appropriate entry to record the payment of $1,000 in salaries should include:

    a. a debit to Salaries Expense of $1,000.
    b. a debit to Salaries Expense of $700.
    c. a debit to Salaries Expense of $1,300.
    d. a debit to Salaries Payable for $300.

DEMONSTRATION PROBLEMS

DP-1 DelMar Corporation had the following adjusted trial balance on December 31:

Cash	$ 1,000	
Accounts receivable	1,500	
Land	4,500	
Accounts payable		$ 2,000
Wages payable		500
Capital stock		4,000
Retained earnings		1,400
Dividends	400	
Service revenue		3,500
Rent expense	500	
Wages expense	1,700	
Utilities expense	1,800	
	$11,400	$11,400

a. For each account in the adjusted trial balance, indicate whether it should be extended to the income statement debit column, income statement credit column, balance sheet debit column, or balance sheet credit column of a work sheet.

b. Consider the contents of the income statement columns of a work sheet and determine the company's net income or net loss.

c. Prepare the closing entries that the company would record on December 31.

DP-2 Specialty Research provides you with information about its various account balances.

Insurance expense	$ 2,200
Advertising expense	4,800
Capital stock	40,000
Beginning retained earnings	70,400
Supplies	5,200
Equipment	40,000
Depreciation expense	6,600
Taxes payable	3,400
Salaries payable	2,000
Long-term investments	10,000
Patents	15,000
Miscellaneous expense	2,600
Accumulated depreciation: equipment	20,800
Land	15,500
Supplies expense	1,600
Bank loan payable	20,000
Copyrights	5,000
Cash	58,400
Accounts receivable	51,600
Dividends	7,800
Salaries expense	64,200
Service revenue	112,400
Prepaid insurance	2,800
Accounts payable	24,300

Prepare complete financial statements (including a detailed classified balance sheet) for the company for the year ended December 31, 19X1.

DP-3 Bellmeade Company began operations on January 1, 19X1. The accounting records reveal that salaries paid during the year totaled $82,000. Further, the firm incurred additional wages of $3,700 that will disbursed to employees on January 7, 19X2. Total payroll on January 7 will amount to $6,300. The Company uses reversing entries and employs the accrual basis of accounting.

    a.   Compute total wage expense for 19X1.
    b.   Record the necessary adjusting and closing entries on December 31, 19X1.
    c.   Record the necessary reversing entry on January 1, 19X2.
    d.   Record the entry to disburse the payroll on January 7, 19X2.

SOLUTIONS TO SELF TESTS

FULFILLMENT OF LEARNING OBJECTIVES

1(a) Net loss
1(b) False
2(a) Nominal accounts
2(b) Balance sheet accounts
3(a) Posting
3(b) After closing
4(a) Longer
4(b) Long-term investments
5(a) 3:1
5(b) Working capital
6(a) Correct
6(b) True

FILL IN THE BLANKS

1. Work sheet
2. Income statement, balance sheet
3. Temporary, nominal
4. Real
5. Income Summary
6. Dividends
7. Post-closing trial balance
8. Operating cycle
9. Liquidity
10. Intangible
11. Current liabilities, current assets
12. Reversing entry

MULTIPLE CHOICE QUESTIONS

1. a. Formal financial statements can be prepared from the work sheet, therefore the work sheet lays the groundwork for their preparation. The work sheet is not a financial statement and does not include details about notes. The work sheet would be prepared at the end of an "accounting cycle" -- not an "operating cycle."

2. b. A net loss is represented in the work sheet by debits exceeding credits in the subtotal of the income statement columns. To complete (i.e., balance) the income statement columns necessitates a credit to the income statement columns and a debit to the balance sheet columns. Therefore, the amount of a net loss is computed and entered in the credit column of the income statement columns of the work sheet.

3. d. Retained Earnings is a balance sheet account and is not closed. Temporary accounts (like Income Summary, Dividends, and Revenue) are closed "to" retained earnings.

4. b. Closing a debit balance in Income Summary is accomplished by crediting Income Summary. The corresponding debit is applied to Retained Earnings.

5. a. A post-closing trial balance is prepared after all closing entries are complete, not "prior to" closing entries. Formal financial statements are prepared from a work sheet, and adjusting entries are recorded in the journal and posted to the ledger.

6. c. Current assets are those which management intends to convert into cash or consume within one year or the operating cycle, whichever is longer.

7. a. The correct ordering of major categories on a classified balance sheet is current assets; long-term investments; property, plant, and equipment; intangible assets; and other assets.

8. c. A current ratio of 0.5:1 signifies that the company has twice as many current liabilities as current assets. Therefore, working capital is a negative amount (i.e., current assets minus current liabilities is negative).

9. a. Reversing entries are an optional tool to assist in the bookkeeping function. Whether or not they are used, identical account balances and financial statements should result. Reversing entries are often used for accrued revenues, and other similar items that will involve future cash flows. Reversing entries are prepared at the beginning of a new accounting period, and closing entries are prepared at the end of an accounting period. Closing entries must be prepared whether or not the company elects to use reversing entries.

10. a. When reversing entries are used, the journal entry on the payment date will record the full amount paid as a debit to Salaries Expense. The net impact is that salaries expense will equal the correct $700 amount related to the new year (i.e., $1,000 paid less $300 related to the prior year). This results because the reversing entry would establish a $300 credit to Salaries Expense and the payroll journal entry enters a $1,000 debit to Salaries Expense.

DEMONSTRATION PROBLEMS

DP-1

(a)
Cash	Balance sheet debit column
Accounts receivable	Balance sheet debit column
Land	Balance sheet debit column
Accounts payable	Balance sheet credit column
Wages payable	Balance sheet credit column
Capital stock	Balance sheet credit column
Dividends	Balance sheet debit column
Service revenue	Income statement credit column
Rent expense	Income statement debit column
Wages expense	Income statement debit column
Utilities expense	Income statement debit column

(b) The income statement columns would include total credits of $3,500 and total debits of $4,000 ($500 + $1,700 + $1,800). This indicates a net loss of $500 ($3,500 - $4,000).

(c)
Dec.	31	Service Revenue	3,500	
		Income Summary		3,500
		To close revenues		
	31	Income Summary	4,000	
		Rent Expense		500
		Wages Expense		1,700
		Utilities Expense		1,800
		To close expenses		
	31	Retained Earnings	500	
		Income Summary		500
		To close Income Summary		
	31	Retained Earnings	400	
		Dividends		400
		To close Dividends account		

DP-2

SPECIALTY RESEARCH
INCOME STATEMENT
FOR THE YEAR ENDED DECEMBER 31, 19X1

Service revenue		$112,400
Less expenses		
Insurance	$ 2,200	
Advertising	4,800	
Depreciation	6,600	
Miscellaneous	2,600	
Supplies	1,600	
Salaries	64,200	
Total expenses		82,000
Net income		$ 30,400

SPECIALTY RESEARCH
STATEMENT OF RETAINED EARNINGS
FOR THE YEAR ENDED DECEMBER 31, 19X1

Beginning balance, Jan. 1	$ 70,400
Add: Net income	30,400
	$100,800
Deduct: Dividends	7,800
Ending balance, Dec. 31	$ 93,000

SPECIALTY RESEARCH
BALANCE SHEET
DECEMBER 31, 19X1

Assets

Current assets			
Cash		$ 58,400	
Accounts receivable		51,600	
Supplies		5,200	
Prepaid insurance		2,800	
Total current assets			$118,000
Long-term investments			10,000
Property, plant, & equipment			
Land		$ 15,500	
Equipment	$40,000		
Less: Accumulated depreciation	20,800	19,200	
Total property, plant, & equipment			34,700
Intangible assets			
Copyrights		$ 5,000	
Patents		15,000	20,000
Total assets			$182,700

Liabilities & Stockholders' Equity

Current liabilities		
Accounts payable	$ 24,300	
Salaries payable	2,000	
Taxes payable	3,400	
Total current liabilities		$ 29,700
Long-term liabilities		
Bank loan payable		20,000
Total liabilities		$ 49,700
Stockholders' equity		
Capital stock	$ 40,000	
Retained earnings	93,000	
Total stockholders' equity		133,000
Total liabilities & stockholders' equity		$182,700

DP-3

(a) Wages paid during 19X1 $82,000
     Wages owed at end of 19X1   3,700
     Total wage expense $85,700

(b) Dec. 31 Wages Expense   3,700
                 Wages Payable   3,700
              Adjusting entry

         31   Income Summary   85,700
                 Wages Expense   85,700
              To close Wages Expense

(c) Jan. 1   Wages Payable   3,700
                 Wages Expense   3,700
              Reversing entry

(d) Jan. 7   Wages Expense   6,300
                 Cash   6,300
              Paid wages

CHAPTER 5

ACCOUNTING/REPORTING FOR MERCHANDISING OPERATIONS

LEARNING OBJECTIVES

After studying this chapter, you should be able to:

1. Account for typical transactions of sellers and buyers of merchandise.

2. Compare and contrast the gross and net methods of accounting for purchases.

3. Compute cost of goods sold and gross profit, and prepare the financial statements and work sheet for a merchandising concern.

4. Prepare the closing entries for a merchandising enterprise.

5. Distinquish between single- and multiple-step income statements.

CHAPTER HIGHLIGHTS

I. **MEASURING MERCHANDISING INCOME** and reporting it on the income statement involves the computation and presentation of an amount called gross profit. Gross profit is the difference between sales and cost of goods sold, and is reported on the income statement as an intermediate amount:

Sales	$90,000
Cost of goods sold	60,000
GROSS PROFIT	$30,000
Operating expense	5,000
Net income	$25,000

A. The **SALES** account is a **REVENUE** account used strictly for recording cash and credit sales of merchandise.

1. If a customer returns merchandise, the preferred accounting method (rather than canceling the sale in the accounts) is to debit **SALES RETURNS AND ALLOWANCES** and credit Accounts Receivable (if the sale was on account) or Cash (if a cash refund is granted). The Sales Returns and Allowances account is a contra-revenue account that is deducted from sales; sales less sales returns and allowances is sometimes called "net sales":

```
              SALES                              $90,000
              LESS: RETURNS & ALLOWANCES           2,000
              NET SALES                          $88,000
              Cost of goods sold                  60,000
              Gross profit                       $28,000
              Operating expense                    5,000
              Net income                         $23,000
```

Importantly, this presentation reveals information about the relative level of returns and provides a measure of customer satisfaction or dissatisfaction. Sales returns (on account) are typically documented by the creation of an instrument known as a credit memorandum. The credit memorandum indicates that a customer's account receivable balance has been credited (reduced), and that payment for the returned goods is not expected.

2. Various types of discounts are extended to customers, **TRADE DISCOUNTS** being one example. A trade discount is a percentage reduction from the catalog or list price. Ultimately, the purchaser is responsible for the invoice price, that is, the list price less the applicable trade discount. Trade discounts are not entered in the accounting records (i.e., the amount recorded as a sale is the invoice price).

3. **CASH DISCOUNTS** are another type of discount (from the seller's viewpoint, cash discounts are known as sales discounts). Cash discounts are expressed in a unique manner, such as 2/10, n/30 -- which means that a 2% discount (from invoice price) is available if the invoice is paid within 10 days, otherwise the net amount is expected to be paid within 30 days. The appropriate journal entries to record a $100 sale on account, terms 2/10, n/30, follow:

    On the date of sale:

    Accounts Receivable   100
        Sales   100
    Sale on account, terms 2/10, n/30

    If the customer pays in time to take the discount:

    Cash   98
    Sales Discounts   2
        Accounts Receivable   100
    Collection on account; discount taken

    If the customer does not take the discount:

    Cash   100
        Accounts Receivable   100
    Collection on account; discount missed

Sales discounts is another contra-revenue account, and is deducted from sales to arrive at net sales on the income statement.

B. The cost of units sold to customers during an accounting period is deducted from sales and is appropriately termed **COST OF GOODS SOLD**. Cost of goods sold is computed by adding beginning inventory and net purchases (resulting in a subtotal known as goods available for sale), and subtracting ending inventory.

Sales		$90,000
COST OF GOODS SOLD		
BEGINNING INVENTORY	$10,000	
ADD: NET PURCHASES	70,000	
GOODS AVAILABLE FOR SALE	$80,000	
LESS: ENDING INVENTORY	20,000	
COST OF GOODS SOLD		60,000
Gross Profit		$30,000
Operating expense		5,000
Net income		$25,000

C. **ACCOUNTING FOR MERCHANDISE ACQUISITIONS** begins with the recording of purchases. Specifically, the Purchases account is debited and Cash or Accounts Payable is credited. The Purchases account is used strictly for purchases of merchandise.

    1. **PURCHASES RETURNS AND ALLOWANCES** are handled similar to sales returns and allowances. When purchased merchandise is returned to a supplier a debit memorandum is prepared. The debit memorandum indicates that the purchaser is debiting their Accounts Payable account; the corresponding credit is to Purchases Returns and Allowances. Purchases returns and allowances are subtracted from purchases to calculate the amount of net purchases for a period.

    2. Cash discounts (called **PURCHASES DISCOUNTS** from the purchaser's perspective) must again be considered. Discounts (like 2/10, n/30) are typically very favorable to the purchaser, as they are designed to encourage early payment.

        a. The purchaser may account for purchases discounts using the **GROSS METHOD**. With this method, the initial purchase is recorded at invoice amount. Subsequent journal entries depend on the taking of the discount:

On the date of purchase:

Purchases	100	
Accounts Payable		100

Purchase on account, terms 2/10, n/30

If payment occurs within the discount period:

Accounts Payable	100	
Purchases Discounts		2
Cash		98

Paid on account; discount taken

If the discount is lost due to late payment:

Accounts Payable	100	
Cash		100

Paid on account; discount missed

b. In the alternative, the **NET METHOD** can be utilized. With this method, the initial purchase is recorded by debiting Purchases and crediting Accounts Payable for the amount of the purchase less the available discount. Subsequent journal entries depend on the taking of the discount:

On the date of purchase:

Purchases	98	
Accounts Payable		98

Purchase on account, terms 2/10, n/30

If payment occurs within the discount period:

Accounts Payable	98	
Cash		98

Paid on account; discount taken

If the discount is lost due to late payment:

Accounts Payable	98	
Purchases Discounts Lost	2	
Cash		100

Paid on account; discount missed

In evaluating the gross and net methods, notice that the Purchases Discounts Lost account (used only with the net method) indicates the total amount of discounts missed during a particular period. The presence of this account draws attention to the fact that discounts are not being taken; frequently an unfavorable situation. The Purchases Discounts account (used only with the gross method) identifies the amount of discounts taken, but does not indicate if any discounts were missed. For reporting purposes, purchases discounts are subtracted from purchases to arrive at net purchases, while purchases discounts lost are recorded as an expense of the particular period.

3. **FREIGHT CHARGES** are a significant cost related to the purchase of merchandise. The party responsible for paying freight charges (i.e., the purchaser or seller) is a negotiated term of the sale, and may be determined by reference to the F.O.B. terms ("free on board"). If goods are sold F.O.B. shipping point, the purchaser is responsible for paying freight costs incurred in transporting the merchandise from the point of shipment to its destination. F.O.B. destination means that the seller is responsible for costs incurred in moving the goods to their desired destination.

   a. Freight cost incurred by a purchaser is called **FREIGHT-IN, AND** is added to purchases in calculating net purchases. Freight cost incurred by the seller is called **FREIGHT-OUT**, and is reported as a selling expense which is subtracted from gross profit in calculating net income. Note that the party responsible for freight charges may not be the party which initially pays the freight bill. Imagine, for example, that goods are shipped F.O.B. shipping point; the seller might prepay the trucking company as an accommodation to the purchaser. This prepaid freight would increase the accounts receivable of the seller. That is, the seller would expect payment for the merchandise and a reimbursement for the freight. The purchaser would record this transaction by debiting Purchases for the amount of the purchase, debiting Freight-In for the amount of the freight, and crediting Accounts Payable for the combined amount due to the seller.

II. There are several ways to maintain **INVENTORY ACCOUNTING** records. At this point, the text is based on a periodic inventory system. With the periodic system, purchases are recorded in the Purchases account and the Inventory account is not updated as purchases and sales occur. At the end of the accounting period, the Inventory account must be updated to reflect the proper amount of goods owned by the firm. An alternative system is the perpetual system. The perpetual system maintains a continuous accounting for units in stock. As purchases and sales occur the Inventory account is increased and decreased; no purchases account is used. A more detailed presentation of the perpetual system is presented in a subsequent chapter.

III. The **FINANCIAL STATEMENTS OF A MERCHANDISING CONCERN** are similar to the financial statements presented in earlier chapters. However, there are several noteworthy modifications.

   A. The **INCOME STATEMENT** includes unique components related to net sales, cost of goods sold (including the computation of net purchases), gross profit, various operating expenses, and net income. A comprehensive example is presented in the text.

   B. The **STATEMENT OF RETAINED EARNINGS** for a merchandising business is identical to that presented in earlier chapters for a service business.

   C. The **BALANCE SHEET** of a merchandising business is also similar to that of a service business. However, an important addition is the Inventory account. Inventory is an asset which would be shown in the current asset section of the balance sheet.

IV. **GOING BEHIND THE SCENES: THE WORK SHEET** can be prepared for a merchandising concern just as it can for a service business. Several different (but similar) formats can be ued to prepare this work sheet -- the text focuses on the closing entry method. The text includes an example of a work sheet prepared by the closing entry method; it appears very similar to that presented in the previous chapter. The distinguishing characteristic of this work sheet is the inclusion in the adjusted trial balance of amounts related to merchandising activities: sales, sales discounts, sales returns and allowances, purchases, freight-in, purchases discounts, purchases returns and allowances, freight-out, and inventory (beginning balance). Notice that each of these accounts is extended from the adjusted trial balance columns to the income statement columns of the work sheet. In addition, ending inventory is entered as a credit in the income statement columns and a debit in the balance sheet columns. This configuration results in a net credit to the income statement columns for the amount of net sales (i.e., a credit for sales and debits for sales discounts and sales returns and allowances), and a net debit for the amount of cost of goods sold (i.e., debits for beginning inventory, purchases, and freight-in, and credits for purchases discounts, purchases returns and allowances, and ending inventory -- this equates to the familiar computation for cost of goods sold: beginning inventory plus net purchases minus ending inventory). Also, freight-out is extended as a debit (an expense). Note that the debit to the balance sheet columns for the correct amount of ending inventory provides the proper valuation for preparing the balance sheet as of the end of the period. All other work sheet procedures are identical to those presented in the earlier chapter.

- A. The preparation of **ADJUSTING ENTRIES** for merchandising firms is performed in a manner similar to that presented in the previous chapter.

- B. **CLOSING ENTRIES** involve debiting Income Summary and crediting accounts included in the income statement columns of the work sheet with debit balances. Next, accounts from the income statement column with credit balances are debited, with a corresponding credit to Income Summary. Importantly, note that the beginning amount of inventory is closed to Income Summary (by debiting Income Summary and crediting Inventory) and the amount of inventory on hand at the end of the period is established in the accounts (by debiting Inventory and crediting Income Summary). After performing the aforementioned procedures, the balance of the Income Summary account is the net income (credit) or net loss (debit) for the period. As a final closing step, recall that the balances of the Income Summary and Dividends account are closed to the Retained Earnings account.

V. The procedures for **INCOME REPORTING** reveal that the income statement can take various formats.

- A. **SINGLE- AND MULTIPLE-STEP STATEMENTS** are two of the more popular approaches. Under the single-step approach, one section is established for all revenues, another section for all costs and expenses. The difference between the two sections is, of course, income before taxes. From this amount, taxes are subtracted to arrive at net earnings. Other businesses use a multiple-step approach in which accounts are presented by association. This reveals important relationships. For example, cost of goods sold is subtracted from net sales to arrive at gross profit. Operating expenses are subtracted from gross profit to arrive at income from operations. Income from operations is then increased or decreased by other revenues, expenses, and income taxes. The text includes a detailed example of a multiple-step income statement. In general, the single-step income statement is thought to be easier to understand, while the multiple-step approach is believed to enhance disclosure by revealing important subtotals.

  1. The operating expenses on a multiple-step income statement are frequently subdivided into **SELLING AND ADMINISTRATIVE EXPENSES**. Selling expenses are those associated with the sale of merchandise; administrative costs are incurred in the management of the business.

2. The **OTHER REVENUES AND EXPENSES** not related to normal business activity are normally shown as a separate nonoperating category on the multiple-step income statement.

    a. **GAINS AND LOSSES** impact profitability and are therefore disclosed on the income statement. They are typically disclosed as a separate line item rather than being merged with other revenues.

3. Since **INCOME TAX EXPENSE** is dependent on the amount of net income, it is typically reported separately, as a deduction from income before tax.

CLASS NOTES

CLASS NOTES

CLASS NOTES

CLASS NOTES

CLASS NOTES

SELF TESTS

FULFILLMENT OF LEARNING OBJECTIVES

Circle the appropriate response.

L.O. 1(a)   Sales returns and allowances should be recorded by:

         debiting Sales Returns and Allowances
         or
         debiting Sales

L.O. 1(b)   Which of the following types of discounts would be recorded in a Sales Discounts account?

         trade discounts   or   cash discounts

L.O..1(c)   Sales returns and allowances and sales discounts are known as:

         contra-revenue accounts   or   expense accounts

L.O. 1(d)   Under which of the following terms would the purchaser be responsible for freight charges?

         F.O.B. destination   or   F.O.B. shipping point

L.O. 1(e)   Who would initially pay the freight charges under the following terms: F.O.B. shipping point, freight prepaid?

         buyer   or   seller

L.O. 2 (a)   The Purchases Discounts Lost account would be utilized under the:

         gross method   or   net method

L.O. 2 (b)   If the gross method is utilized to record purchases and available cash discounts are taken, how many accounts would be affected by the appropriate journal entry to record payment of the invoice?

         two   or   three

L.O. 3(a)   Beginning inventory plus net purchases equals:

         goods available for sale   or   cost of goods sold

L.O. 3(b)   Net purchases equals gross purchases plus freight-in minus purchase discounts and purchase returns and allowances.

         true   or   false

L.O. 3(c) The total cost of goods available for sale should be allocated to:

cost of goods sold and ending inventory
or
gross profit

L.O. 3(d) The amount of ending inventory on a work sheet for a merchandising concern that uses the closing entry method should be entered in the:

credit column of the income statement columns
or
credit column of the balance sheet columns

L.O. 3(e) If the closing entry method is used, the amount of beginning inventory can be found in the debit column of the adjusted trial balance columns of the work sheet.

true or false

L.O. 4(a) Sales Discounts and Sales Returns and Allowances are credited, and Purchases Discounts and Purchases Returns and Allowances are debited as part of the closing process.

true or false

L.O. 4(b) The net amount of debits and credits in the Income Summary account is closed to the Retained Earnings account.

true or false

L.O. 5(a) Which of the following income statement formats is justified on the grounds of simplicity and ease of understanding?

single-step approach or multiple-step approach

L.O. 5(b) Gross profit and income from operations are important subtotals on a multiple-step income statement.

correct or incorrect

FILL IN THE BLANKS

1. Goods acquired by a retailer for resale to others is called _____ _____.

2. The _____ account is used strictly to record revenues that relate to cash and credit sales of merchandise.

3. Once a return or allowance is authorized, the seller documents the transaction on a form known as a _____ _____.

4. The Sales Returns and Allowances account and the Sales Discount account are known as _____ revenue accounts.

5. List price minus trade discounts equals _____ _____.

6. A _____ _____ might be expressed as 2/10, n/30.

7. Beginning inventory plus net _____ equals _____ _____ _____ _____. The later amount less _____ _____ equals cost of goods sold. Sales minus cost of goods sold equals _____ _____.

8. _____ and _____ are caused by factors such as arrival of merchandise in damaged condition, late arrival of ordered goods, and receipt of goods not ordered.

9. The _____ _____ account is unique to the gross method of recording purchases (in contrast to the net method).

10. Under the net method of recording purchases, a missed discount would be recorded to the Purchases Discounts Lost account with a _____ at the time of _____.

11. If the buyer is to incur all freight charges, the terms are F.O.B. _____ _____.

12. An inventory system which maintains up-to-date account balances for inventory at all times is termed a _____ system.

13. Using the closing entry method, the amount of ending inventory on a work sheet for a merchandising concern is entered in the _____ column of the income statement columns and the _____ column of the balance sheet columns.

14. An income statement approach which presents accounts by association (i.e., sales and cost of goods sold, etc.) is termed the _____-_____ format.

15. _____ expenses are those associated with the sale of merchandise, and _____ expenses are those pertaining to management of the business.

MULTIPLE CHOICE QUESTIONS

Circle the appropriate response.

1. The Sales account and Purchases account should include:

   a. only cash sales and cash purchases of merchandise.
   b. only credit sales and credit purchases of merchandise.
   c. both cash and credit sales and cash and credit purchases of merchandise.
   d. not only merchandise transactions, but also purchases and sales of other assets used in the business.

2. Purchasers of merchandise may be dissatisfied with the quality of goods purchased on account, and return the goods to the seller with an indication that payment will not be forthcoming. In such case, the document prepared by the purchaser is called:

   a. a debit memorandum.
   b. a credit memorandum.
   c. a receiving report.
   d. an invoice.

3. Bergstrom accepted the return of merchandise by a customer. The merchandise had been sold on account, and payment had not been received on the date of return. The returned goods retailed for $400, but cost Bergstrom only $300. The appropriate journal entry for Bergstrom is:

   a. Accounts Receivable   400
          Sales Returns & Allowances   400
   b. Sales Returns & Allowances   400
          Accounts Receivable   400
   c. Sales   400
          Purchases   300
          Accounts Receivable   100
   d. Sales Returns & Allowances   400
          Purchases   300
          Accounts Receivable   100

4. Which of the following statements is true?

   a. Cash discounts are used to reduce the invoice price below the stated list price.
   b. The expression 2/30, n/60, means that a 2% cash discount is available if the invoice is paid within 30 to 60 days.
   c. Cash discounts may not be used in conjunction with trade discounts.
   d. Cash discounts normally apply to the invoice price of the merchandise, excluding freight charges.

5. Lux had net purchases of $50,000, ending inventory of $25,000, net sales of $100,000, and gross profit of $32,000. How much was Lux's beginning inventory?

   a. $7,000
   b. $43,000
   c. $93,000
   d. $143,000

6. On February 1, Crown Company purchased $2,000 of merchandise, terms 2/10, n/30. Crown uses the gross method of recording purchases. Payment of the accounts payable was made on February 26. Which of the following journal entries is appropriate for the February 26 transaction?

    a. Purchases   2,000
        Accounts Payable   2,000
    b. Accounts Payable   1,960
        Cash   1,960
    c. Accounts Payable   1,960
        Purchases Discounts Lost   40
        Cash   2,000
    d. Accounts Payable   2,000
        Cash   2,000

7. On March 1, Zekew Company purchased $1,000 of merchandise, terms 1/10, n/30. Zekew uses the net method of recording purchases. Payment of the accounts payable was made on March 4. Which of the following journal entries is appropriate for the March 4 transaction?

    a. Purchases   990
        Cash   990
    b. Accounts Payable   990
        Cash   990
    c. Accounts Payable   1,000
        Purchases Discounts   10
        Cash   990
    d. Accounts Payable   1,000
        Cash   1,000

8. The work sheet of a merchandising concern (which uses the closing entry method) would include a separate line item for which of the following accounts?

    a. Purchases
    b. Income Summary
    c. Cost of Goods Sold
    d. Ending Retained Earnings

9. A multiple-step income statement is thought to be more beneficial to financial statement users because of the revelation of important relationships. Which of the following is not separately identified on a multiple-step income statement?

    a. Gross profit
    b. Net income
    c. Income taxes
    d. Total costs and expenses

10. Dodd Company utilizes the closing entry method for its periodic inventory accounting system. Dodd had beginning inventory of $59,000, ending inventory of $37,000, and net purchases of $123,000. Which of the following accounts should be debited by Dodd at the end of its accounting year?

   a. Purchases, for $123,000
   b. Inventory, for $59,000
   c. Inventory, for $37,000
   d. All of the above

DEMONSTRATION PROBLEMS

DP-1   Hamilton Corporation purchased $5,000 of merchandise on account on May 1, terms 3/10, n/40.

    a.   Assuming that Hamilton uses the gross method of recording purchases, prepare journal entries to record:
        (1)   The purchase on May 1.
        (2)   Payment, if payment occurs on May 5.
        (3)   Payment, if payment occurs on May 30.

    b.   Repeat part (a), assuming that Hamilton uses the net method of recording purchases.

DP-2   Power Source Software Store provides information about the following merchandise purchases:

Purchase 1: $1,500 gross purchase; $100 returned within three days; F.O.B. shipping point; terms 2/10, n/30; freight of $50 was prepaid by the seller; payment of the invoice occurred 26 days from the date of purchase

Purchase 2: $3,000 gross purchase; F.O.B. destination; terms 1/20, n/60; freight of $10 was paid by the seller; payment of the invoice occurred 11 days from the date of purchase

Purchase 3: $9,500 gross purchase; F.O.B. destination; terms 2/10, n/30; freight of $100 was collected from Power Source Software Store at the time of delivery; payment of the invoice occurred 5 days from the date of purchase

Determine the amount of cash Power Source Software Store paid to the seller for each of the three purchases.

DP-3 Larry Otis, manager of Payless Outlet Store, provided the following information:

Purchases	$123,600
Salary expense	35,700
Freight-out	600
Freight-in	1,200
Rent expense	13,000
Utilities expense	4,100
Sales discounts	800
Merchandise inventory, Jan. 1	45,000
Merchandise inventory, Dec. 31	37,400
Sales	293,400

Prepare an abbreviated multiple-step income statement for Payless Outlet Store, and prepare all end-of-period adjusting and closing entries which would impact the Income Summary account using the closing entry method.

SOLUTIONS TO SELF TESTS

FULFILLMENT OF LEARNING OBJECTIVES

1(a) Debiting Sales Returns and Allowances
1(b) Cash discounts
1(c) Contra-revenue accounts
1(d) F.O.B. shipping point
1(e) Seller
2(a) Net method
2(b) Three
3(a) Goods available for sale
3(b) True
3(c) Cost of goods sold and ending inventory
3(d) Credit column of the income statement columns
3(e) True
4(a) True
4(b) True
5(a) Single-step approach
5(b) Correct

FILL IN THE BLANKS

1. Merchandise inventory
2. Sales
3. Credit memorandum
4. Contra-
5. Invoice price
6. Cash discount
7. Purchases, goods available for sale, ending inventory, gross profit
8. Returns, allowances
9. Purchases Discounts
10. Debit, payment
11. Shipping point
12. Perpetual
13. Credit, debit
14. Multiple-step
15. Selling, administrative

MULTIPLE CHOICE QUESTIONS

1. c. The Sales and Purchases accounts are used strictly for cash and credit sales and purchases of merchandise.

2. a. The purchaser prepares a debit memorandum to indicate that they are "debiting" their Accounts Payable; this means that they don't intend to pay for the returned goods. Credit memorandums are prepared by sellers of merchandise; indicating that the seller does not expect payment for returned items (i.e., crediting Accounts Receivable). A receiving report is prepared by a purchaser to document the receipt of ordered goods and an invoice is a document prepared by a seller to inform the purchaser of the amount due for a particular transaction (i.e., a bill).

3. b. To record the acceptance of returned goods requires an increase in Sales Returns and Allowances (a contra-revenue account which is increased with a debit) and a reduction of Accounts Receivable (credit). The Purchases account is not impacted.

4. d. Cash discounts are generally not available on freight. Trade discounts are used to reduce the invoice price below the stated list price. The expression 2/30, n/60, means that a 2% discount is available if the invoice is paid within 30 days, otherwise the net amount is due within 60 days. A single transaction may involve both cash and trade discounts.

5. b. Sales - cost of goods sold = gross profit;
$100,000 - cost of goods sold = $32,000;
Cost of goods sold = $68,000

Goods available for sale - ending inventory = cost of goods sold;
Goods available for sale - $25,000 = $68,000;
Goods available for sale = $93,000

Beginning inventory + purchases = goods available for sale;
Beginning inventory + $50,000 = $93,000;
Beginning inventory = $43,000

6. d. The payment of the invoice did not occur within the discount period. Therefore, $2,000 of cash was disbursed in settlement of the accounts payable. The accounts payable was originally established at its $2,000 gross amount. Choice "b" is the correct entry if payment had been made within the discount period and the net method was utilized. Choice "c" is the correct entry if payment had been made outside the discount period and the net method was utilized. Choice "a" is the correct entry to record the purchase on February 1 (using the gross method).

7. b. The payment of the invoice was within the discount period. Therefore, $990 of cash was disbursed in settlement of the accounts payable. The accounts payable was originally established at its $990 net amount. Choice "c" is the correct entry if payment had been made within the discount period and the gross method was utilized. Choice "d" is the correct entry if payment had been made outside the discount period and the gross method was utilized. Choice "a" is the correct entry if the purchase was a cash purchase with a 1% discount from invoice.

8. a. Purchases is an account included in the work sheet. Income Summary arises in the closing process, and is not listed in the work sheet. Cost of goods sold can be calculated from information in the work sheet, but is not listed separately. The work sheet includes retained earnings before income and dividends -- not the ending balance.

9. d. Because of the reporting of expenses according to their nature (i.e., cost of goods sold, selling and administrative expenses, other expenses, etc.) a single total for all expenses cannot be separately identified (as might be the case with a single-step presentation). Gross profit, net income, and income taxes are each listed separately in a multiple-step presentation.

10. c. Part of the end-of-period entries is to establish the ending balance of the Inventory account (by debiting Inventory and crediting Income Summary); choice "c" is the appropriate entry to accomplish this objective. Choice "b" is backwards -- the beginning inventory needs to be removed from the accounts by crediting Inventory and debiting Income Summary. Purchases is closed by crediting the account, and debiting Income Summary; therefore, "a" is not correct.

DEMONSTRATION PROBLEMS

DP-1

(a) May 1 Purchases   5,000
              Accounts Payable   5,000
           Purchased merchandise on account

    5   Accounts Payable   5,000
              Purchases Discounts   150
              Cash   4,850
           Paid on account; discount taken

    30   Accounts Payable   5,000
              Cash   5,000
           Paid on account; discount missed

(b) May 1 Purchases   4,850
              Accounts Payable   4,850
           Purchased merchandise on account

    5   Accounts Payable   4,850
              Cash   4,850
           Paid on account; discount taken

    30   Accounts Payable   4,850
           Purchases Discounts Lost   150
              Cash   5,000
           Paid on account; discount missed

DP-2

(1) $1,500 - $100 = $1,400; $1,400 + $50 = $1,450 payment

(2) $3,000 - ($3,000 X 1%) = $2,970 payment

(3) $9,500 - ($9,500 X 2%) = $9,310; $9,310 - $100 (seller's freight cost paid by Power Source Software Store) = $9,210 payment

DP-3

PAYLESS OUTLET STORE
INCOME STATEMENT
FOR THE YEAR ENDED DECEMBER 31, 19XX

Revenues			
Sales			$293,400
Less: Sales discounts			800
Net sales			$292,600
Cost of goods sold			
Beginning inventory		$ 45,000	
Add: Purchases	$123,600		
Freight-in	1,200	124,800	
Goods available for sale		$169,800	
Less: Ending inventory		37,400	
Cost of goods sold			132,400
Gross profit			$160,200
Expenses			
Rent expense		$ 13,000	
Salaries expense		35,700	
Freight-out		600	
Utilities expense		4,100	
Total expenses			53,400
Net income			$106,800

Dec.	31	Income Summary	224,000	
		Inventory		45,000
		Sales Discounts		800
		Purchases		123,600
		Freight-in		1,200
		Rent Expense		13,000
		Salaries Expense		35,700
		Freight-out		600
		Utilities Expense		4,100
		To remove beginning inventory and close income statement accounts having debit balances		
	31	Inventory	37,400	
		Sales	293,400	
		Income Summary		330,800
		To record ending inventory and close income statement accounts having credit balances		
	31	Income Summary	106,800	
		Retained Earnings		106,800
		To close Income Summary		

CHAPTER 6

ACCOUNTING SYSTEMS AND INTERNAL CONTROL

LEARNING OBJECTIVES

After studying this chapter, you should be able to:

1   Appreciate the role and importance of a good accounting system.

2   Explain the relationship between control accounts and subsidiary ledgers.

3   Recognize the features of a typical microcomputer-based accounting software package.

4   Describe the tasks performed by the general ledger, accounts receivable, and accounts payable modules.

5   Explain the nature of internal control and identify various internal control procedures.

CHAPTER HIGHLIGHTS

I. A good accounting system generates information for reporting, planning, controlling, and decision-making activities. This information is developed by processing data (facts, figures, transactions, and so forth) into a usable format. A firm's **TRANSACTION PROCESSING** ability is likely to be adversely impacted by growth unless system refinements are made.

   A. **SYSTEM REFINEMENTS** can take many forms, from the simple to the elaborate, with computers likely playing a major role. However, even in a manual accounting environment certain improvements (to the basic accounting system introduced in earlier chapters) must occur.

   1. Whenever a firm sells or buys on account, the basic accounting system should be enriched to include **SUBSIDIARY LEDGERS AND CONTROL ACCOUNTS**. Consider that the recording of a sale on account requires a debit to Accounts Receivable (and a purchase on account requires a credit to Accounts Payable), thereby maintaining a ledger account for the total of all receivables (and payables). But, how can the amount due from a specific customer (or due to a specific supplier) be determined? Additional records, called subsidiary ledger accounts, provide the answer. The main general ledger accounts related to receivables and payables are called the control accounts; the additional set of records maintained for each customer or supplier are the subsidiary accounts. The subsidiary accounts are not part of the general ledger, financial statements, or trial balances. To explain, whenever a debit or credit is recorded to Accounts Receivable or Accounts Payable, a like amount should be

entered in the subsidiary account of the specific customer or supplier. In this way, the control accounts maintain a balance equal to the total receivables and payables, while the subsidiary accounts provide information about amounts due to or from specific parties (note that the combined balances of all the individual subsidiary accounts should equal the corresponding control account balance). The text includes a graphic demonstration of the relationships between subsidiary and control accounts.

2. As growth occurs and more information is desired, companies must seek other forms of **PROCESSING REDUCTION IN A MANUAL SYSTEM**. Techniques for reducing the tedium include such simple things as carbon paper (a system whereby the preparation of a document simultaneously updates other underlying accounting records), and other more involved elements such as the utilization of special journals.

3. **SPECIAL JOURNALS** handle specific types of recurring transactions in ways that significantly decrease recording and posting procedures. Special journals are sometimes used for sales of merchandise on account, purchases of merchandise on account, cash receipts, and cash disbursements. Appendix B of the text provides a detailed look at the operation of a manually maintained special journal system.

II. Rapid advances in computer technology have ushered in an era where **COMPUTERIZED ACCOUNTING SYSTEMS** are rapidly replacing traditional manual systems. Low cost software is readily available for most accounting tasks, although many users still find it necessary to develop customized applications.

   A. For the most part, the **FEATURES OF MICROCOMPUTER SYSTEM SOFTWARE** tend to parallel the function and objective of manual accounting systems. Both types of systems process transactions by using debits and credits, maintain ledger accounts, and produce financial statements. However, a computerized system replaces the traditional journals and ledgers with files and records maintained on a storage medium. Tasks such as posting, preparing reports, and report generation are fully automated.

   B. Another characteristic of computerized systems is **THE CONCEPT OF MODULAR ACCOUNTING**. Specific tasks are grouped and processed in the most efficient manner. For instance, sales on account may be processed through a specialized module that requests information peculiar to a sale on account (amount of sale, customer information, etc.). It is likely that the computer operator will merely respond to information requests, rather than preparing the traditional debit/credit journal entry; the computer program is conditioned to translate the input to processable form. Modules also facilitate division of accounting tasks among different individuals, and lead to greater efficiency by grouping like activities.

      1. The modules in a microcomputer accounting system are accessed via the main menu. The main menu provides a listing of available processing modules. **ACCESSING THE** specific **MODULES** requires selecting the module of choice and pressing an appropriate key on the keyboard.

      2. The **GENERAL LEDGER MODULE** is at the heart of a computerized accounting system. This module houses the general ledger accounts, and provides the means by which journal entries are entered, posted, and processed into financial statements.

a. Some programs provide **EDIT ROUTINES** that allow changes to be made to previously entered data. Other programs block such changes, and may require a "correcting" entry for any revisions of prior input. The diversity exists because some system managers prefer simplicity; others want a complete documented record of all data entry activity.

b. The general ledger module typically provides for **FINANCIAL STATEMENT/REPORT GENERATION**. These reports are usually printable on either the computer screen or paper. Typical reports include the chart of accounts, general journal, general ledger, trial balance, and financial statements.

c. The **CLOSING ROUTINE** that you learned in previous chapters is highly mechanical, and easily automated. When this routine is invoked, the computer will reset temporary accounts to zero and update Retained Earnings. Because specific transaction data is likely to be lost in the process, the computer usually warns the operator before completion of closing.

3. For many businesses, sales on account constitute a significant portion of business activity. Therefore, they are likely to use a separate **ACCOUNTS RECEIVABLE MODULE** for processing sales and collections on account. In addition to maintaining basic information about sale, the module also facilitates the creation of customer invoices, sales journals, sales reports, cash receipts journals, subsidiary ledgers, monthly statements, and so forth.

4. The **ACCOUNTS PAYABLE MODULE** is similar to the accounts receivable module, except that it is used to process purchase transactions. The module is capable of producing a purchases journal, cash payments journal, subsidiary ledgers, various reports, as well as checks for payment of amounts owed.

C. **ARE COMPUTERIZED SYSTEMS ALWAYS THE ANSWER?** No. Computers are not the answer to all business processing problems. Computers are capable of producing huge amounts of information which can obscure important feedback. In addition, the costs and benefits of office automation must be weighed.

D. Accounting related computer applications are almost endless. **OTHER MICROCOMPUTER APPLICATIONS** include tax return preparation, data base searches (e.g., court cases, tax laws, etc.), statistical sampling applications (for audit purposes), and others. A primary tool used by accountants is the electronic spreadsheet. This tool is helpful because the program is flexible, and allows rapid computation and recomputation of key amounts.

III. **INTERNAL CONTROL** is defined as the various measures adopted by an organization to safeguard its assets, check the reliability and accuracy of accounting information, ensure compliance with management policies, and evaluate operating performance and efficiency.

A. **THE INTERNAL CONTROL STRUCTURE** of a business is dependent on the accounting system, the control environment, and the control procedures. The control environment pertains to the combined effect of a firm's policies and attitudes toward control implementation. Control procedures are specifically integrated into the accounting system and relate to the features noted hereafter.

1. One important control is **LIMITED ACCESS TO ASSETS**. This control feature assures that only authorized and responsible employees can obtain access to key assets. For example, a supplies stock area may be accessible only to department supervisors.

2. **SEPARATION OF DUTIES** is another important control. Activities like transaction authorization, transaction recording, and asset custody should be performed by different employees. Separating functions reduces the possibility of errors (because of cross-checking of accounting records to assets on hand, etc.) and fraud (because of the increased need for collusion among employees).

3. A number of **ACCOUNTABILITY PROCEDURES** can be implemented to improve the degree of internal control.

    a. **DUTY AUTHORIZATION** is a control feature which requires that certain functions be performed by a specific person (e.g., customer returns of merchandise for credit can be approved only by a sales manager).

    b. **PRENUMBERED DOCUMENTS** allow ready identification of missing items. For example, checks are usually prenumbered so that missing checks can be identified rapidly.

    c. Independent **VERIFICATION OF RECORDS** is another control procedure. Examples include comparing cash in a cash register with the sales recorded on that register and periodic reconciliation of bank accounts.

4. A company may engage an accounting firm or CPA to provide an **INDEPENDENT REVIEW** of the company's accounting records and internal controls. The accountant may offer suggestions for improvement and test the established system to determine if it is functioning as planned.

5. In designing and implementing an internal control system, careful attention should be paid to the **COSTS AND BENEFITS** of the system. It is folly to develop a system which costs more to establish and maintain than it is worth to the company.

B. **INTERNAL CONTROLS IN A COMPUTERIZED ENVIRONMENT** must receive special attention. Data are collected, processed, and stored in a way that is not visible to the human eye. As such, problems with record and file management, hard-copy documentation, and the possibility of data alteration or destruction must all be considered.

   1. Computers can be used to to conduct a fraud or embezzlement. The lack of adequate controls may allow a dishonest employee to divert funds or commit other criminal acts. Such **COMPUTER FRAUD** often goes undetected or unreported.

CLASS NOTES

CLASS NOTES

CLASS NOTES

CLASS NOTES

SELF TESTS

FULFILLMENT OF LEARNING OBJECTIVES

Circle the appropriate response.

L.O. 1   The accounting system adopted by a firm should allow for rapid growth, without the need for future refinements or system revisions.

true   or   false

L.O. 2(a)   Which of the following types of accounts would be the fundamental general ledger account?

control account   or   subsidiary account

L.O. 2(b)   The total of individual subsidiary ledger account balances should equal the balance of the corresponding control account.

correct   or   incorrect

L.O. 2(c)   A separate journal entry is needed to record amounts into the subsidiary ledger.

true   or   false

L.O. 3(a)   With a microcomputer accounting system, posting is automated and the closing process is often performed by pressing a single key on a computer's keyboard.

true   or   false

L.O. 3(b)   To streamline the data entry and processing process a computerized accounting system often divides tasks into specific processing:

targets   or   modules

L.O. 4(a)   In a computerized environment, the general ledger routine is the heart of the system. Which general ledger task is most frequently used?

report generation   or   enter/edit entry

L.O. 4(b)   Which specific general ledger task is most likely to erase old data?

edit   or   close

L.O. 4(c)   Different programs have different features. A feature that assists users in locating a previous entry from a data file is facilitated by the assignment of:

windows   or   reference numbers

L.O. 4(d)   Which functional area is most likely to be capable of producing a remittance advice?

accounts receivable   or   accounts payable

L.O. 4(e)   A tool that is especially useful to accountants because it allows rapid recomputation of important figures is the:

electronic spreadsheet   or   telephone data base

L.O. 5(a)   The separation of duties, accountability procedures, and sound personnel practices are all part of a properly designed internal control system.

true   or   false

L.O. 5(b)   Microcomputers reduce the possibility of fraud in an accounting system.

true   or   false

FILL IN THE BLANKS

1. The general ledger account for Accounts Receivable is called the _____ account, and is supported by information about individual customer account balances in the _____ ledger.

2. Meaningful reduction of processing can be achieved in a manual system through the use of _____ journals that handle specific recurring transactions.

3. Accounting data are stored in computers by using _____ (e.g., information about one employee) and _____ (e.g., information about a group of employees).

4. A _____ is a listing on a computer screen of the various program options available to the user.

5. The _____ _____ module is the portion of a typical computerized accounting system that houses the general ledger accounts and facilitates report generation.

6. Specific transaction data is likely to be erased whenever the _____ routine is utilized.

7. Both the _____ journal and the _____ _____ journal are apt to be prepared by the accounts receivable module.

8. To minimize the probability of error occurrence and improve the credibility of financial statements and reports, features known as _____ _____ are built into accounting systems.

9. A company's _____ _____ represents the combined effect of many factors on implementing, evaluating, and improving the effectiveness of specified firm policies.

10. _____ _____ _____ means that incompatible duties like transaction authorization, transaction recording, and asset custody are performed by different employees within an organization.

11. Important forms such as checks, sales invoices, and purchase orders are usually serially _____.

12. An _____ _____ is a computerized work sheet consisting of columns and rows that are filled with report headings, financial data, and computational formulas.

13. _____ _____ involves the use of computers to aid in fraud or embezzlement.

MULTIPLE CHOICE QUESTIONS

Circle the appropriate response.

1. The subsidiary accounts payable ledger accounts should be:

    a. debited for a number of individual amounts totaling the balance of all payments on account.
    b. credited for a number of individual amounts totaling the balance of all merchandise purchases on account.
    c. have an aggregate balance equal to the accounts payable balance in the general ledger.
    d. All of the above.

2. One of the major benefits of special journals is that they:

    a. do away with the need for a general ledger.
    b. reduce the amount of posting that is necessary to process transactions.
    c. do away with the need for financial statements.
    d. incorporate carbon paper to reduce the recording of redundant information.

3. Which of the following characteristics would not be appropriate to describe the rationale for utilization of a microcomputer accounting system?

    a. The reduction of posting errors.
    b. The availability of continuously up-to-date inventory levels and inventory control techniques.
    c. The ability to do "what-if" analysis through electronic spreadsheet software.
    d. The elimination of employee fraud.

4. Which of the following terms is used to describe the various program options available to the user?

    a. Menu
    b. Module
    c. Window
    d. Spreadsheet

5. The general ledger module is at the heart of a computerized accounting system. Which of the following routines is least likely to be included in the general ledger module?

   a. Edit routine
   b. Financial statement preparation routine
   c. Closing routine
   d. Account statement routine

6. Which of the following reports or documents are not likely to be produced in a computerized accounting environment?

   a. General ledger
   b. General journal
   c. Chart of accounts
   d. Work sheet

7. A well designed computerized accounting system should detect an out-of-balance journal entry via:

   a. the preparation of a trial balance.
   b. the rejection of input at the time of data entry.
   c. the preparation of an out of balance financial statement.
   d. the automated closing process.

8. The accounts payable module can be used to produce:

   a. checks.
   b. monthly statements.
   c. the sales journal.
   d. All of the above.

9. Which of the following features is central to the control environment?

   a. Checks and other important documents are prenumbered.
   b. Two signatures are required on checks.
   c. Management's philosophy and operating style.
   d. Approved purchase orders must be on file before accepting delivery of merchandise from a supplier.

10. Which of the following would constitute an internal control weakness?

    a. The company requires use of prenumbered documents.
    b. Preparation of periodic bank reconciliations are performed by employees otherwise unaffiliated with the cash receipt and disbursement process.
    c. Centralization of incompatible duties is required.
    d. Limited access to assets is enforced at all times.

DEMONSTRATION PROBLEMS

DP-1   Morris Manufacturing maintains a subsidiary ledger of the amounts due from individual customers. A review of the accounting records at the end of April revealed the following balances:

Jones	$6,000
Hilcraft	3,500
Manard	1,500
Lorenzo	8,100

- a. How much should appear in the balance sheet for accounts receivable?
- b. Would the subsidiary ledger normally serve as the answer to part (a)? Explain.
- c. What procedure should Morris follow to help ensure that the subsidiary ledger balances are relatively error free?
- d. If a $100 collection on account occurred on May 7, what should Morris do to keep the accounting records in balance?

DP-2　　Imagine that you are providing accounting and consulting services to a client. The client has asked you to:

    a.   explain the advantages of a microcomputer accounting system.
    b.   identify some of the features associated with a good internal control system.

DP-3 Perkin's Packing House uses a computerized accounting system that is identical to that described in the text. The system consists of a general ledger module, accounts receivable module, and accounts payable module. Identify the module that should be used to record the following transactions or accomplish the stated tasks:

a. Collected cash on account from Barbara Martinez, a customer.
b. Prepared checks to various suppliers.
c. Prepared month-end financial statements.
d. Closed the accounting records at the end of the month.
e. Sold goods on account.
f. Prepared customer invoices.
g. Recorded depreciation expense for the month.

SOLUTIONS TO SELF TESTS

FULFILLMENT OF LEARNING OBJECTIVES

1	False
2(a)	Control account
2(b)	Correct
2(c)	False
3(a)	True
3(b)	Modules
4(a)	Enter/edit entry
4(b)	Close
4(c)	Reference numbers
4(d)	Accounts payable
4(e)	Electronic spreadsheet
5(a)	True
5(b)	False

FILL IN THE BLANKS

1. Control, subsidiary
2. Special
3. Records, files
4. Menu
5. General ledger
6. Closing
7. Sales, cash receipts
8. Internal control
9. Control environment
10. Separation of duties
11. Prenumbered
12. Electronic spreadsheet
13. Computer fraud

MULTIPLE CHOICE QUESTIONS

1. d. Each of the characteristics pertain to the subsidiary accounts payable ledger.

2. b. Special journals greatly reduce the amount of posting. General ledgers and financial statements remain an important feature of the accounting system, even if special journals are used. Carbon paper is used in "write it once" type systems, but these systems do not necessarily use special journals.

3. d. Employee fraud is not eliminated by computers. However, computers do reduce posting errors, make continuously up-to-date inventory records available, and allow what-if analysis via electronic spreadsheet software.

4. a. The menu is used to reveal the various program options available. A module is an element of the program that handles a specific component of the overall accounting process. A window is a an overlay screen of additional information that can be accessed at any time. A spreadsheet is a specific type of program that facilitates computations in an organized format.

5. d. An account statement would typically be prepared in the accounts receivable module. The other functions are normally associated with the general ledger module.

6. d. The work sheet is not needed, as the computations normally performed on a work sheet are all performed by the program. However, the other documents are at the core of the accounting system.

7. b. A good program will not accept an out-of-balance entry. If an such entries are systematically blocked, then the trial balance and financial statements will be in balance.

8. a. Checks to vendors are sometimes produced through the accounts payable module. Monthly statements and the sales journal are normally associated with the accounts receivable module.

9. c. Management attitude is the most critical element in a control environment.

10. c. Separation of incompatible duties is a hallmark of good internal control. To centralize incompatible duties invites errors and irregularities into the accounting process. Typical internal control strengths include use of prenumbered documents, preparation of bank reconciliations by employees otherwise unaffiliated with the cash receipt and disbursement process, and limited access to assets.

DEMONSTRATION PROBLEMS

DP-1

(a) $19,100, which is the total of the amounts due from the individual customers.

(b) No. Normally the total due from customers would be determined by reference to the general ledger control account.

(c) Periodically, the total of the subsidiary ledger accounts should be compared to the general ledger control account, and any differences must be resolved.

(d) Morris must record an entry to reduce Accounts Receivable and increase Cash. In addition, the paying customer's subsidiary account must also be reduced.

DP-2

(a) A microcomputer can process large volumes of data quickly and more efficiently than is possible with a manual system. Error reduction is also likely to occur, as (1) the machine is not subject to fatigue or boredom and (2) computerized accounting systems may have controls that examine data validity before transactions are accepted as input.

(b) Limited access to assets, separation of duties, and accountability procedures (e.g., duty authorization, prenumbered documents, and verification of records) are all fundamental control features.

DP-3

(a) Accounts receivable

(b) Accounts payable

(c) General ledger

(d) General ledger

(e) Accounts receivable

(f) Accounts receivable

(g) General ledger

CHAPTER 7

CASH AND SHORT-TERM INVESTMENTS

LEARNING OBJECTIVES

After studying this chapter, you should be able to:

1 Describe the composition of cash and how cash is presented on a balance sheet.

2 Explain cash management and identify the controls and procedures related to cash receipts and disbursements.

3 Reconcile a bank account.

4 Establish and operate a petty cash system.

5 Account for short-term investments under the historical-cost and the lower-of-cost-or-market methods.

CHAPTER HIGHLIGHTS

I. To be included on the balance sheet as **CASH**, an item must be acceptable to a bank for deposit and be free from restrictions (i.e., available for use in satisfying current debts). Cash typically includes coins, currency, funds on deposit with a bank, checks, and money orders. Items like certificates of deposit, postdated checks, IOUs, travel advances, and postage stamps are typically not classified as cash.

   A. The appropriate **BALANCE SHEET PRESENTATION** for cash is in the current asset section (unless special restrictions exist). The existence of compensating balances (amounts that must be left on deposit and cannot be withdrawn) should be disclosed.

   B. **CASH MANAGEMENT** is important to ensure that sufficient cash is available to meet obligations, and to make sure that idle cash is appropriately invested to maximize the return to the company.

   1. **CASH PLANNING** systems consist of those procedures adopted to properly manage cash. A major component of a cash planning system is the cash budget; that is, the overall plan of activity that depicts cash inflows and outflows.

   2. **CASH CONTROL** systems are the procedures adopted to safeguard an organization's funds.

a. **INTERNAL CONTROL FOR CASH** is based on the same general control features introduced in the earlier chapter; access to cash should be limited to a few authorized personnel, incompatible duties should be separated, and accountability features (like prenumbered checks, etc.) should be developed.

b. The control of **RECEIPTS FROM CASH SALES** should begin at the point of sale and continue through to deposit at the bank. Specifically, electronic point-of-sale terminals should be used, actual cash on hand at the end of the day should be compared to amounts calculated by the point-of-sale terminals, and daily bank deposits should be made. Any cash shortages or excesses should be identified and recorded in a Cash Short & Over account.

c. Control of **RECEIPTS FROM CUSTOMERS ON ACCOUNT** begins when payments are received (in the mail or otherwise). The person opening the mail should prepare a listing of checks received and forward the list to the accounting department. The checks are forwarded to a cashier who prepares a daily bank deposit. The accounting department enters the information from the listing of checks into the accounting records, and compares the listing to a copy of the deposit slip prepared by the cashier.

d. The controls over **CASH DISBURSEMENTS** include procedures that allow only authorized payments for actual expenditures and maintenance of proper separation of duties. Control features include requiring that significant disbursements be made by check, performance of periodic bank reconciliations, proper utilization of petty cash systems, and verification of supporting documentation before disbursing funds.

3. Periodic **BANK RECONCILIATIONS** should be performed to assess the accuracy of the Cash account. The reconciliation involves a systematic comparison of the Cash account with the bank statement.

    a. The amount of cash shown on monthly **BANK STATEMENTS** (the documents received from a bank which summarize deposits and other credits, and checks and other debits) **VERSUS** the amount of cash in the general ledger **CASH ACCOUNTS** frequently differ. Some differences are caused by items reflected on company records but not yet recorded by the bank; examples include deposits in transit (a receipt entered on company records but not processed by the bank) and outstanding checks (checks written which have not cleared the bank). Other differences relate to items noted on the bank statement but not recorded by the company; examples include nonsufficient funds (NSF) checks (checks previously deposited but which have been returned for nonpayment), bank service charges, notes collected by the bank, and interest.

b. The following illustration highlights **THE RECONCILIATION PROCESS**:

Ending balance per bank statement	$XXX
Add: Deposits in transit (and similar receipts entered on company records but not yet reported on the bank statement)	XXX
	$XXX
Deduct: Outstanding checks (and similar disbursements entered on company records but not reported on the bank statement)	XXX
Adjusted cash balance: bank	$XXX
Ending balance per company records	$XXX
Add: Interest (and similar receipts reported on the bank statement but not entered on company records)	XXX
	$XXX
Deduct: NSF checks (and similar disbursements reported on the bank statement but not entered on company records)	XXX
Adjusted cash balance: company records	$XXX

In reviewing this example, note that the balance per the bank statement is reconciled to the "correct" amount of cash; likewise, the balance per company records is reconciled to the "correct" amount. Once the correct adjusted cash balance is satisfactorily calculated, journal entries must be prepared for all items identified in the reconciliation of the ending balance per company records to the adjusted cash balance. These entries serve to record the transactions and events which impact cash but have not been previously journalized (e.g., NSF checks, bank service charges, interest income, and so on).

c. The text provides **AN EXAMPLE** of a complete bank reconciliation, and the related discussion demonstrates the appropriate journal entries.

4. A **PETTY CASH** system is a fund established for use in making small payments which are impractical to pay by check. Examples include postage due, reimbursement to employees for purchases of small office supplies, and numerous similar items. The establishment of a petty cash system begins by making out a check to cash, cashing it, and placing the cash in a petty cash box. The journal entry for this activity simply debits Petty Cash and credits Cash.

a. **MAKING DISBURSEMENTS FROM THE FUND** is the responsibility of a petty cash custodian who must obtain a receipt for each cash disbursement. These receipts (also known as petty cash vouchers) are placed in the petty cash box, so that cash in the box plus receipts in the box equals the amount of the petty cash fund (i.e., the amount of cash originally placed in the fund).

b. As expenditures occur, cash in the box will be depleted and must be replenished. **REPLENISHING THE PETTY CASH FUND** involves writing out a check to cash, cashing it, and placing the cash in the petty cash box. At the same time the receipts are removed from the petty cash box and formally recorded as expenses. The journal entry for all of this activity involves debits to appropriate expense accounts as represented by the receipts, and a credit to Cash for the amount of the replenishment. Notice that the Petty Cash account is not impacted -- it was originally established as a base amount and its balance has not been changed by virtue of this activity.

c. **ERRORS IN THE PETTY CASH FUND** will occur. That is, receipts plus cash on hand will not always equal the base amount established for the petty cash fund. In this event, the journal entry to record full replenishment may require an additional debit (for shortages) or credit (for overages) to Cash Short & Over.

II. **SHORT-TERM INVESTMENTS** (sometimes called marketable securities) include investments in stock of corporations, certificates of deposit, treasury securities, and so forth. To be reported as a short-term investment in the current asset section of the balance sheet, these items must be readily salable, and acquired with the intent to convert them into cash within the operating cycle or one year, whichever is longer.

A. Accounting for all short-term investments begins by **RECORDING** them at their **INITIAL COST** (which includes transaction costs like brokerage commissions), **AND** the subsequent accounting for **CHANGES IN VALUE** depends on the method selected.

1. One method of accounting typically used for short-term investments in debt securities is the **HISTORICAL-COST METHOD**. With this method, the investment is maintained in the accounting records at cost, and changes in value are ignored (except for possible disclosure via notes to the financial statements). Earnings on these investments (e.g., interest received) is reported as revenue.

2. Another technique to account for short-term investments is the **LOWER-OF-COST-OR-MARKET METHOD**. Investments are entered in the accounting records at cost, and the short-term investments portfolio is subsequently reported on the balance sheet at the lower of aggregate cost or aggregate market value. Decreases in the aggregate market value of a short-term investment portfolio below aggregate cost are reported as losses, and recoveries of previously recognized declines in aggregate market value are reported as revenue. Note that a portfolio of investments is never reported at more than its aggregate cost, and the amount of revenue from a recovery cannot exceed previously recognized losses. Any dividends received are reported as dividend revenue.

a. The journal entry to record **DECLINES IN MARKET VALUE** involves a debit to Unrealized Loss on Short-term Investments and a credit to Allowance for Decline in Market Value of Short-term Investments. The Unrealized Loss account is reported as a loss on the income statement, while the Allowance account is a contra-asset account. On the face of the balance sheet, the short-term investments would be reported as follows:

Current assets
 Short-term investments in stock $50,000
 Less: Allowance for decline in market
  value of short-term investments   3,000
 Short-term investments at the lower of
  cost or market $47,000

In this manner, a financial statement user can readily assess not only the cost of the investments, but also the current market value.

 b. **RECORDING RECOVERIES** simply involves a debit to the Allowance account and a credit to Recovery in Value of Short-term Investments. If a recovery in market value causes fair value to equal or exceed the cost of the portfolio, then the Allowance account would be "zeroed" out and the investments would be reported as follows:

Current assets
 Short-term investments in stock $50,000

Otherwise, the investments would be presented net of whatever balance still remained in the Allowance account (as shown in IIA2a of this outline). The Recovery account is reported as a gain or revenue item within the income statement for the period when the recovery occurred.

 c. **JUSTIFICATION FOR LOWER OF COST OR MARKET** is based on the accounting convention of conservatism, which holds that measurement practices be employed that are least likely to overstate assets and/or income.

B. The **SALE OF STOCK INVESTMENTS** is accounted for by comparing original cost to sales price, with the difference representing a gain or loss. Lower-of-cost-or-market considerations are ignored (because they are applied only to the aggregate portfolio at the end of each period).

CLASS NOTES

CLASS NOTES

CLASS NOTES

CLASS NOTES

CLASS NOTES

SELF TESTS

FULFILLMENT OF LEARNING OBJECTIVES

Circle the appropriate response.

L.O. 1(a)   The items reported in the Cash account on the balance sheet must be acceptable to a bank for deposit and free from restrictions for use in satisfying current debts.

true   or   false

L.O. 1(b)   The Cash account is listed on the balance sheet in the current asset section, and all cash items are normally combined and reported as a single figure.

correct   or   incorrect

L.O. 2(a)   A cash shortage identified by comparing cash in a cash register to the total cash sales per the register's tape would be recorded in the Cash Short & Over account with a:

debit   or   credit

L.O. 2(b)   The accounting department should have exclusive control over the functions of cash collection, bank deposits, recording appropriate journal entries, and preparing periodic bank reconciliations.

true   or   false

L.O. 3(a)   Which of the following items would be subtracted from the balance per bank statement in adjusting to the correct adjusted cash balance?

outstanding checks   or   NSF checks

L.O. 3(b)   The reconciliation of the cash balance per company records to the correct adjusted cash balance would indicate the need for journal entries.

true   or   false

L.O. 3(c)   Monthly bank service charges are subtracted in the reconciliation of a certain "amount" to the correct adjusted cash balance. What is the "amount" in question?

ending balance per bank statement
or
ending balance per company records

L.O. 4(a)   The original amount of a petty cash fund should be equal to cash remaining in the fund plus:

cash short and over   or   petty cash vouchers

L.O. 4(b) The replenishment of a petty cash fund involves a credit to which of the following accounts?

Cash   or   Petty Cash

L.O. 5(a) The initial recording of short-term investments is not dependent on the choice of the historical-cost or lower-of-cost-or-market methods.

correct   or   incorrect

L.O. 5(b) Lower-of-cost-or-market adjustments are determined by comparing investment cost to market on what basis?

aggregate   or   individual

FILL IN THE BLANKS

1. _____ includes coins, currency, and money orders, but not _____ _____ _____ (known as CD's) or checks that become payable on a future date (known as _____ _____).

2. Deposits that must be maintained as a condition of a loan are known as _____ _____.

3. The _____ _____ is a major component of a cash planning system, and represents the overall plan of activity that depicts cash inflows and outflows for a stated period of time.

4. Cash receipts should be deposited at the bank on a _____ basis.

5. _____ _____ _____ arise when receipts have been entered on the company records but not as yet posted by the bank.

6. The bank reconciliation is based on the Cash account and a document called a _____ _____.

7. The receipts accumulated in a petty cash box are frequently called _____ _____ _____.

8. The key element in deciding whether an investment should be presented as a short-term investment in the current asset section is _____ _____.

9. The _____-_____ method is typically employed for short-term debt investments.

10. Under the lower-of-cost-or-market method, short-term investments should be presented at the lower of _____ cost or market value.

11. The unrealized loss appears on the _____ _____, while the allowance for decline in value appears on the _____ _____.

MULTIPLE CHOICE QUESTIONS

Circle the appropriate response.

1. The cash account on the balance sheet should not include which of the following items?

    a. Travel advances to employees
    b. Currency
    c. Money orders
    d. Deposits in transit

2. A credit memorandum accompanying a bank statement would occur for which of the following items?

    a. A previously deposited customer check that was returned NSF.
    b. Bank service charges for the month.
    c. The proceeds of a note collected by the bank are deposited to the account.
    d. Each of the above.

3. When reconciling the ending cash balance per the bank statement to the correct adjusted cash balance, how would deposits in transit be handled?

    a. Added to the balance per the bank statement.
    b. Subtracted from the balance per the bank statement.
    c. Added to the balance per company records.
    d. Ignored.

4. A bank reconciliation sometimes points to the need for adjusting entries. In general, the source of the adjustments is:

    a. the reconciliation of the ending balance per the bank statement to the adjusted cash balance.
    b. the reconciliation of the cash balance per the company records to the adjusted cash balance.
    c. both a and b.
    d. none of the above.

5. Malory Company provides the following information about the month-end bank reconciliation:

Ending cash per bank statement	$1,367
Ending cash per company records	7,383
Monthly bank service charge	25
Deposits in transit at month-end	8,345
Outstanding checks at month-end	2,399
Customer check returned NSF	45

The correct ending cash balance is:

a. $4,914
b. $7,268
c. $7,313
d. $7,383

6. Malory Company provides the following information about the month-end bank reconciliation:

Ending cash per bank statement	$1,367
Ending cash per company records	7,383
Monthly bank service charge	25
Deposits in transit at month-end	8,345
Outstanding checks at month-end	2,399
Customer check returned NSF	45

What journal entry should be recorded to cause the company records to be correct?

a. Cash   70
       Cash Short & Over   70
b. Miscellaneous Expense   70
       Cash   70
c. Miscellaneous Expense   25
   Accounts Receivable   45
       Cash   70
d. Miscellaneous Expense   2,399
       Cash   2,399

7. The short-term investments owned by a company should be reported as a current asset on the balance sheet if they are readily salable and are:

a. acceptable to a bank for deposit.
b. intended to be converted into cash within one year or the operating cycle, whichever is longer.
c. satisfactory for settlement of current debts.
d. capable of being converted into cash within one year or the operating cycle, whichever is longer.

8. During its first year of operation, Lenton Company acquired three short-term investments in marketable equity securities. Investment A cost $50,000 and had a year-end market value of $60,000. Investment B cost $35,000 and had a year-end market value of $17,000. Investment C cost $26,000 and had a year-end market value of $24,000. What amount should be reported as a charge against income in Lenton's income statement for the first year of operation?

   a. $0
   b. $10,000
   c. $20,000
   d. $30,000

9. During its first year of operation, Lenton Company acquired three short-term investments in marketable equity securities. Investment A cost $50,000 and had a year-end market value of $60,000. Investment B cost $35,000 and had a year-end market value of $17,000. Investment C cost $26,000 and had a year-end market value of $24,000. The journal entry to record the lower-of-cost-or market adjustment would include:

   a. a debit to Unrealized Loss on Short-term Investments.
   b. a credit to Recovery in Value of Short-term Investments.
   c. a debit to Allowance for Decline in Market Value of Short-term Investments.
   d. At least two of the above.

10. Amerivest held a short-term investment in Wagon Corporation stock. The investment was acquired at $7 per share, had a market value of $5 per share on the last balance sheet date prior to the date of sale, and was sold for $6.50 per share. How much gain or loss would be recognized on the sale of the stock?

    a. $0.50 loss
    b. $1.00 gain
    c. $2.00 loss
    d. $1.50 gain

DEMONSTRATION PROBLEMS

DP-1 The following information related to cash was taken from the accounting records and end-of-month bank statement of Glen Company for the month of April.

Balance per bank	$1,921.58
Balance per company records	1,976.00
Note collected by the bank during the month	400.00
Interest on note collected during the month	20.00
Bank service charge for the month	43.28
NSF check returned with bank statement	215.57
Outstanding checks	616.42
Deposit in transit	831.99

a. Prepare a bank reconciliation for Glen Company.
b. Prepare any journal entries necessitated by Glen Company's bank reconciliation.

Bank

1921.58
+ 831.99
− 616.42
_____
2137.15

Company

1976.00
+ 400.00
+ 20.00
− 43.28
− 215.57
_____
2137.15

Cash   420.00
  N/R   400.00
  I/R   20.00

A/R   215.57
S/C   43.28
  Cash   258.85

148 Cash and Short-Term Investments

DP-2 Warren Company established and operated a petty cash fund during April of 19X2. Prepare the petty cash related journal entries for the activity described hereafter.

April 11 The fund was established at $200

April 17 Cash in the fund was $82, and receipts for office supplies amounted to $108. The fund was fully replenished.

April 30 Cash in the fund was $103, and receipts for office supplies amounted to $97. The fund was fully replenished and increased to $500.

Petty Cash   200
   Cash   200

Expenses   108
Cash Short & Over   10
   Cash   118

Expense   97
Petty Cash 300
   Cash   397

DP-3 Bekins Company was formed during 19X1 and invested $50,000 in stocks of various corporations. The stocks were readily salable and management intends to sell the stocks whenever the firm is in need of cash. The accompanying table gives the cost and year-end values for the aggregate portfolio of short-term investments:

	19X1	19X2
Cost	$50,000	$50,000
Market Value	47,000	53,000

a. Present the company's 19X1 and 19X2 year-end journal entries to value the short-term investments at lower-of-cost-or-market.
b. Show how the securities would appear on the company's 19X1 and 19X2 balance sheets.

a) Unrealized loss   3000
    Allowance for Decline
    in Market Value   3000

Allowance for Decline   3000
in Market Value
    Short term investment
    recovery   3000

b) Current assets
    Short term investment   50,000
    Less: Allowance for Decline
    in Market Value   3,000
    Short term investment at LofCoM   47,000

Current assets
    Short term investments   50,000

SOLUTIONS TO SELF TESTS

FULFILLMENT OF LEARNING OBJECTIVES

1(a)   True
1(b)   Correct
2(a)   Debit
2(b)   False
3(a)   Outstanding checks
3(b)   True
3(c)   Ending balance per company records
4(a)   Petty cash vouchers
4(b)   Cash
5(a)   Correct
5(b)   Aggregate

FILL IN THE BLANKS

1. Cash, certificates of deposit, postdated checks
2. Compensating balances
3. Cash budget
4. Daily
5. Deposits in transit
6. Bank statement
7. Petty cash vouchers
8. Managerial intent
9. Historical-cost
10. Aggregate
11. Income statement, balance sheet

MULTIPLE CHOICE QUESTIONS

1. a. Travel advances to employees are really a nontrade receivable -- the employee either has to return the money or provide an accounting to indicate how the money was spent. Currency and money orders are both cash because they are acceptable to a bank for deposit and can be used to satisfy debts. Deposits in transit are cash, the bank simply has not posted the deposit to a specific account.

2. c. A credit memorandum issued by a bank indicates that a bank account has been increased. Of the noted items, only answer "c" relates to a transaction which increases cash.

3. a. Deposits in transit must be added to the balance per the bank statement. These are amounts of cash which belong to the company, but which have not as yet been recorded by the bank. The balance per company records should already include these amounts, so answer "c" is incorrect.

4. b. The cash balance per company records is the amount of cash in the general ledger account before the reconciliation. The correct amount of cash actually possessed by the firm is the adjusted cash balance, per the reconciliation. Logically, the reconciliation of the cash balance per company records to the correct amount of cash points to the need for a journal entry to update the Cash account.

5. c. The correct ending cash balance is $7,313:

Ending balance per bank statement		$1,367
Add:		
Deposits in transit		8,345
		$9,712
Deduct:		
Outstanding checks		2,399
Adjusted cash balance: bank		$7,313
Ending balance per company records		$7,383
Deduct:		
Bank service charge	$25	
NSF check	45	70
Adjusted cash balance: company records		$7,313

6. c. The correct entry is based on the reconciliation of the ending cash balance per company records to the adjusted cash balance:

Miscellaneous Expense	25	
Accounts Receivable	45	
Cash		70

Bank service charge and NSF check charged against account by bank

7. b. This choice is the second criterion for classification of marketable securities as a short-term investment. Both choices "a" and "c" pertain to the definition of cash. Choice "d" ignores the fact that managerial intent is critical to the balance sheet classification of marketable securities.

8. b. Aggregate cost equals $111,000 ($50,000 + $35,000 + $26,000). Aggregate market value equals $101,000 ($60,000 + $17,000 + $24,000). The $10,000 difference is a decline which is reported as an unrealized loss.

9. a. The appropriate entry is to debit Unrealized Loss on Short-term Investments and credit Allowance for Decline in Market Value of Short-term Investments for $10,000. Choice "a" is the only correct choice.

10. a. $0.50 loss. The loss is computed by comparing the cost to the sales price. Lower-of-cost-or-market considerations are ignored.

DEMONSTRATION PROBLEMS

DP-1

(a)
Ending balance per bank statement			$1,921.58
Add:			
Deposit in transit			831.99
			$2,753.57
Deduct:			
Outstanding checks			616.42
Adjusted cash balance: bank			$2,137.15
Ending balance per company records			$1,976.00
Add:			
Note collected by bank		$400.00	
Interest revenue on note		20.00	420.00
			$2,396.00
Deduct:			
Bank service charge		$ 43.28	
NSF check		215.57	258.85
Adjusted cash balance: company records			$2,137.15

(b)
Cash	420.00	
Notes Receivable		400.00
Interest Revenue		20.00
Note and interest collected by bank		
Miscellaneous Expense	43.28	
Accounts Receivable	215.57	
Cash		258.85
Bank service charge and NSF check charged against account by bank		

DP-2

April	11	Petty Cash	200	
		Cash		200
		To establish petty cash fund		
	17	Office Supplies Expense	108	
		Cash Short & Over	10	
		Cash		118
		To replenish petty cash fund		
	30	Office Supplies Expense	97	
		Petty Cash	300	
		Cash		397
		To replenish and increase petty cash fund		

DP-3

(a) <u>19X1</u>

Unrealized Loss on S-T Investments	3,000	
Allowance for Decline in Market Value		
of S-T Investments		3,000
To record decline in market value of		
short-term investment portfolio		

<u>19X2</u>

Allowance for Decline in Market		
Value of S-T Investments	3,000	
Recovery in Value of S-T Investments		3,000
To record recovery in value of short-term		
investment portfolio		

(b) <u>19X1</u>

Current assets	
Short-term investments	$50,000
Less: Allowance for decline in market value	
of short-term investments	3,000
Short-term investments at the lower of cost or market	$47,000

<u>19X2</u>

Current assets	
Short-term investments (market value, $53,000)	$50,000

CHAPTER 8

RECEIVABLES

LEARNING OBJECTIVES

After studying this chapter, you should be able to:

1. Distinguish between trade and nontrade receivables.

2. Account for uncollectible receivables by using both the direct write-off and the allowance methods.

3. Calculate uncollectible accounts expense by using the income statement and balance sheet approaches.

4. Account for credit card sales.

5. Demonstrate the computations and journal entries for notes receivable and interest, including discounted and dishonored obligations.

CHAPTER HIGHLIGHTS

I. **RECEIVABLES** arise from a variety of claims against customers and others, and are classified as current or noncurrent based on expectations about the amount of time it will take to collect them. The majority of receivables are classified as trade receivables, which arise from the sale of products or services to customers.

II. **ACCOUNTS RECEIVABLE** represent the amounts due from credit sales. Unfortunately, some accounts may prove to be uncollectible, necessitating the need to develop a system to account for these "bad debts."

　　A. A simple, but generally unacceptable method to account for uncollectible accounts is the **DIRECT WRITE-OFF METHOD**. Under this technique, specific accounts receivable are removed from the accounting records and uncollectible accounts expense is recorded when the accounts are determined to be uncollectible.

　　B. A better matching of revenue and expense is achieved by recording an estimate of future uncollectible accounts in the same accounting period that related credit sales are made. This is possible under the **ALLOWANCE METHOD**.

　　　　1. One type of allowance method establishes uncollectibles in **RELATIONSHIP TO SALES**: the **INCOME STATEMENT APPROACH**. With this technique, an estimated percentage of sales or credit sales is debited to Uncollectible Accounts Expense and

credited to the Allowance for Uncollectible Accounts each period. Importantly, this technique merely adds the estimated amount to the Allowance account.

2. Another allowance technique establishes uncollectibles in **RELATIONSHIP TO ACCOUNTS RECEIVABLE: the BALANCE SHEET APPROACH**. This approach begins with an estimate of the balance which should be in the Allowance account (for example, 3% of accounts receivable), and is completed by determining the necessary journal entry to adjust from the existing allowance balance (either debit or credit) to the desired balance (credit).

   a. One specific way to estimate the balance which should be in the allowance account is via an **AGING OF ACCOUNTS RECEIVABLE**. This method categorizes individual accounts according to the length of time outstanding, and a historically developed percentage is then applied to each age category to determine the estimated amount uncollectible.

3. **WRITING OFF UNCOLLECTIBLE ACCOUNTS** as they are specifically determined to be uncollectible is accomplished by debiting the Allowance for Uncollectible Accounts and crediting Accounts Receivable. Importantly, observe that no income statement impact occurs with this entry -- the income statement impact resulted in the period of sale when the Allowance was established.

4. **COLLECTION OF AN ACCOUNT PREVIOUSLY WRITTEN OFF** is recorded by reversing the entry made to write off the account, and then recording the collection in an ordinary manner.

5. The rate of bad debt experience varies significantly between businesses and provides **INSIGHTS INTO BUSINESS OPERATIONS**.

C. Many retailers engage in **CREDIT CARD SALES**. While some large firms offer their own credit cards, others find it cost effective to accept widely recognized cards. In exchange for a fee (usually a percentage of the amount charged), the merchant is able to avoid most credit risks and need not maintain their own credit department.

   1. The accounting for credit card sales depends on whether the underlying transactions are **BANK CARD VERSUS NONBANK CARD SALES**. Some cards are "bank cards," (e.g., MasterCard) and are essentially regarded as cash sales for the amount of the sale (less the applicable service charge). Other "nonbank" card sales (e.g., American Express) should normally be recorded as credit sales; when collection from the credit card company occurs, the receivable is removed from the accounts (and any resulting service charge is expensed).

D. Many companies which sell on account will grant extended payment terms. The terms allow customers to pay amounts gradually. The resulting **INSTALLMENT RECEIVABLES** are initially established in the accounting records at the sales price. As payments are collected, the receivable is gradually reduced (and any interest collected is recognized as income).

III. **NOTES RECEIVABLE** are written promises from clients or customers to pay a definite amount of money on a specific future date. The maker of the note is the party promising to make payment, the payee is the party to whom payment will be made, the principal is the stated amount of the note, and the maturity date is the day the note (and interest) will be due.

   A. Interest is the charge imposed on the borrower of funds for the use of money. **THE NATURE OF INTEREST** is such that the amount depends on the size, rate, and duration of the note. In mathematical form: Interest = Principal X Rate X Time. For example, a $1,000, 60-day note, bearing interest at 12% per year, would result in interest of $20 ($1,000 X 12% X 60/360).

   B. The **ACCOUNTING FOR NOTES AND INTEREST** is such that Notes Receivable is initially debited for the face amount. Subsequently, interest received is credited to Interest Revenue (accrued interest revenue not collected by the end of an accounting period would be recognized with an adjusting entry). At maturity, collected notes are removed from the accounts and any previously unrecorded interest is recognized.

   C. **DISCOUNTING NOTES RECEIVABLE** means that money is borrowed with a specific note receivable serving as collateral.

      1. Proper accounting requires that careful consideration be given to **THE DETAILS BEHIND DISCOUNTING**. At the time of discounting, Cash is debited for the amount received, Notes Receivable is credited, and the difference is recorded as Interest Expense (if a debit is needed to balance the entry) or Interest Revenue (if a credit is needed). The amount of cash received from discounting is computed as: Maturity Value - Discount = Proceeds. The discount is computed as: Maturity Value X Discount Rate X Discount Period = Discount.

   D. Importantly, the party discounting a note may remain contingently liable for the note. That is, if the maker of the note fails to pay at maturity, the party that discounted the note will instead have to pay. In situations which involve the **DISHONORING** of **A NOTE**, the accounting is simple; the party making payment will merely debit Accounts Receivable and credit Cash. The amount will be the maturity value plus any incidental service charges. The debit to Accounts Receivable reflects the hope of eventually collecting from the dishonoring party.

      1. Some **NOTES NOT YET DISCOUNTED** may also be dishonored. In this instance, the note should be removed from the accounts, accrued interest recorded, and an account receivable established for the amount due. This treatment again reflects the hope of an eventual collection from the dishonoring party.

CLASS NOTES

CLASS NOTES

CLASS NOTES

CLASS NOTES

CLASS NOTES

SELF TESTS

FULFILLMENT OF LEARNING OBJECTIVES

Circle the appropriate response.

L.O. 1(a)   The majority of receivables are trade receivables.

               true   or   false

L.O. 1(b)   Accrued receivables, advances to employees, and deposits with utilities are examples of:

               trade receivables
               or
               nontrade receivables

L.O. 2(a)   Does the allowance method or the direct write-off method achieve a better matching of revenues and expenses?

               allowance   or   direct write-off

L.O. 2(b)   A separate allowance account is established under the direct write-off method.

               correct   or   incorrect

L.O. 3(a)   Which approach to estimating uncollectible accounts utilizes computation techniques like aging of accounts receivable or percentage of outstanding accounts receivable (in contrast to percentage of sales)?

               income statement   or   balance sheet

L.O. 3(b)   The income statement approaches to estimating uncollectible accounts result in computations which reveal the balance which should be in the Allowance for Uncollectible Accounts account.

               true   or   false

L.O. 4   When is a sale normally recognized if a customer uses a nonbank credit card?

               at the time of sale
               or
               at the time of collection from
               the credit card company

L.O. 5(a)   Notes receivable would initially be recorded at their maturity value.

               true   or   false

L.O. 5(b) The difference between the proceeds from discounting a note and the note's carrying value would be recorded as interest revenue if the carrying value was greater than the discounting proceeds.

correct   or   incorrect

FILL IN THE BLANKS

1. _____ receivables arise from the sale of goods and services to customers on account.

2. Under the _____ _____-_____ method, uncollectible accounts are recognized when the actual loss is confirmed.

3. The _____ _____ _____ is the amount of cash expected to be collected from accounts receivable balances.

4. The allowance method that places emphasis on the matching principle is called the _____ _____ approach.

5. Individual accounts receivable are categorized according to the length of time outstanding under a process known as _____ _____ _____ _____.

6. _____ receivables arise when customers purchase goods on a deferred payment plan.

7. The _____ promises to pay a stipulated amount of a note to the payee.

8. _____ is the charge imposed on the borrower of funds, and can be computed as _____ X _____ X _____.

9. A _____ _____ is a potential obligation which may become an actual obligation based on future events and circumstances.

10. The maturity value of a note is the amount due on the maturity date and includes _____ plus _____.

MULTIPLE CHOICE QUESTIONS

Circle the appropriate response.

1. Trade accounts receivable:

   a. arise from the sale of a company's products or services.
   b. are reported in the noncurrent asset section of the balance sheet.
   c. include deposits with utilities.
   d. generally comprise the minority of the total receivables balance.

2. Lundstrom Company began making sales on credit during 19X1. The company used the direct write-off method for uncollectible accounts. A material amount of uncollectible accounts resulting from sales made during 19X1 were written off during 19X2. What was the effect of this write-off on net income for 19X1 and 19X2?

	19X1	19X2
a.	Overstate	Overstate
b.	Overstate	Understate
c.	Understate	Overstate
d.	Understate	Understate

3. Taylor Company uses the direct write-off method of recording uncollectible accounts receivable. Recently, a customer informed Taylor that he would be unable to pay $300 owed to Taylor. Taylor's proper journal entry to reflect this event would be:

a.	Uncollectible Accounts Expense	300	
	Allowance for Uncollectible Accounts		300
b.	Allowance for Uncollectible Accounts	300	
	Accounts Receivable		300
c.	Uncollectible Accounts Expense	300	
	Accounts Receivable		300
d.	Sales	300	
	Accounts Receivable		300

4. Malcom's financial statements revealed uncollectible accounts expense of $8,000, accounts receivable of $140,000, and allowance for uncollectible accounts of $12,000. The net realizable value of Malcom's accounts receivable is:

   a. $128,000
   b. $132,000
   c. $136,000
   d. $152,000

5. Branz Company had credit sales during the current year which amounted to $700,000. Historically, 3% of credit sales are uncollectible. If Branz uses the allowance method of recording uncollectible accounts, a proper journal entry for the year would be:

a.	Accounts Receivable	21,000	
	Allowance for Uncollectible Accounts		21,000
b.	Uncollectible Accounts Expense	21,000	
	Accounts Receivable		21,000
c.	Uncollectible Accounts Expense	21,000	
	Allowance for Uncollectible Accounts		21,000
d.	Allowance for Uncollectible Accounts	21,000	
	Accounts Receivable		21,000

6. Lindy Company uses an allowance method to account for uncollectible accounts. Lindy estimates that 5% of the outstanding accounts receivable will be uncollectible. At the end of the year, Lindy has outstanding accounts receivable of $750,000, and a debit balance in the Allowance for Uncollectible Accounts account of $9,000. Lindy should record uncollectible accounts expense of:

   a. $28,500
   b. $37,500
   c. $46,500
   d. $55,500

7. Flynn Company uses an allowance method for recording uncollectible accounts. Flynn determined that $4,000 due from Mitchell will not be collected. The entry Flynn should record to write off the Mitchell account is:

   a. Uncollectible Accounts Expense   4,000
        Accounts Receivable   4,000
   b. Sales   4,000
        Accounts Receivable   4,000
   c. Uncollectible Accounts Expense   4,000
        Allowance for Uncollectible Accounts   4,000
   d. Allowance for Uncollectible Accounts   4,000
        Accounts Receivable   4,000

8. John Company uses an allowance method for recording uncollectible accounts. John was notified by Paul that payment on a $1,000 receivable would be forthcoming. John had previously written off the receivable from Paul. The proper journal entry for John to record to reinstate the receivable into the accounts is:

   a. Accounts Receivable   1,000
        Allowance for Uncollectible Accounts   1,000
   b. Allowance for Uncollectible Accounts   1,000
        Sales   1,000
   c. Accounts Receivable   1,000
        Sales   1,000
   d. Accounts Receivable   1,000
        Uncollectible Accounts Expense   1,000

9. Interest on a loan may be computed by which of the following formulas?

   a. (principal x rate)/time
   b. (principal x rate x time)
   c. (principal x time)/rate
   d. (principal x time)/time

10. Vivian Howell is the payee of $10,000, 180-day, 8% note. After holding the note 120 days, Vivian discounted the note with her bank at a 12% rate. How much cash did Vivian receive for discounting the note?

    a. $ 9,800
    b. $10,000
    c. $10,192
    d. $10,208

DEMONSTRATION PROBLEMS

DP-1 The following data are available for Gerald Company:

Cash sales	$800,000
Credit sales	300,000
Accounts receivable	120,000
Allowance for uncollectible accounts	3,000 (credit)

All information is as of December 31, before adjusting entries.

a. Prepare the journal entries necessary to record uncollectible accounts expense assuming:
   (1) Uncollectible accounts are estimated to be 3% of credit sales.
   (2) Uncollectible accounts are estimated to be 6% of accounts receivable.

b. How would accounts receivable appear on the December 31 balance sheet under:
   (1) Assumption (1) of part (a)?
   (2) Assumption (2) of part (a)?

a1) 300,000
    × .03
    ─────
    9000

Uncollectable Accts Exp.   9000
    Allowance for Uncoll. accts   9000

a2) 120,000
    × .06
    ─────
    7200
    -3000
    ─────
    4200

Uncollectable Accts. Exp   4200
    Allowance for Uncoll. Accts   4200

b1) Accts. Receivable   120,000
    Less: Allow. for Uncoll. accts 12,000
                                 ────────
                                 108,000

b2) Accts. Receivable   120,000
    Less: Allow. for Uncoll. Accts   7,200
                                 ────────
                                 112,800

DP-2   Castel Company provides the following information about accounts receivable.

    Accounts receivable $200,000
    Less: Allowance for uncollectible accounts   15,000
                                                 $185,000

Castel also notes that a customer is unable to pay $5,000 owed on account.

   a.   Prepare the journal entry to record the write-off of the $5,000 account.
   b.   Subsequent to the write-off, the customer manages to pay the full $5,000. Prepare the journal entry for the payment.

Uncollectable Accts Expense   5000
    A/R   5000

A/R   5000
    Un Acct Exp   5000

Cash   5000
    A/R   5000

DP-3 On April 1 of the current year, Bennigan Company accepted a $24,000, 90-day, 12% note on account from Mac Corporation. On May 31, Bennigan discounted the note at the bank at a 10% discount rate.

    a.   Prepare the appropriate journal entry to record the receipt of the note on April 1.
    b.   Prepare the appropriate journal entry to record the discounting on May 31.
    c.   On July 1, Bennigan received notification that Mac dishonored the note. Prepare the appropriate journal entry for Bennigan assuming a protest fee of $10.

a) N/R   24,000
    A/R   24,000
    90 Day 12%

720-Int

b) Cash   24,514
    N/R   24,000
    Interest Rev.   514

c) A/R   24,730
    Cash   24,730

SOLUTIONS TO SELF TESTS

FULFILLMENT OF LEARNING OBJECTIVES

1(a)	True
1(b)	Nontrade receivables
2(a)	Allowance
2(b)	Incorrect
3(a)	Balance sheet
3(b)	False
4	At the time of sale
5(a)	False
5(b)	Incorrect

FILL IN THE BLANKS

1. Trade
2. Direct write-off
3. Net realizable value
4. Income statement
5. Aging of accounts receivable
6. Installment
7. Maker
8. Interest, principal, rate, time
9. Contingent liability
10. Principal, interest

MULTIPLE CHOICE

1. a. Trade receivables arise from the sale of products or services to customers. They typically comprise the majority of total receivables and are reported as current assets. Trade receivables contrast with nontrade receivables which arise from advances to employees, deposits with utilities, and so forth.

2. b. Generally accepted accounting principles require the use of an allowance method if bad debts are material in amount. Lundstrom's use of the direct write-off approach resulted in recording no uncollectible accounts expense in 19X1, even though the credit sales which triggered the uncollectible accounts were recorded in that year. 19X1 income was thereby overstated. 19X2's income was reduced for the write-offs attributable to 19X1 sales, and accordingly was understated.

3. c. Answers "a" and "b" both relate to the allowance methods -- establishing the allowance and writing off an account against the allowance. Under the direct write-off method, expense is recorded at the same time the receivable is written off, as demonstrated by answer "c." Answer "d" is not a typical journal entry.

4. a. $128,000. The net realizable value of accounts receivable is $140,000 (the gross accounts receivable) less $12,000 (the allowance amount), or $128,000.

5. c. The journal entry reflects the recording of expense and the establishment of an allowance for $21,000 ($700,000 X 3%). The allowance is increased for the calculated amount because the percentage of sales (i.e., income statement approach) technique is in use.

6. c. $46,500. The desired balance in the Allowance account is $37,500 ($750,000 X 5%). The Allowance account should be a credit balance; therefore, an adjustment of $46,500 is needed to convert from a $9,000 debit balance to a $37,500 credit balance. This adjustment would occur by debiting Uncollectible Accounts Expense and crediting the Allowance for Uncollectible Accounts for $46,500.

7. d. Under the allowance method, uncollectible accounts are recorded by writing off the specific account receivable against the Allowance account.

8. a. To reinstate a previously written-off account requires a reversal of the entry which was made at the time of write off.

9. b. The formula is the amount of the loan (principal) times the interest rate per period (rate) times the number of periods (time).

10. c. $10,192. The maturity value equals $10,000 plus interest of $400 ($10,000 X 8% X 180/360), or $10,400. The discount equals $208 ($10,400 X 12% X 60/360). Note that the fraction (60/360) is based on the remaining 60 days until maturity (i.e., 180 - 120 days). The proceeds equal $10,400 maturity value less the $208 discount, or $10,192.

DEMONSTRATION PROBLEMS

DP-1

(a) 1. Credit sales $300,000
Estimate X 0.03
$ 9,000

Uncollectible Accounts Expense 9,000
    Allowance for Uncollectible Accounts 9,000

2. Accounts receivable $120,000
Estimate X 0.06
Required balance in allowance $ 7,200
Present balance in allowance 3,000
$ 4,200

Uncollectible Accounts Expense 4,200
    Allowance for Uncollectible Accounts 4,200

(b) 1. Accounts receivable $120,000
Less: Allowance for uncollectible accounts 12,000
$108,000

2. Accounts receivable $120,000
Less: Allowance for uncollectible accounts 7,200
$112,800

DP-2

(a) Allowance for Uncollectible Accounts   5,000
    Accounts Receivable   5,000
To write-off uncollectible account

(b) Accounts Receivable   5,000
    Allowance for Uncollectible Accounts   5,000
To reinstate account

Cash   5,000
    Accounts Receivable   5,000
To record collection on account

DP-3

(a) Apr. 1 Notes Receivable   24,000
    Accounts Receivable   24,000
Received note on account

(b) May 31 Cash   24,514
    Notes Receivable   24,000
    Interest Revenue   514
Proceeds from discounted note

Proceeds = maturity value (($24,000 X 12% X 90/360) + $24,000) - discount ($24,720 X 10% X 30/360) = $24,720 - $206 = $24,514

(c) July 1 Accounts Receivable   24,730
    Cash   24,730
To record payment to the bank from note default

CHAPTER 9

INVENTORY

LEARNING OBJECTIVES

After studying this chapter, you should be able to:

1. Explain the ownership issues related to goods in transit and goods on consignment.

2. Identify the effects of inventory errors on financial statements.

3. Demonstrate use of the specific identification, FIFO, LIFO, and weighted-average inventory methods.

4. Recognize the factors that are considered when selecting an inventory method and the effects of such a selection on financial statements.

5. Apply the lower-of-cost-or-market rule of inventory valuation.

6. Explain the importance of inventory estimates and use both the gross profit and retail methods.

7. Contrast the features of the periodic and perpetual inventory systems.

CHAPTER HIGHLIGHTS

I. **WHAT IS INVENTORY?** For a merchandising business, the goods available for resale to customers constitute the bulk of inventory. However, for a manufacturer, inventories include more than just finished goods completed and awaiting sale; also included is work in process (goods being manufactured but not yet completed) and raw materials (goods to be used in the manufacture of products). Inventories are typically classified as current assets on the balance sheet.

   A. Determining which goods to include in inventory often involves assessment of **OWNERSHIP PROBLEMS**.

   1. Technically, **GOODS IN TRANSIT** belong to the party holding legal ownership. Ownership depends on the F.O.B. terms. Goods sold F.O.B. shipping point become property of the purchaser once shipped by the seller. Goods sold F.O.B. destination do not belong to the purchaser until they arrive at their final destination. Therefore, when determining the amount of inventory owned at year end, goods in transit (both purchased and sold) must be considered in light of the F.O.B. terms.

   2. **GOODS ON CONSIGNMENT** are goods where the party holding physical possession is not the legal owner. The consignee (the person with physical possession) merely

acts as a sales agent. The consignor (legal owner) includes consigned goods in inventory; the consignee does not.

3. No matter how effective a company's accounting system, the **TAKING** of **A PHYSICAL INVENTORY** should occur at least once each year. This counting process allows the company to determine the actual level of goods on hand and adjust the accounting records accordingly.

II. In accounting for inventory and physically counting inventory, it is possible that errors will occur. Accountants and business persons should understand the **EFFECTS OF INVENTORY ERRORS ON FINANCIAL STATEMENTS**. A general rule of thumb is that overstatements of ending inventory cause overstatements of income, while understatements of ending inventory cause understatements of income; likewise retained earnings is overstated or understated. This general rule of thumb presumes that the purchase was recorded, but the ending inventory was incorrectly counted.

A. Inventory errors tend to be **COUNTERBALANCING ERRORS**. That is, one year's ending inventory error becomes the next year's beginning inventory error. The general rule of thumb is that overstatements of beginning inventory cause that year's income to be understated, while understatements of beginning inventory cause overstatements of income. For example, overstating ending inventory in Year 1 overstates income for that year. The overstatement in beginning inventory in Year 2 causes Year 2's income to be understated. Hence, for the two year period, the total income would be correct. However, the amount for each year is critically flawed.

III. As you might suspect from the preceding discussion, **INVENTORY VALUATION AND INCOME MEASUREMENT** are interwoven.

A. **MATCHING: THE KEY OBJECTIVE** of inventory accounting is valuing ending inventory and measuring the cost of goods sold which must be subtracted from (i.e., matched with) sales on the income statement. Accounting for inventory is a basic process of summing beginning inventory and net purchases to arrive at goods available for sale, then subtracting ending inventory to arrive at cost of goods sold. One critical factor is determining the cost of ending inventory.

B. **COST DETERMINATION** for inventory requires consideration of invoice cost, transportation charges, insurance, and similar carrying charges.

C. Once the unit cost of inventory is determined, **COSTING METHODS** must be applied to allocate the cost of goods available for sale to ending inventory and cost of goods sold.

1. One costing method is **SPECIFIC IDENTIFICATION**. This method requires a business to identify each unit of merchandise with the unit's cost and retain that identification until the inventory is sold. Once the inventory item is sold, the cost of the unit is assigned to cost of goods sold. Specific identification requires tedious record keeping and is only used for small inventories of uniquely identifiable goods (e.g., automobiles, fine jewelry, and so forth).

D. As an alternative to specific identification, **COST FLOW ASSUMPTIONS** may be used. The assumptions bear no relation to the physical flow of goods; they are merely used to assign costs to inventory units.

1. Two widely used inventory valuation techniques are the first-in, first-out (FIFO) and last-in, first-out (LIFO) methods. These methods are based on a different underlying assumption about which units are sold first from the total stock of goods available for sale during a period. **A GENERAL INTRODUCTION TO FIFO AND LIFO** reveals that FIFO is based on the premise that the oldest units are sold first (and their related costs become part of cost of goods sold). Conversely, LIFO assumes the newest units are sold first.

2. More specifically, with **FIRST-IN, FIRST-OUT CALCULATIONS**, the oldest cost (i.e., the first in) is matched against revenue. The costs of the most recent purchases are assigned to units in ending inventory.

3. With **LAST-IN, FIRST-OUT CALCULATIONS** the reverse occurs; recent costs are assigned to goods sold while the oldest costs remain in inventory.

4. The **WEIGHTED AVERAGE** method relies on average unit cost to calculate cost of units sold and ending inventory. Average cost is determined by dividing total cost of goods available for sale by total units available for sale.

5. A **COMPARISON AND EVALUATION OF ALTERNATIVE INVENTORY VALUATION METHODS** reveals that LIFO results in the lowest income during a period of rising prices, FIFO the highest, and weighted average an amount in between.

6. **WHICH METHOD SHOULD BE SELECTED?** Selecting an inventory method depends on careful consideration of income tax consequences and financial statement results.

    a. In recent years, **INCOME TAXES** have generally been reduced by utilization of the LIFO method. This resulted because LIFO tended to give lower income (therefore lower taxes) due to rising prices.

    b. Some argue that **FINANCIAL STATEMENT PRESENTATION** is enhanced by LIFO because it matches recently incurred costs with the recently generated revenues. Others maintain that FIFO is better because recent costs are reported in inventory on the balance sheet.

7. No matter which method is selected, **CONSISTENCY IN METHOD APPLICATION** should be maintained. This does not mean that changes cannot occur; however, changes should only be made if financial accounting is improved.

IV. Conservatism requires that **LOWER OF COST OR MARKET** be utilized for inventory valuation.

   A. **MEASURING THE DECLINE IN VALUE** requires evaluating the difference between inventory cost and market value. Market value is defined as replacement cost, not to exceed net realizable value (selling price minus completion and disposal costs), nor to be less than net realizable value minus a normal profit margin.

   B. **APPLICATION OF THE LOWER-OF-COST-OR-MARKET RULE** can occur for each item in inventory, or for the aggregate inventory. Once a write-down is deemed necessary, the loss should be recognized in income and inventory should be reduced. Once reduced, the Inventory account becomes the new basis for valuation and reporting purposes.

- C. **WHAT ABOUT INCREASES IN VALUE?** If inventory that was previously reduced recovers in value, it nevertheless stays written down. Simply, recoveries in value are not recognized.

V. If a physical count of inventory is not possible, then **INVENTORY ESTIMATES** must be used.

- A. The **GROSS PROFIT METHOD** is an estimation technique in which the normal gross profit rate is multiplied times sales to estimate gross profit. Sales minus estimated gross profit equals estimated cost of goods sold, and goods available for sale minus estimated cost of goods sold provides an estimate of ending inventory.

- B. The **RETAIL METHOD** is widely used by merchandising firms to value or estimate ending inventory. The cost-to-retail percentage is multiplied times ending inventory at retail (which may be determined by physical count and valuation or by subtracting sales from goods available for sale at retail) to arrive at the cost of ending inventory.

VI. **PERIODIC AND PERPETUAL INVENTORY SYSTEMS** are alternative techniques to accumulate and maintain inventory information. With the periodic system, recall that the Inventory account is not affected as purchases and sales occur (beginning inventory is maintained in the account throughout the period). Purchases are recorded in a Purchases account, and ending inventory is determined by a physical count. Beginning inventory, purchases, and ending inventory are used to calculate cost of goods sold.

- A. **PERPETUAL SYSTEMS** maintain continuous records of inflows and outflows of merchandise; the Inventory account is constantly updated.

- B. An **ILLUSTRATION OF A PERPETUAL SYSTEM** reveals that a running balance for inventory and cost of goods sold is constantly maintained. The running balance of inventory and cost of goods sold can be maintained on a FIFO basis.

    1. **GENERAL LEDGER UPDATING** of Inventory and Cost of Goods Sold occur as purchases and sales occur. Specifically, Inventory is debited as purchases occur and credited as sales occur. As Inventory is credited, Cost of Goods Sold is debited. The Purchases account is not needed in a perpetual system.

VII. **APPENDIX**: The **LIFO AND AVERAGE COSTING** methods can also be used **UNDER A PERPETUAL INVENTORY SYSTEM**.

- A. With **LIFO**, as each sale occurs, the cost of the units sold is based on the most recent purchase(s) of goods.

- B. A **MOVING AVERAGE** perpetual approach is considerably more involved, as a new average unit cost must be computed with each purchase.

CLASS NOTES

CLASS NOTES

CLASS NOTES

CLASS NOTES

SELF TESTS

FULFILLMENT OF LEARNING OBJECTIVES

Circle the appropriate response.

L.O. 1(a)   Goods in transit should never be included in the buyer's inventory.

true   or   false

L.O. 1(b)   Goods on consignment should be included in the accounts of the:

consignee   or   consignor

L.O. 2(a)   Overstating ending inventory would have what effect on income for that year?

overstate   or   understate

L.O. 2(b)   The impact of inventory errors on income tends to be counterbalanced by offsetting errors in the following accounting period.

correct   or   incorrect

L.O. 3(a)   Under which inventory cost-flow assumption would the most recent cost be assigned to the Inventory account on the balance sheet?

LIFO   or   FIFO

L.O. 3(b)   Under the weighted-average inventory method, the average unit cost of inventory is determined by dividing the sum of the individual purchase prices by the number of purchases which occurred during the year.

correct   or   incorrect

L.O. 3(c)   The specific identification method would be used for inventory which involves many similar homogeneous items.

true   or   false

L.O. 4(a)   During a period of rising prices, which inventory method would tend to minimize tax liability?

FIFO   or   LIFO

L.O. 4(b)   During a time of rising prices, the LIFO technique causes inventory on the balance sheet to bear what relationship to its fair value?

greater than   or   less than

L.O. 5(a)   In determining inventory's lower-of-cost-or-market valuation, market is defined as:

sales price   or   replacement cost

L.O. 5(b)   The lower-of-cost-or-market rule can be applied item-by-item or to the aggregate inventory.

true   or   false

L.O. 5(c)   Recoveries of value for inventory previously reduced by lower-of-cost-or-market rule adjustments should be recognized.

correct   or   incorrect

L.O. 6(a)   Under the gross profit method, ending inventory is determined by multiplying net purchases by the estimated gross profit percentage.

true   or   false

L.O. 6(b)   Under the retail inventory method, the estimated ending inventory can be determined by multiplying the cost-to-retail percentage times the:

retail value of goods available for sale
or
estimated ending inventory at retail

L.O. 7(a)   In a perpetual inventory system, which account is not utilized?

Purchases   or   Cost of Goods Sold

L.O. 7(b)   Which inventory method produces the same results under both the perpetual and periodic inventory systems?

FIFO   or   LIFO

FILL IN THE BLANKS

1. For a manufacturer, inventories can be divided into categories such as _____ _____, _____ _____ _____, and _____ _____.

2. Legal ownership of inventory is dependent on freight terms, namely F.O.B. _____ _____ and F.O.B. _____.

3. The _____ is the legal owner of goods on consignment.

4. The process of counting an inventory is called taking a _____ _____.

5. Understating beginning inventory would cause income for that year to be _____.

6. _____ _____ plus _____ _____ equals _____ _____ _____ _____, which can be divided into _____ _____ _____ _____ for reporting on the income statement and _____ _____ for reporting on the balance sheet.

7. The _____ _____ method requires a business to identify each unit of merchandise with the unit's cost, and retain that identification until the inventory is sold.

8. Under the _____ inventory method, the most recent costs incurred are assigned to cost of goods sold on the income statement.

9. The _____ inventory method would cause income to be the highest during a period of rising prices.

10. _____ requires that accounting and valuation methods be used on a regular basis from year to year.

11. Under the lower-of-cost-or-market method, market is defined as _____ _____ not to exceed _____ _____ _____ nor to be less than _____ _____ _____ minus a _____ _____ _____.

12. The _____ _____ method estimates inventory on the basis of a company's gross profit rate.

13. The _____ _____ is widely used by merchandising firms to value or estimate ending inventory.

14. The perpetual inventory system can be executed under the _____ method, _____ method, or _____-_____ method.

15. Under the perpetual system, when inventory is sold, the _____ _____ _____ _____ account is debited and _____ is credited. The _____ account, which is used with a periodic system, is not used with the perpetual system.

MULTIPLE CHOICE QUESTIONS

Circle the appropriate response.

1. Inventory accounts should be classified in which section of a balance sheet?

    a. Current assets
    b. Investments
    c. Property, plant, and equipment
    d. Intangible assets

2. Ritz Company agreed to purchase certain inventory items from Hostess Corporation. Hostess shipped the goods F.O.B. destination. On December 31, Ritz's accounting year-end, Ritz was aware that the goods had been shipped and would be received any day.

   a. Ritz should include the goods in its inventory calculated on December 31.
   b. Ritz should include the goods in its inventory calculated on December 31, but should not record the obligation to pay for them.
   c. Ritz should not include the goods in its inventory calculated on December 31, but should include the related payable on its balance sheet at December 31.
   d. Ritz should not include the goods in its inventory calculated on December 31, and should not include the related payable on its balance sheet at December 31.

3. Wonder Corporation failed to record the purchase of merchandise on account. The merchandise and related accounts payable should have been recorded but were not. What is the effect of these errors on assets, liabilities, retained earnings, and net income, respectively?

   a. Understated, understated, no effect, no effect
   b. Understated, understated, understated, understated
   c. Understated, overstated, overstated, understated
   d. Overstated, overstated, understated, overstated

4. Hefty Company wants to know the effect of different inventory methods on financial statements. Given below is information about beginning inventory and purchases for the current year.

January 2	Beginning Inventory, 500 units at $3.00
April 7	Purchased 1,100 units at $3.20
June 30	Purchased 400 units at $4.00
December 7	Purchased 1,600 units at $4.40

   Sales during the year were 2,700 units at $5.00. If Hefty used the first-in, first-out method, ending inventory would be:

   a. $2,780
   b. $3,960
   c. $9,700
   d. $10,880

5. Hefty Company wants to know the effect of different inventory methods on financial statements. Given below is information about beginning inventory and purchases for the current year.

    January 2   Beginning Inventory, 500 units at $3.00
    April 7   Purchased 1,100 units at $3.20
    June 30   Purchased 400 units at $4.00
    December 7   Purchased 1,600 units at $4.40

    Sales during the year were 2,700 units at $5.00. If Hefty used the last-in, first-out method, cost of goods sold would be:

    a. $2,780
    b. $3,960
    c. $9,700
    d. $10,880

6. Hefty Company wants to know the effect of different inventory methods on financial statements. Given below is information about beginning inventory and purchases for the current year.

    January 2   Beginning Inventory, 500 units at $3.00
    April 7   Purchased 1,100 units at $3.20
    June 30   Purchased 400 units at $4.00
    December 7   Purchased 1,600 units at $4.40

    Sales during the year were 2,700 units at $5.00. If Hefty used the weighted-average method, gross profit would be:

    a. $3,255
    b. $3,415
    c. $10,245
    d. $13,500

7. Bernstein Corporation recently experienced a fire which destroyed all of its inventory. The following data have been reconstructed from partial accounting information, and pertain to the year up to the date of the fire.

Beginning inventory	$20,000
Net purchases	45,000
Sales	80,000
Gross profit rate	40%

    Using the gross profit method, estimate the dollar amount of inventory which was destroyed in the fire.

    a. $17,000
    b. $33,000
    c. $48,000
    d. $65,000

8. Gerber Department Store utilizes the retail inventory method. Gerber's beginning inventory cost $140,000 and retailed for $280,000. Purchases for the period amounted to $390,000 and were priced to sell at twice that amount. Sales for the period, all at normal retail, were $600,000. How much is the cost of Gerber's estimated ending inventory?

    a. $115,000
    b. $150,000
    c. $230,000
    d. $300,000

9. Which of the following inventory methods will always produce the same results under both a periodic and perpetual system?

    a. FIFO
    b. LIFO
    c. Average
    d. All of these

10. An inventory pricing procedure in which the oldest costs incurred rarely have an effect on the ending inventory valuation is:

    a. FIFO
    b. LIFO
    c. Retail
    d. Weighted-average

DEMONSTRATION PROBLEMS

DP-1 The following information is available for the Baird Company for the month of June:

Beginning inventory	700 units at $7.00	4900
June 6	Purchased 1,000 units at $7.20	7200
June 19	Purchased 1,500 units at $7.50	11250
June 30	Purchased 900 units at $8.00	7200
		30550

2900 – sold
4100

After considering the purchase which occurred on June 30, there were 1,200 units unsold and remaining in stock at the end of the month. Baird Company uses a periodic inventory system. Determine the ending inventory balance under each of the following valuation methods.

a. First-in, first-out
b. Last-in, first-out
c. Weighted-average (round per unit cost computations to the nearest cent)

a) 700 @ 7.00 = 4900
   1000 @ 7.20 = 7200
   1200 @ 7.50 = 9000
   ─────
   2900   21100

Goods avail for sale   30550
Less: Ending Inv.   21100
                        ─────
Cost of Goods Sold   9450

b) 900 @ 8.00 = 7200
   1500 @ 7.50 = 11250
   500 @ 7.20 = 3600
   ─────
   2900   22050

Goods avail for sale   30550
Less: Ending Inv.   22050
                        ─────
Cost of Goods Sold   8500

c) 7.45 × 1200 = 8940

DP-2 Pepperidge Corporation operates a retail store. Pepperidge uses the retail inventory valuation method. The following information is available for the year ended December 31, 19X1.

	Cost	Retail
Inventory, January 1	$ 50,000	$ 75,000
Purchases, January-December	600,000	900,000
Sales from January-December	400,000	600,000

A physical count revealed ending inventory of $339,000 at retail. Using the retail inventory method, estimate the cost of stolen and lost inventory.

Beg Inv   50,000   75,000
Add: Purchases   600,000   900,000
Goods Av. Sale   650,000   975,000

$$\frac{650,000}{975,000} = 66\%$$

Less: Net Sales   600,000
Est. ending Inv retail   375,000
Est. ending Inv cost   250,000

DP-3 Cheddar Company had a beginning inventory on January 1 of 1,000 units at $3.00. Purchases and sales throughout the year were as follows:

Purchases:
- February 6 — 1,500 units at $4.00
- November 7 — 2,000 units at $4.40

Sales:
- May 7 — 1,800 units at $20.00
- December 4 — 1,500 units at $21.00

Cheddar Company uses a perpetual inventory system.

a. Calculate ending inventory if the FIFO cost flow assumption is used.
b. Calculate ending inventory if the LIFO cost flow assumption is used.
c. Calculate ending inventory if the moving-average cost flow assumption is used (round per unit computations to the nearest cent).
d. Prepare journal entries to reflect purchase and sale activities under the perpetual FIFO system.

FIFO

Date	Units Bought	Sold	Unit Cost	Total Cost	Ending Inv Units	Ending Inv Cost
Beg Inv	1000		3.00	3000	1000	3000
Feb 6	1500		4.00	6000	2500	9000
May 7		1800	1000@3.00 / 800@4.00	6200	700	2800
Nov 7	2000		4.40	8800	2700	11600
Dec		1500	700@4.00 / 800@4.40	2800 / 3520	1200	5280

LIFO

Date	Units Bought	Units Sold	Unit Cost	Total Cost	Ending Inv Units	Ending Inv Cost
Beg Inv	1000		3.00	3000	1000	3000
Feb 6	1500		4.00	6000	2500	9000
May 7		1800	1500@4.00 / 300@3.00	6000 / 900	700	2100
Nov 7	2000		4.40	8800	2700	10900
Dec 7		1500	1500@4.40	6600	1200	4300

SOLUTIONS TO SELF TESTS

FULFILLMENT OF LEARNING OBJECTIVES

1(a) False
1(b) Consignor
2(a) Overstate
2(b) Correct
3(a) FIFO
3(b) Incorrect
3(c) False
4(a) LIFO
4(b) Less than
5(a) Replacement cost
5(b) True
5(c) Incorrect
6(a) False
6(b) Estimated ending inventory at retail
7(a) Purchases
7(b) FIFO

FILL IN THE BLANKS

1. Raw materials, work in process, finished goods
2. Shipping point, destination
3. Consignor
4. Physical inventory
5. Overstated
6. Beginning inventory, net purchases, goods available for sale, cost of goods sold, ending inventory
7. Specific identification
8. LIFO
9. FIFO
10. Consistency
11. Replacement cost, net realizable value, net realizable value, normal profit margin
12. Gross profit
13. Retail method
14. FIFO, LIFO, moving-average
15. Cost of Goods Sold, Inventory, Purchases

MULTIPLE CHOICE QUESTIONS

1. a. Inventory is appropriately classified as a current asset because it will be used or sold and converted to cash within the operating cycle.

2. d. Ritz should not include the goods in its inventory until the goods are received, as evident from the freight terms which specified F.O.B. destination. The obligation would not be recorded until the inventory was received.

3. a. Assets are understated because the inventory was not recorded. Liabilities are understated because the accounts payable was not recorded. The error has no impact on income; both purchases and ending inventory are understated, resulting in cost of goods sold being correctly stated:

Beginning inventory	Correct
Plus: purchases	Understated
Goods available for sale	Understated
Less: ending inventory	Understated
Cost of goods sold	Correct

Because cost of goods sold is correct, income is correct. Likewise, since income is correct, retained earnings is correct.

4. b. $3,960. Ending inventory consisted of 900 units ((500 + 1,100 + 400 + 1,600) - 2,700). The value for these items is based on the last purchase at $4.40 each (900 X $4.40).

5. d. $10,880. Cost of goods sold consisted of the last 2,700 units purchased ((1,600 X $4.40) + (400 X $4.00) + (700 X $3.20)).

6. a. $3,255. Sales minus cost of goods sold equals gross profit. Sales are $13,500 (2,700 X $5.00). Cost of goods sold is $10,245, calculated as weighted-average cost per unit (((500 units X $3) + (1,100 units X $3.20) + (400 units X $4.00) + (1,600 units X $4.40))/(500 + 1,100 + 400 + 1,600)) times the 2,700 units sold.

7. a. $17,000. Cost of goods sold up to the date of the fire was $48,000 ($80,000 sales minus cost of goods sold equals the gross profit of $32,000 ($80,000 X 40%)). Beginning inventory ($20,000) plus net purchases ($45,000) is goods available for sale ($65,000). Goods available for sale minus cost of goods sold is the estimated ending inventory lost to fire.

8. c. $230,000. Cost of goods available for sale is $530,000 ($140,000 + $390,000). The retail value of the goods is $1,060,000 ($280,000 + $780,000), resulting in a cost to retail percentage of 50%. Ending inventory at retail is $460,000 ($1,060,000 - $600,000); therefore, the estimated cost of ending inventory is $230,000 ($460,000 X 50%).

9. a. FIFO valuations do not depend on the choice of a periodic or perpetual system. As sales occur, the cost is always presumed to be from the oldest goods in stock. This occurs whether the computation is made only once at the end of the period or throughout the period. The other methods would yield different results under a periodic versus a perpetual system, as the units presumed to be sold are sensitive to the timing of the sale.

10. a. With FIFO, the oldest costs are almost always charged to cost of goods sold. With LIFO, the oldest costs are likely to remain in inventory. Average and retail methods tend to blend costs, so that the oldest costs impact both cost of goods sold and ending inventory.

DEMONSTRATION PROBLEMS

DP-1

(a) FIFO:

900 units at $8.00 =	$7,200
300 units at $7.50 =	2,250
	$9,450

(b) LIFO:

700 units at $7.00 =	$4,900
500 units at $7.20 =	3,600
	$8,500

(c) Weighted-average:

700 units at $7.00 =	$ 4,900
1,000 units at $7.20 =	7,200
1,500 units at $7.50 =	11,250
900 units at $8.00 =	7,200
4,100 units	$30,550

$30,550/4,100 units = $7.45 per unit;

$7.45 X 1,200 units = $8,940

DP-2

	Cost	Retail
Beginning inventory, Jan. 1	$ 50,000	$ 75,000
Purchases	600,000	900,000
Goods available for sale	$650,000	$975,000

Ratio of cost to retail prices: ($650,000/$975,000 = 66.66%)

Less: Net sales		600,000
Estimated ending inventory at retail		$375,000
Estimated ending inventory at cost ($375,000 X 66.66%)	$250,000	

Estimated ending inventory at cost ($250,000) less actual ending inventory at cost ($339,000 X 66.66% = $226,000) yields the cost of unaccounted for inventory ($24,000).

DP-3

(a) FIFO

	Purchases	Sales	Balance
Beginning			1,000 @ $3.00
Feb. 6	1,500 @ $4.00		1,000 @ $3.00 1,500 @ $4.00
May 7		1,000 @ $3.00 800 @ $4.00	700 @ $4.00
Nov. 7	2,000 @ $4.40		700 @ $4.00 2,000 @ $4.40
Dec. 4		700 @ $4.00 800 @ $4.40	1,200 @ $4.40

Ending inventory is $5,280 (1,200 units X $4.40).

(b) LIFO

	Purchases	Sales	Balance
Beginning			1,000 @ $3.00
Feb. 6	1,500 @ $4.00		1,000 @ $3.00 1,500 @ $4.00
May 7		1,500 @ $4.00 300 @ $3.00	700 @ $3.00
Nov. 7	2,000 @ $4.40		700 @ $3.00 2,000 @ $4.40
Dec. 4		1,500 @ $4.40	700 @ $3.00 500 @ $4.40

Ending inventory is $4,300 ((700 units X $3.00) + (500 units X $4.40)).

(c) Moving-average

	Purchases	Sales	Balance	
Beginning			1,000 @ $3.00	
Feb. 6	1,500 @ $4.00		1,000 @ $3.00 = 1,500 @ $4.00 = 2,500	$ 3,000 6,000 $ 9,000
			$9,000/2,500 = $3.60	
May 7		1,800 @ $3.60	700 @ $3.60	
Nov. 7	2,000 @ $4.40		700 @ $3.60 = 2,000 @ $4.40 = 2,700	$ 2,520 8,800 $11,320
			$11,320/2,700 = $4.19	
Dec. 4		1,500 @ $4.19	1,200 @ $4.19	

Ending inventory is $5,028 (1,200 units X $4.19).

(d)
Feb. 6	Inventory		6,000	
	Accounts Payable			6,000
	Purchased 1,500 units at $4			
May 7	Accounts Receivable		36,000	
	Sales			36,000
	Sold 1800 units at $20			
	Cost of Goods Sold		6,200	
	Inventory			6,200
	Sold 1,800 shirts ((1,000 at $3) + (800 at $4))			
Nov. 7	Inventory		8,800	
	Accounts Payable			8,800
	Purchased 2,000 units at $4.40			
Dec. 4	Accounts Receivable		31,500	
	Sales			31,500
	Sold 1,500 units at $21			
	Cost of Goods Sold		6,320	
	Inventory			6,320
	Sold 1,500 units ((700 at $4) + (800 at $4.40))			

CHAPTER 10

PROPERTY, PLANT, AND EQUIPMENT/NATURAL RESOURCES/INTANGIBLES

LEARNING OBJECTIVES

After studying this chapter, you should be able to:

1. Differentiate between capital and revenue expenditures.

2. Account for cash and lump-sum purchases of property, plant, and equipment.

3. Explain the concept of depreciation and use various depreciation methods (e.g., straight-line, units-of-output, declining-balance, and sum-of-the-years'-digits).

4. Identify the financial reporting and tax issues related to depreciation.

5. Account for property, plant, and equipment costs incurred after asset acquisition.

6. Record disposals and exchanges of property, plant, and equipment.

7. Calculate natural resource cost and depletion.

8. Recognize the various types of intangible assets and compute amortization.

CHAPTER HIGHLIGHTS

I. The approach for **DETERMINING THE COST OF PROPERTY, PLANT, AND EQUIPMENT** is to identify those expenditures which are ordinary and necessary to get the equipment in place and in condition for its intended use. Such amounts are known as capital expenditures and would include the purchase price, freight, ordinary installation, and so forth. Expenditures that benefit only the immediate period are known as revenue expenditures and should be expensed as incurred. An example is repair of abnormal damage caused during installation of equipment. Also, note that interest cost incurred to finance the purchase of property, plant, and equipment is expensed; an exception is interest incurred on funds borrowed to finance construction of plant and equipment. Interest related to the period of active construction is a capital expenditure.

   A. Property, plant, and equipment is often acquired via a **CASH PURCHASE**. In this case, the purchase price is easy to determine. It consists of the negotiated price (not list price), less available cash discounts, plus freight, and plus normal installation.

B. Sometimes property, plant, and equipment may be acquired in a **LUMP-SUM PURCHASE**. In this instance, the total cost of the package of assets is readily determinable from the purchase price. However, allocating the purchase price to individual assets requires a pro-rata allocation. This occurs because the sum of the appraised values of the individual assets may not equal the price paid for the package of assets. Simply, if land, building, and equipment were acquired as a package, and if the appraised value of the land was 30% of the total appraised value of all of the items in the package, then 30% of the purchase price would be debited to the Land account.

C. An expedient approach to account for **SMALL ITEMS OF PROPERTY, PLANT, AND EQUIPMENT** is to expense the cost at the time of purchase.

    1. In determining whether an outlay should be expensed or capitalized, consideration should be given to the cost of maintaining precise accounting records, the benefits of that precision, and the materiality of the amounts involved. Such **COST/BENEFIT AND MATERIALITY** considerations are generally a matter of professional judgment.

II. The process used to allocate the cost of long-lived assets to the accounting periods benefited is known as **DEPRECIATION**. Depreciation is a process of allocation, not valuation.

  A. **DETERMINING** the **SERVICE LIFE** of an asset is an essential first step in calculating the amount of depreciation attributable to a specific period. Service life is not necessarily equal to physical life; three factors must be considered.

    1. **PHYSICAL DETERIORATION** is sometimes termed "wear and tear," and usually establishes an outer limit on the service life of an asset.

    2. **OBSOLESCENCE** is the shortening of service life due to technological advances that render an asset out of date and less desirable.

    3. **INADEQUACY** is an economic determinant of service life which is relevant when an asset is no longer fast enough or large enough to fill the competitive and productive needs of a company.

    4. The **RELATIVE SIGNIFICANCE OF THE THREE FACTORS** on service life depends on the specific situation. In some cases, all three factors must be considered. In other cases, one factor alone may control the determination of service life.

  B. There are several acceptable **METHODS OF DEPRECIATION**. The four methods used most often are straight-line, units-of-output, declining-balance, and sum-of-the-years'-digits.

    1. The **STRAIGHT-LINE METHOD** is simple and popular. The annual depreciation is calculated by dividing the depreciable base (cost - residual value) by the service life in years. The appropriate journal entry to record depreciation is to debit Depreciation Expense and credit Accumulated Depreciation (recall that this is a contra asset account). Annual depreciation expense is reported on the income statement. The balance sheet reveals the cost of assets minus the amount of depreciation taken to date (i.e., accumulated depreciation); the net of these amounts is called book value.

a. When assets are acquired at other than the beginning of an accounting period, depreciation must be calculated for **PARTIAL PERIODS**. The straight-line method amount for a partial period is just a fraction of the annual amount. For example, an asset acquired on the first day of April would be used for only nine months during the first calendar year. Therefore, year one depreciation would be 9/12 of the annual amount. Companies may assume that assets are acquired on the first or last day of the month or year (based on whether they are acquired in the first or last half of the month or year); however, such assumptions should be consistently applied.

2. Calculating the depreciation rate under the **UNITS-OF-OUTPUT METHOD** involves dividing the depreciable base by the service life in units of output (e.g., machine hours). The resulting rate is then multiplied by the usage (i.e., output) during a period to arrive at the depreciation expense.

3. **ACCELERATED DEPRECIATION METHODS** result in relatively large amounts of depreciation in early years of asset life and small amounts in later years. These methods can be justified if the quality of service produced by an asset declines over time, or if repair and maintenance costs will rise over time to offset the declining depreciation amount.

    a. A fixed percentage of the straight-line rate (e.g., 200%) is multiplied times the remaining book value of an asset (as of the beginning of the year) to determine depreciation under the **DECLINING-BALANCE METHOD**. As time passes, book value and annual depreciation decrease. For assets used only part of a year, the depreciation would be the declining-balance rate times book value times the fraction of the year in use.

    b. Annual depreciation under the **SUM-OF-THE-YEARS'-DIGITS METHOD** requires that the depreciable base be multiplied by a fraction. The numerator is a digit relating to the year of use (e.g., the digit for an asset with a ten-year life would be 10 for the first year of use, 9 for the second, and so on) and the denominator is the sum-of-the-years' digits (e.g., 10 + 9 + 8 + ... + 2 + 1 = 55). Depreciation for partial years is more complex, requiring a layering calculation for each year of use (e.g., if a ten-year asset is acquired on July 1, 19X1, depreciation for 19X1 is the depreciable base times 10/55 times 6/12 (relating to six months of use); depreciation for 19X2 is the depreciable base times 10/55 times 6/12, plus the depreciable base times 9/55 times 6/12).

4. **SELECTION OF A DEPRECIATION METHOD** depends on a number of factors, including usage, efficiency, obsolescence, and the timing of repair cost. In theory, the method selected should be the one which best matches revenues and expenses.

C. From time to time, **REVISIONS OF DEPRECIATION** calculations are needed to reflect new estimates of service life and residual value. Rather than correct prior periods' financial statements, such revisions are made prospectively (over the future) so that the remaining depreciable base is spread over the remaining life.

D. **DEPRECIATION AND THE TAX LAWS** have changed over the years with Congress occasionally introducing special techniques to speed or slow the permissible rate of depreciation (a policy tool used to stimulate investment or otherwise regulate the economy). One example is the Modified Accelerated Cost Recovery System (MACRS). MACRS allows the cost of certain assets to be allocated over a specific number of years (regardless of actual useful life) according to a predefined schedule. The schedules indicate the percentage of asset cost to be assigned to each year. For example, 3-year property is recovered (i.e., written off) at the rate of 33.3% for the first year, 44.4% the second year, 14.8% the third year, and 7.5% the fourth year (the fourth year amount arises because of the "half-year convention," as discussed in the text).

III. **PLANT AND EQUIPMENT COSTS SUBSEQUENT TO ASSET ACQUISITION** are treated as capital expenditures if future economic benefits result from the expenditure. Future economic benefits occur if the service life of an asset is prolonged, the quantity of services expected from an asset are increased, or the quality of services expected from an asset are improved. Expenditures not meeting at least one of these criteria should be accounted for as a revenue expenditure and be expensed as incurred.

　　A. Amounts spent to maintain the normal operating condition of an asset are termed **REPAIRS** and should be expensed as incurred.

　　B. **ADDITIONS** are items that provide future benefits and are affixed to existing assets. An example is the addition of an air conditioning unit to a truck previously having none. In the case of additions, criteria relating to capitalization are satisfied.

　　C. **BETTERMENTS** are expenditures that improve or increase future service potential of an asset. Betterments qualify for capitalization (and may actually be recorded by crediting Cash and debiting Accumulated Depreciation).

　　D. **ASSESSMENTS** result when charges are made by a municipality for permanent improvements to property (e.g., curbs, sidewalks, and street improvements). Assessments are normally added to the Land account.

IV. **DISPOSALS OF PROPERTY, PLANT, AND EQUIPMENT** are inevitable. A preliminary step is to update depreciation to the date of disposal.

　　A. After depreciation is updated, the **REMOVAL OF ASSETS FROM THE ACCOUNTS** consists of eliminating the cost of the asset from the books, removing the related accumulated depreciation, and recording a loss to balance the journal entry. The loss equals the asset's book value if no proceeds were received from the disposal.

　　B. Accounting for the **SALE OF DEPRECIABLE ASSETS** requires that the appropriate asset account be credited (for the asset's cost), Accumulated Depreciation be debited, Cash (or other consideration received from the sale) be debited, and the balancing amount of loss or gain be debited or credited. Simply stated, the loss or gain (if any) is the difference between the proceeds received from the sale and the book value of the asset sold.

　　C. Productive assets are sometimes exchanged or traded for newer assets. The accounting for **EXCHANGES AND TRADE-INS OF ASSETS** depends on the nature of the exchange -- is the transaction an exchange of similar or dissimilar assets?

1. Accounting for **EXCHANGES OF SIMILAR ASSETS** depends on whether a gain or loss is indicated -- losses are recognized and gains are not.

    a. To account for the **LOSS SITUATION** necessitates removing the old asset (and any additional consideration paid) from the accounts, recording the new equipment at its fair value, and debiting Loss on Exchange to balance the journal entry. This loss should equal the difference between the fair value of the asset received and the book value of the asset(s) given.

    b. To account for the **GAIN SITUATION** necessitates removing the old asset (and any additional consideration paid) from the accounts, and recording the new asset at the book value of the asset(s) relinquished. No gain is recorded.

2. Accounting for **EXCHANGES OF DISSIMILAR ASSETS** is simple: the old asset (and any additional consideration paid) is removed from the accounts, the new asset is recorded at its fair value, and any resulting gain (credit needed to balance the journal entry) or loss (debit needed to balance the journal entry) is recorded.

3. **FEDERAL INCOME TAX PROCEDURES** for exchanges are different than the financial accounting rules. Under the tax law, neither gains nor losses are recognized on exchanges of similar assets. Furthermore, the new asset should be recorded at the book value of the old asset (plus any cash paid or to be paid). In contrast gains and losses tend to be recognized on the exchange of a dissimilar asset.

V. **NATURAL RESOURCES** are sometimes called wasting assets and include items like oil and gas wells, mineral deposits, and standing timber. Natural resources should be entered into the accounting records at the cost of the resource plus related items like legal fees, surveying costs, and exploration and development costs.

   A. Like depreciation of property, plant, and equipment, the cost of natural resources must be allocated over the periods benefited. This allocation is termed **DEPLETION**. The calculation of depletion begins by dividing the cost of the natural resource (less any expected residual value) by the estimated units in the resource deposit; the resulting amount is depletion per unit. If all of the resource extracted during a period is sold, then depletion expense equals depletion per unit times the number of units extracted and sold. If a portion of the extracted resources are not sold, then the cost of those units (i.e., number of units times depletion per unit) should be carried on the balance sheet as inventory.

      1. **REVISION OF DEPLETION RATES** is identical to revision of depreciation; the remaining depletable base is spread over the remaining units.

   B. The equipment used to extract natural resources should be accounted for as property, plant, and equipment, and be depreciated. Sometimes **DEPRECIABLE ASSETS RELATED TO NATURAL RESOURCES** cannot be removed from the natural resource site at project completion. As a result, the useful life of the equipment is the shorter of the equipment's life or the life of the natural resource.

VI. Long-lived assets that lack physical existence and contribute to the earnings capability of a company are termed **INTANGIBLE ASSETS**. Examples include patents, copyrights, and franchises. Intangible assets are entered into the accounting records at cost, which includes all expenditures necessary to place the intangible in a service-producing capacity. Intangibles are presented on the balance sheet in a separate section immediately following property, plant, and equipment.

A. **PATENTS** give their owners exclusive rights to use or manufacture a particular product. The cost of a patent should be amortized over its useful life (not to exceed its legal life of 17 years). Importantly, the cost of a patent does not include the research and development costs incurred in seeking the knowledge necessary for the patent. Such costs are required to be expensed. The amount included in the Patent account includes only the cost of a purchased patent and/or incidental costs related to the registration of a patent (like legal fees).

B. **COPYRIGHTS** provide their owners with the exclusive right to produce or sell an artistic or published work. A copyright has a legal life equal to the life of the creator plus 50 years; the economic life is usually shorter. The economic life is the period of time over which the cost of a copyright should be amortized.

C. **FRANCHISES** give their owners the right to manufacture or sell certain products or perform certain services on an exclusive or semi-exclusive basis. The cost of a franchise is reported as an intangible asset, and should be amortized over the estimated useful life (not to exceed 40 years).

D. **TRADEMARKS** are another important intangible asset, the cost of which should be spread over a period not to exceed 40 years. The legal life of a trademark is 20 years, with unlimited renewal options.

E. When a lessee improves property leased from a lessor, the expenditures related to the improvement are called **LEASEHOLD IMPROVEMENTS**. Such amounts may be shown as an intangible asset, and should be amortized over the shorter of the life of the lease or the life of the improvement.

F. **GOODWILL** is a unique intangible asset. Goodwill is the excess of the purchase price paid for another company over the fair value of the identifiable assets acquired. Such excess may be paid because of the acquired company's outstanding management, earnings record, or other similar features.

   1. The proper **ACCOUNTING FOR GOODWILL** begins with its initial recording. Goodwill is debited for the difference between (1) the cash and other consideration paid and liabilities assumed (the credits) and (2) the fair value of the assets acquired (the debits).

G. Like depreciation and depletion, the cost of intangible assets must also be allocated over time through a process known as **AMORTIZATION OF INTANGIBLES**.

   1. **AMORTIZATION PROCEDURES** consist of allocating the cost of an intangible asset over its useful life, not to exceed 40 years. In determining useful life, both legal life and economic life must be considered.

   2. **AN EXAMPLE** of the amortization process reveals that the annual amortization amount is debited to Amortization Expense and credited to the specific intangible asset (rather than accumulated amortization).

CLASS NOTES

CLASS NOTES

CLASS NOTES

CLASS NOTES

SELF TESTS

FULFILLMENT OF LEARNING OBJECTIVES

Circle the appropriate response.

L.O. 1(a) Incidental expenditures incurred when purchasing equipment (e.g., freight, installation, etc.) which are ordinary and necessary for the acquisition are referred to as:

capital expenditures   or   revenue expenditures

L.O. 1(b) Revenue expenditures should be expensed in the period incurred.

true   or   false

L.O. 2(a) The cash purchase of an item of property, plant, and equipment should ordinarily be reported at the list price of the item.

true   or   false

L.O. 2(b) In an apportionment of the amount paid to acquire a package of assets, the amount assigned to a specific asset is based on its relative appraised value. The approach described relates to a:

cash purchase   or   lump-sum purchase

L.O. 3(a) The process used to allocate the cost of long-lived assets to the accounting periods benefited is known as:

obsolescence   or   depreciation

L.O. 3(b) Depreciation is a process of:

valuation   or   allocation

L.O. 3(c) The term "service life" is synonymous with:

physical life   or   economic life

L.O. 3(d) Business growth may cause certain items of depreciable property, plant, and equipment to become deficient in their service capabilities. Such action is termed:

physical deterioration   or   inadequacy

L.O. 3(e) Asset cost minus residual value is termed:

book value   or   depreciable base

L.O. 3(f) Under the units-of-output depreciation method, the depreciable base is divided by the service life:

in years or in output

L.O. 3(g) Under double-declining balance depreciation, salvage value is ignored in the preliminary depreciation calculation.

true or false

L.O. 3(h) Sum-of-the-years'-digits depreciation for an asset acquired during the middle of a year may involve the utilization of two different fractional rates in determining depreciation for a full year.

true or false

L.O. 3(i) The straight-line method generally results in the highest possible (as compared to accelerated depreciation methods) depreciation expense during an asset's early years of usage.

true or false

L.O. 3(j) For an asset with a five-year life, depreciation expense during the third year will be the same under the straight-line and:

sum-of-the-years'-digits method
or
double-declining balance method

L.O. 4(a) The process to adjust depreciation for a change in service life entails spreading the remaining depreciable base over the remaining useful life.

correct or incorrect

L.O. 4(b) A company must utilize the same depreciation methods for financial reporting and taxes purposes.

correct or incorrect

L.O. 5(a) Which of the following expenditures meet at least one of the criteria for capitalization?

repairs or assessments

L.O. 5(b) For costs incurred subsequent to asset acquisition, capitalization will occur only if the service life of an asset is prolonged.

true or false

L.O. 6(a)   The difference between the book value of an asset and the proceeds received from its sale should be reported as a gain or loss.

true or false

L.O. 6(b)   If an asset with a book value of $1,000 is abandoned, a $1,000 loss will be recognized in the income statement.

correct or incorrect

L.O. 6(c)   Briefly stated, which of the following should be recognized on the exchange of similar assets?

gains or losses

L.O. 6(d)   For Federal income tax purposes, gains and losses on exchanges of similar assets are not recognized. Also, new assets received in the exchange are recorded at the cash paid or to be paid plus:

the fair value of the new asset
or
the book value of the old asset

L.O. 7(a)   The total amount of depletion for a given period is necessarily charged to expense in the income statement.

true or false

L.O. 7(b)   When a revision of depletion rates occurs, the basic principle is to spread the remaining book value (less residual value) over the remaining number of units.

correct or incorrect

L.O. 8(a)   Intangible assets should be carried in the accounting records at their:

cost less amortization or market value

L.O. 8(b)   The amortization period for intangible assets is generally considered to be the economic life of the property, not to exceed:

20 years or 40 years

FILL IN THE BLANKS

1. Expenditures that fail to provide benefits to future periods are commonly known as _____ _____.

2. A _____-_____ _____ occurs when a package of assets are acquired for a single purchase price amount.

3. The cost/benefit theme is consistent with the concept of _____, which refers to the significance of a particular item or transaction.

4. Another name for economic or useful life is _____ _____.

5. In determining an asset's useful life, consideration must be given to three factors: _____ _____, _____, and _____.

6. One of the most popular depreciation methods is the _____-_____ method.

7. Cost minus residual value is known as _____ _____, whereas cost minus accumulated depreciation is known as _____ _____.

8. An accelerated depreciation method that involves applying a fixed depreciation rate to the remaining book value of an asset is known as the _____-_____ method.

9. Tax laws permit asset cost to be charged against specific years via use of the _____ _____ _____ _____.

10. With the MACRS, one-half of a year's depreciation is deducted in the year of asset acquisition (regardless of the specific date of purchase) because of the _____-_____ _____.

11. _____, also known as improvements or extraordinary repairs, generally improve or increase future service potential of an asset.

12. If a cash sale of an item of depreciable property occurs, and the journal entry to record the sale is balanced by the recording of a debit, then a _____ should be recognized.

13. Briefly stated, _____ on the exchange of similar assets are ignored while _____ are recognized.

14. _____ gains _____ losses are recognized on the exchange of dissimilar assets.

15. For tax purposes, the exchange of similar assets will normally result in no _____ or _____.

16. _____ is the allocation of natural resource cost to the resources extracted during an accounting period.

17. Patents, copyrights, and franchises are examples of _____ _____.

18. Improvements made on leased property are sometimes called _____ _____, and should be accounted for as intangible assets.

19. _____ occurs when the value of a company as an operating entity exceeds the value of its individual identifiable assets and liabilities.

20. The process of charging the cost of an intangible to expense is known as _____.

MULTIPLE CHOICE QUESTIONS

Circle the appropriate response.

1. Lancer Corporation purchased a parcel of land as a factory site for $150,000. An old building on the property was demolished, and construction began immediately on a new building. Costs incurred are as follows:

Demolition of old building	$ 30,000
Architect's fees	25,000
Legal fees for land purchase contract	2,000
Construction costs	250,000

    Lancer should record the cost of the new land and building, respectively, at:

    a. $150,000 and $250,000
    b. $152,000 and $275,000
    c. $180,000 and $250,000
    d. $182,000 and $275,000

2. Omni Corporation purchased a new vehicle on January 1, 19X1. The vehicle cost $100,000, has a five-year life, and a $20,000 residual value. Omni has a December 31 year-end. If Omni depreciates the truck by the double-declining balance method, how much should be recorded as depreciation expense during 19X4?

    a. $0
    b. $1,600
    c. $8,640
    d. $40,000

3. Realistic Company purchased a new truck on January 1, 19X1. The truck cost $20,000, has a four-year life, and a $4,000 residual value. The company has a December 31 year-end. If Realistic Company depreciates the truck by the sum-of-the-years'-digits method, how much should Realistic report as the book value of the truck at the end of 19X3?

    a. $1,600
    b. $2,000
    c. $5,600
    d. $14,400

4. On July 1, 19X1, Clem Company purchased factory equipment for $50,000. Residual value was estimated to be $2,000. The equipment will be depreciated over ten years using the sum-of-the-years'-digits depreciation method. Clem has a December 31 year-end, and during 19X1, one-half of a year's depreciation expense was recorded. How much depreciation expense should be recorded for 19X2? (round computations to the nearest dollar)

    a. $7,855
    b. $8,291
    c. $8,636
    d. $8,727

5. On July 1, 19X1, Robinson Company purchased a new machine for $200,000. The machine is estimated to have a service-life of 10 years with an estimated residual value of $5,000. Robinson uses the straight-line depreciation method. During 19X5, it became apparent that the machine would not be efficient to operate after December 31, 19X7. Furthermore, the machine would have no scrap value on that date. How much should be charged to depreciation expense in 19X5 under generally accepted accounting principles? (round computations to the nearest dollar)

    a. $19,500
    b. $42,250
    c. $43,917
    d. $65,000

6. Cross Country Trucking Company recently replaced the oil filter on one of its cross country rigs. How should one account for this cost?

    a. As a repair and maintenance expense.
    b. As an increase in the cost of the truck.
    c. As a reduction in accumulated depreciation associated with the truck.
    d. As an intangible asset.

7. A machine that cost $18,000, with a book value of $4,000, is sold for $3,400. Which of the following is true concerning the journal entry to record the sale?

    a. Accumulated Depreciation is debited for $4,000.
    b. Machinery is credited for $4,000.
    c. Loss on sale of machinery is credited for $600.
    d. Accumulated Depreciation is debited for $14,000.

8. Cash of $500 and equipment costing $2,500 with accumulated depreciation of $2,125 is exchanged for a similar asset with a fair value of $625. How much is the gain or loss on this transaction?

    a. A gain of $250 should be recognized.
    b. A loss of $250 should be recognized.
    c. A loss of $500 should be recognized.
    d. No gain or loss should be recognized.

9. Cash of $500 and equipment costing $2,500 with accumulated depreciation of $2,125 is exchanged for a dissimilar asset with a fair value of $1,000. At what amount should the new asset be recorded?

    a. $500
    b. $875
    c. $1,000
    d. $3,000

10. Deep Gold Mining Company recognizes $4 of depletion for each ton of ore mined. This year, 300,000 tons of ore were mined but only 180,000 were sold. The amount of depletion which should be deducted from revenue this year is:

    a. $0
    b. $480,000
    c. $720,000
    d. $1,200,000

DEMONSTRATION PROBLEMS

DP-1   Miranda Company purchased an automobile on January 1, 19X1. The auto cost $19,500, and Miranda paid $500 of freight on the purchase. The automobile was estimated to have a five-year service life and a residual value of $4,000. Plans call for the automobile to be driven 15,000 miles annually. Compute 19X2 depreciation expense using each of the following methods:

     a.   Units of output, assuming that 18,000 miles are driven during 19X2.
     b.   Straight-line.
     c.   Sum-of-the-years'-digits.
     d.   Double-declining balance.

DP-2 Rotor Craft Company purchased a new lathe on May 1, 19X1, that will be depreciated over a service life of four years. The lathe cost $100,000 and has a $20,000 estimated residual value. Calculate depreciation expense for 19X2 by using the:

a. Straight-line method.
b. Double-declining balance method.
c. Sum-of-the-years'-digits method.

DP-3   Barretta Company purchased a truck on January 1, 19X1. The cost of the truck was $90,000, and the truck had a service life of four years. Estimated residual value was set at $8,000. Barretta used the straight-line method of depreciation. Respond to the following fact situations, assuming each is independent of the others.

   a.   Barretta sold the truck on January 1, 19X3, for $75,000. Compute the gain or loss on the sale.
   b.   If the truck had been destroyed in an accident on July 1, 19X4, how much would be recorded as a loss?
   c.   If the truck and $15,000 cash were exchanged on January 1, 19X5, for a new truck with a fair value of $24,000, what journal entry would Barretta record?

SOLUTIONS TO SELF TESTS

FULFILLMENT OF LEARNING OBJECTIVES

1(a)	Capital expenditures
1(b)	True
2(a)	False
2(b)	Lump-sum purchase
3(a)	Depreciation
3(b)	Allocation
3(c)	Economic life
3(d)	Inadequacy
3(e)	Depreciable base
3(f)	In output
3(g)	True
3(h)	True
3(i)	False
3(j)	Sum-of-the-years'-digits method
4(a)	Correct
4(b)	Incorrect
5(a)	Assessments
5(b)	False
6(a)	True
6(b)	Correct
6(c)	Losses
6(d)	The book value of the old asset
7(a)	False
7(b)	Correct
8(a)	Cost less amortization
8(b)	40 years

FILL IN THE BLANKS

1. Revenue expenditures
2. Lump-sum purchase
3. Materiality
4. Service life
5. Physical deterioration, obsolescence, inadequacy
6. Straight-line
7. Depreciable base, book value
8. Declining-balance
9. Modified accelerated cost recovery system
10. Half-year convention
11. Betterments
12. Loss
13. Gains, losses
14. Both, and
15. Gain, loss
16. Depletion

17. Intangible assets
18. Leasehold improvements
19. Goodwill
20. Amortization

MULTIPLE CHOICE QUESTIONS

1. d. $182,000 and $275,000. The $182,000 consists of $150,000 site cost, $30,000 demolition cost, and $2,000 legal fees. The $275,000 amount equals the architect's fees and construction costs.

2. b. 19X1 depreciation = $100,000 X 40% = $40,000
   19X2 depreciation = $60,000 X 40% = $24,000
   19X3 depreciation = $36,000 X 40% = $14,400
   19X4 depreciation = $21,600 X 40% = $8,640

   However, 19X4 depreciation is limited to the amount to reduce net book value to the $20,000 salvage value; therefore, 19X4 depreciation is only $1,600.

3. c. $5,600. The book value equals cost ($20,000) minus accumulated depreciation ($14,400). The accumulated depreciation is calculated as follows:

19X1	4/10 X ($20,000 - $4,000) =	$ 6,400
19X2	3/10 X ($20,000 - $4,000) =	4,800
19X3	2/10 X ($20,000 - $4,000) =	3,200
		$14,400

4. b. $8,291. 19X2 depreciation is calculated as follows:

10/55 X 1/2 X $48,000 =	$4,363.64
9/55 X 1/2 X $48,000 =	3,927.27
	$8,290.91

5. c. $43,917. The book value on January 1, 19X5, is $131,750. The book value reflects 3.5 years of depreciation at $19,500 per year ($200,000 cost minus accumulated depreciation of $68,250 ($19,500 X 3.5)). Because there is no residual value, the remaining book value must be depreciated over the remaining life of 3 years ($131,750/3 = $43,917).

6. a. Repair and maintenance expense is recorded because this is a relatively small expenditure benefiting only the immediate period. If it qualified as a capital expenditure, it might be recorded as described in choices "b" or "c." This is clearly not an intangible asset.

7. d. The appropriate journal entry to record the sale is:

Cash	3,400	
Loss	600	
Accumulated Depreciation	14,000	
Machine		18,000

The only choice consistent with this entry is "d."

8. b. The consideration given ($500 + ($2,500 - $2,125) = $875) is $250 greater than the value of the asset received ($625), necessitating the recording of a loss.

9. c. $1,000. Because the exchange is for a dissimilar asset, the new asset is recorded at its fair market value. The difference between the asset's fair value and the book value given ($500 + ($2,500 - $2,125) = $875) would be recorded as a gain ($1,000 - $875 = $125 gain).

10. c. $720,000. The deletion that should be deducted from revenue equals the 180,000 units sold times the $4 per ton depletion rate. The depletion on the other 120,000 units (300,000 - 180,000) is reported as inventory (120,000 X $4 = $480,000).

DEMONSTRATION PROBLEMS

DP-1

(a) Units-of-output method:

$$\frac{\$20{,}000 \text{ cost} - \$4{,}000 \text{ residual value}}{75{,}000 \text{ estimated miles}} = \frac{\$16{,}000}{\$75{,}000}$$

= $0.21333/mile; $0.21333 X 18,000 miles = $3,840

(b) Straight-line method:

$$\frac{\$20{,}000 \text{ cost} - \$4{,}000 \text{ residual value}}{5 \text{ years}} = \frac{\$16{,}000}{5} = \$3{,}200$$

(c) Sum-of-the-years'-digits method:

4/15 X ($20,000 cost - $4,000 residual value) = $4,267

(d) Double-declining balance method:

19X1: $20,000 cost X 40%* = $8,000
19X2: ($20,000 - $8,000) X 40% = $4,800

*Straight-line rate (20%) X 2 = 40%

DP-2

(a) Straight-line method:

$$\frac{\$100{,}000 \text{ cost} - \$20{,}000 \text{ residual value}}{4 \text{ years}} = \underline{\$20{,}000}$$

(b) Double-declining balance method:

19X1: $100,000 cost X 50%* X 8/12** = $33,333
19X2: ($100,000 - $33,333) X 50% = $33,333

* Straight-line rate (25%) X 2 = 50%
**During 19X1, the asset was only used for 8 months

(c) Sum-of-the-years'-digits method:

(4/10 X ($100,000 - $20,000) X 4/12)* = $10,667
(3/10 X ($100,000 - $20,000) X 8/12)** =   16,000
                                           $26,667

* For the last four months of the first full year of use.
**For the first eight months of the second full year of use.

DP-3

(a) Jan. 1, 19X1 - Jan. 1, 19X3 = 2 years

Cost	$90,000
Less: Residual value	8,000
Depreciable base	$82,000

Annual depreciation = $82,000/4 years = $20,500

$20,500 X 2 years = $41,000 depreciation taken;
$90,000 - $41,000 = $49,000 book value;
$75,000 sales proceeds - $49,000 = $26,000 gain on sale

(b) Jan. 1, 19X1 - July 1, 19X4 = 3.5 years

$20,500 X 3.5 years = $71,750 depreciation taken;
$90,000 - $71,750 = $18,250 book value;
$0 salvage proceeds - $18,250 = $18,250 loss

(c) Equipment traded in:
    Cost $90,000
    Less: Accumulated depreciation (4 years
        X $20,500 depreciation per year)   82,000
    Book value $ 8,000

Equipment acquired:
    Invoice price $24,000
    Less: Trade-in allowance ($24,000 -$15,000)   9,000
    Cash paid $15,000

Equipment (new)	23,000	
Accumulated Depreciation: Equipment	82,000	
Equipment (old)		90,000
Cash		15,000

To record acquisition of new equipment and trade-in of old equipment

Gains are not recognized on the exchange of similar assets. The old equipment had a book value of $8,000 but was allowed a $9,000 trade-in value (suggesting a $1,000 gain).

CHAPTER 11

CURRENT AND LONG-TERM LIABILITIES

LEARNING OBJECTIVES

After studying this chapter, you should be able to:

1. Explain the occurrence of and accounting for typical current liabilities of a business.

2. Account for notes payable when interest is included in the face value of a note and when interest is recorded separately.

3. Identify typical contingent liabilities and recognize the guidelines that are used for recording such obligations in the accounts.

4. Prepare journal entries for warranty costs.

5. Account for mortgage notes.

6. Recognize the growing importance of leases and the underlying differences between operating and capital leases.

7. Understand the fundamental accounting issues related to pension plans and postretirement health-care benefits.

8. Describe the basic issues related to accounting for income taxes.

9. (Appendix) Calculate and record payroll, including the employer's tax obligation.

CHAPTER HIGHLIGHTS

I. **CURRENT LIABILITIES** are debts or obligations that will be paid within one year or the operating cycle, whichever is longer. Payment of current liabilities typically involve the use of current assets, or the creation of another current liability. Current liabilities include accounts payable, prepayments by customers, amounts collected for and payable to third parties, the portion of long-term debt due within one year or the operating cycle (whichever is longer), accrued liabilities for expenses incurred but not yet paid, notes payable to banks and other parties, and contingent liabilities.

   A. **ACCOUNTS PAYABLE** represent amounts owed to suppliers for the purchase of goods or services.

B. **PREPAYMENTS (ADVANCES) BY CUSTOMERS** arise from transactions such as selling magazine subscriptions in advance, selling tickets in advance, and other similar items. These items represent an obligation on the part of the seller to either return the money or deliver a service in the future.

C. Often, a company will engage in **COLLECTIONS FOR THIRD PARTIES**. The recipient of the cash has an obligation to turn the money over to another entity, such as a tax collection authority. Such amounts are appropriately reflected as a current liability until the funds are remitted to the rightful owner.

D. The **CURRENT PORTION OF LONG-TERM DEBT** is the amount of principal which is to be paid within one year or the operating cycle, whichever is longer. For example, a $100,000 note may be paid in equal annual increments of $10,000, plus accrued interest. At the end of any given year, the $10,000 principal due during the following year should be reported as a current liability (along with any accrued interest), with the remaining balance shown as a long-term liability.

E. **ACCRUED LIABILITIES** include items like accrued salaries and wages, vacation pay, income taxes, interest, and so forth. These items relate to expenses that accumulate with the passage of time, but will be paid in one lump-sum amount.

 1. The cost of employee service accrues gradually with the passage of time. The amount that employees have earned but not been paid is termed **ACCRUED SALARIES** and should be reported as a current liability.

 2. Like accrued salaries, **ACCRUED VACATION PAY** also accumulates with the passage of time. The dollar value of accumulated paid vacation time due to employees should be reported as an accrued liability.

F. Formal short-term borrowings, known as **NOTES PAYABLE**, are often used to finance purchases of equipment, real estate, and other similar assets. These notes are typically due in less than one year, and it is common to report them as a current liability.

 1. **ACCOUNTING FOR NOTES PAYABLE** is straightforward. The amount borrowed is entered in the accounting records by increasing Cash (debit) and Notes Payable (credit). When the note is repaid, the difference between the carrying amount of the note and the cash necessary to repay that note is reported as interest expense (importantly, if any of this interest had been previously accrued, that portion would be a reduction of interest payable rather than recorded as interest expense). Representative journal entries for a $10,000, 10%, one-year note follow:

 To issue a note:

Cash	10,000	
Notes Payable		10,000

To repay the note:

Interest Expense	1,000	
Cash		1,000
Notes Payable	10,000	
Cash		10,000

2. Occasionally, **NOTES** may be issued **WITH INTEREST INCLUDED IN THE FACE VALUE**. For example, $10,000 may be borrowed, but an $11,000 note is established (interest is not separately stated). The $1,000 difference is initially recorded as a discount on notes payable (reported as contra liability; i.e., an $11,000 note payable minus a $1,000 discount, for a net liability equal to the $10,000 borrowed). At maturity, $11,000 is repaid, representing a $10,000 repayment of borrowed amounts and $1,000 interest.

   a. **DISCOUNT AMORTIZATION** should occur to transfer the discount to interest expense. This means that, over the life of the note, the $1,000 discount (from the preceding example) should be recorded as interest expense by debiting Interest Expense and crediting Discount on Notes Payable. In this way, the $11,000 paid at maturity (credit to Cash) can be offset with an $11,000 reduction in the Notes Payable account (debit). In journal entry form:

To issue a note with interest included in the face value:

Cash	10,000	
Discount on Notes Payable	1,000	
Notes Payable		11,000

To repay the note and amortize the discount:

Interest Expense	1,000	
Discount on Notes Payable		1,000
Notes Payable	11,000	
Cash		11,000

Discount amortization occurs not only at the date of repayment, but also at the end of an accounting period (to record interest expense for the amount attributable to the period). In the preceding example, the $1,000 of interest expense may need to be recorded partially in one period and partially in another. A brief comparison of notes issued at face value versus notes issued at a discount reveals that the resulting balance sheets (net amount of liability) are essentially identical; likewise, for interest expense.

G. A company may have potential or **CONTINGENT LIABILITIES**. This occurs when the company might owe some amount to another party, but there is uncertainty about the timing and amount (if any). A lawsuit is an example of a contingent liability.

   1. The **ACCOUNTING RULES FOR CONTINGENCIES** require that a liability be recorded in the accounts when it is probable that the future event will occur and the amount of

the liability can be reasonably estimated. On the other hand, if it is only reasonably possible that the contingent liability will become a real liability, then disclosure via notes to the financial statements is all that is required.

      2. **WARRANTY COSTS** are recorded as a contingent liability because they are probable and can be reasonably estimated. When goods are sold, an estimate of the amount of warranty costs to be incurred on the goods should be recorded as expense, with the offsetting credit to a Warranty Liability account. As warranty work is performed, the Warranty Liability is reduced and Cash (or other resources used) is credited. In this manner, the expense is recorded in the same period as the sale (matching principle).

  H. One appropriate **BALANCE SHEET DISCLOSURE** for current liabilities is to list them according to their due dates, from the earliest to the latest. Another acceptable alternative is to list them by maturity value, from the largest to the smallest.

II. Many financing transactions necessarily involve the creation of **LONG-TERM LIABILITIES**.

  A. Many long-term borrowings are accomplished via **MORTGAGE NOTES**. Mortgage notes are used to finance real estate purchases and similar transactions. The repayment of borrowed funds is secured by the particular property that is financed (i.e., the property is the collateral). Mortgage notes are typically paid in regular installments. Each payment covers the interest that has accumulated since the last payment date, with the excess reducing the balance of the note.

  B. Many businesses acquire needed assets via **LEASES**. With a lease arrangement, the lessee pays money to the lessor for the rights to use an asset for a stated period of time.

      1. Leases may be classified according to two broad categories: **OPERATING LEASES VERSUS CAPITAL LEASES**. An operating lease provides the lessee with the right to use property for a limited period of time, and amounts paid should be recorded as rent expense. In contrast, capital leases are more akin to a financing transaction.

      2. The **ACCOUNTING FOR CAPITAL LEASES** can become quite complex. The basic ingredients, however, are that the lessee records the leased asset as an item of property, plant, and equipment. The asset is then depreciated over its useful life to the lessee. The lessee also records a long-term liability reflecting the obligation to make continuing payments under the lease agreement. As these payments are made, an amount of interest expense is recorded and the liability is reduced. The accounting for the obligation is similar to the accounting for a mortgage note.

  C. Increasingly, companies are providing **PENSION PLANS** that are designed to provide retirement benefits to employees.

      1. **PENSION ACCOUNTING AND REPORTING** adheres to the matching concept; pension expense is recorded during the years an employee works for the company. Also, companies typically fund pension obligations over the employee's active service period by transferring money to a separate pension fund. This pension fund invests monies and makes periodic payments to retired employees. On a company's accounting records, the periodic expense is debited to Pension Expense, and Cash is credited for the amount disbursed to the pension fund. If the amount expensed exceeds the amount contributed to the pension fund, a pension liability is likely to be

reported on the company's balance sheet (importantly, this liability should not be confused with the amount that the pension fund owes to retired employees). Additional pension disclosures are generally required. Finally, note that the payment of retirement benefits by the pension fund does not require an entry on the company's books.

    D.   Only recently did companies begin to be required to report a liability for the future expected costs of **POSTRETIREMENT HEALTH-CARE BENEFITS**. This liability relates to costs that are expected to be incurred in the future because of health insurance that an employer will provide for the benefit of employees after they retire. This obligation can be very substantial, especially in light of health-care cost increases.

    E.   Because financial accounting rules are governed by accounting standards and tax return preparation is governed by tax laws, significant differences often exist between pretax financial income and income reportable to the Internal Revenue Service (known as taxable income). In view of this situation, the taxes paid or due to the government may not be an appropriate measure of a company's tax expense. Hence, the measurement of **LIABILITIES FOR FEDERAL INCOME TAXES** often becomes quite complex.

        1.   **DIFFERENCES BETWEEN TAXABLE INCOME AND FINANCIAL INCOME** are sometimes only temporary. Temporary differences arise when revenues are subject to taxation before being recognized in financial income, revenues are subject to taxation after being recognized in financial income, expenses are deductible for tax purposes before being recognized in financial income, and expenses are deductible for tax purposes after being recognized in financial income. In the alternative, some differences between taxable and financial income are caused by events that have no tax consequences. For example, the payment of fines is an expense on the company's books but is not deductible for tax purposes.

        2.   Temporary differences result in **DEFERRED INCOME TAXES**. To illustrate, existing temporary differences may cause an expectation that a future year's taxable income will exceed financial income. As a result, one will expect that taxes owed in the future will exceed tax expense based on accounting income. Therefore, the deferred tax liability equals the expected difference in income multiplied times the expected future tax rate. The amount of deferred tax is classified as either a current or long-term liability based on the amount of time until the difference is anticipated to reverse.

III.   **APPENDIX: ACCOUNTING FOR PAYROLL** is a significant issue for almost every company.

    A.   A company is required to maintain **EMPLOYEE EARNINGS** records. One important number revealed by these records is total or gross earnings (which, for an hourly employee, is the total hours worked multiplied by the hourly pay rate).

    B.   **DEDUCTIONS FROM EMPLOYEE EARNINGS** cause an employee's take-home pay to be less than gross pay.

        1.   **SOCIAL SECURITY/MEDICARE TAXES (FICA)** are paid by almost all employees. These taxes are computed as a constant percentage of earnings (but are imposed on only designated base amounts of earnings each year).

        2.   Another common deduction relates to **FEDERAL, STATE, AND CITY INCOME TAXES**. Employers are required to withhold these taxes from an employee's pay. The

withheld amounts must be remitted periodically to the government. Withholding amounts are based on the employee's level of income, the frequency of pay, marital status, and the number of withholding allowances claimed (based on the number of dependents). Employees claim withholding allowances by filing a form W-4.

3. There are **OTHER** payroll **DEDUCTIONS** that may occur; insurance, savings bonds, charity, and so forth.

4. The **CALCULATION OF TAKE-HOME PAY** (net pay) requires that deductions be subtracted from gross earnings.

C. Businesses are required to fulfill extensive **PAYROLL RECORDING AND RECORD KEEPING** requirements. A payroll register may be used to accumulate information about gross earnings, deductions, and net pay for each employee. A summary journal entry for the payroll would include a debit to Salaries Expense for the gross pay, credits to various payables related to withheld amounts (Social Security Taxes Payable, Medicare Taxes Payable, Federal Income Taxes Payable, etc.), and a credit to Salaries Payable for the net pay. When the withheld amounts are remitted to the appropriate agency, Cash is credited and the appropriate payable is debited.

1. Shortly after the conclusion of a calendar year, an employer must review their **EMPLOYEE RECORDS** and prepare a summary wage and tax statement (commonly called a W-2). This information is provided to both the employee and the Internal Revenue Service, and helps employees accurately prepare their own annual federal and state income tax returns.

D. Just as the employee must bear certain payroll taxes, **PAYROLL TAXES OF THE EMPLOYER** must also be considered.

1. The amount of **SOCIAL SECURITY/MEDICARE TAX** paid by the employee must be matched by the employer. Therefore, the actual tax to be remitted to the government is twice the amount deducted from an employee's paycheck.

2. **FEDERAL UNEMPLOYMENT TAX** is a tax imposed only on the employer. The amount of the tax is determined by multiplying a specific rate times a base amount of income. Federal unemployment tax rates are reduced significantly in those states (most states) which have their own unemployment program.

3. **STATE UNEMPLOYMENT TAXES** are assessed on a base amount of income at a specified rate (determined on a state-by-state basis). An employer may receive a merit reduction in the imposed rate if the employer has a low incidence of unemployment claims by former employees.

4. **RECORDING THE EMPLOYER'S** payroll **TAXES** requires that the sum total of the payroll taxes be debited to an expense account. The offsetting credits are to various liability accounts, reflecting amounts due to the different taxing authorities.

CLASS NOTES

CLASS NOTES

CLASS NOTES

CLASS NOTES

SELF TESTS

FULFILLMENT OF LEARNING OBJECTIVES

Circle the appropriate response.

L.O. 1(a)   An example of an accrued liability is:

salaries payable
or
the current portion of long-term debt

L.O. 1(b)   Collections for third parties should be recorded as a current liability.

true   or   false

L.O. 1(c)   Which of the following would not be a typical current liability?

prepayments (advances) to suppliers
or
amounts collected for and payable to third parties

L.O. 2(a)   How would the net (or total) liability reported on a balance sheet compare for (1) notes with interest included in the face value and (2) notes where interest is recorded separately?

same   or   different

L.O. 2(b)   A Discount account should be established when interest is included in the face amount of the note.

correct   or   incorrect

L.O. 2(c)   The process of reducing a discount by recognizing interest expense is frequently referred to as discount amortization.

true   or   false

L.O. 3(a)   The guidelines for the recognition of contingent liabilities reflect that they should be recorded in the accounts when it is probable that the future event will occur and the amount of the liability can be reasonably:

estimated   or   isolated

L.O. 3(b)   By definition, contingent liabilities are improbable.

true   or   false

L.O. 4(a)   A warranty liability is a typical contingent liability that meets the guidelines for recording as a liability in the accounts.

correct   or   incorrect

L.O. 4(b)   Warranty expense should be reported in the:

period of sale   or   period of warranty service

L.O. 4(c)   On the payment of monies for the satisfaction of a warranty, which account should be affected?

expense   or   liability

L.O. 5(a)   Mortgage notes are often used to finance the purchase of real estate and are typically paid in monthly installments, with each installment representing the interest and partial payment on the note's:

principal   or   collateral

L.O. 5(b)   The unpaid balance of a mortgage note could be expressed as the original borrowing minus the total payments that have occurred.

true   or   false

L.O. 6(a)   Which party pays the other for the use of property?

lessee   or   lessor

L.O. 6(b)   Under which type of lease does the lessee obtain the rights to use leased property for a limited period of time and treat amounts paid as expense?

operating lease   or   capital lease

L.O. 6(c)   The liability recorded under a capital lease is more like a:

mortgage note
or
note payable with interest included in the face amount

L.O. 7(a)   Pension expense and postretirement health-care costs should be recorded during an employee's active period of:

service   or   retirement

L.O. 7(b)   Differences between pension expense and amounts paid to a pension fund are typically reported as a pension liability in the balance sheet.

correct   or   incorrect

L.O. 8(a)   Income measurement based on income tax regulations is often referred to as:

pretax financial income   or   taxable income

L.O. 8(b)   Differences between taxable income and pretax financial income may be caused by revenues being subject to taxation before being recognized in financial income. This is an example of:

a temporary difference
or
an event having no tax consequence

L.O. 8(c)   Recording of a deferred tax liability indicates that amounts are immediately due the Federal government.

true   or   false

L.O. 9(a)   Which of the following payroll taxes is borne exclusively by the employer?

social security taxes   or   unemployment taxes

L.O. 9(b)   Deductions from employee earnings, plus net pay, equals:

gross earnings   or   gross withholdings

L.O. 9(c)   Withholding allowances are determined by reference to the:

W-4   or   W-2

L.O. 9(d)   Amounts withheld from employees' paychecks are recorded on the employer's books as a:

liability   or   contra liability

FILL IN THE BLANKS

1. _____ _____ are debts or obligations that will be paid within one year or the operating cycle.

2. Sales tax is an example of a collection for a _____ _____.

3. Another name for an accrued liability is an _____ _____.

4. Accrued liabilities for employee service consist of _____ _____ and _____ _____ _____ _____.

5. The discount on notes payable is reported as a _____ _____.

6. The process of reducing the discount by recognizing interest expense is frequently referred to as _____ _____.

7. Liabilities that are not definite and absolute, but instead give rise to potential liabilities, are known as _____ _____.

8. The guidelines for recording contingent liabilities into the accounts stipulate that the future event be _____ and the amount of liability be _____ _____.

9. Warranty costs should be expensed in the period of _____.

10. _____ _____ are often used to finance the purchase of real estate.

11. A lease is an arrangement that allows one party, the _____, to use the assets of another party, the _____, for a stated period of time.

12. Many lease agreements provide a period of use nearly equal to the entire service life of the leased assets. Such agreements frequently contain a provision for the lessee to acquire the property at a bargain purchase price, and are called _____ _____.

13. A _____ _____ is an agreement between a company and its employees that provides for retirement benefits.

14. Employers typically finance retirement plans by making periodic cash payments directly to a _____ _____.

15. _____ _____ result when revenues and expenses are recognized in different accounting periods for income tax and financial reporting purposes.

16. _____ _____ _____ _____ are reported on the financial statements as an obligation, and reflect that taxable income is expected to exceed financial income over future years.

17. The _____ _____ _____ _____ provides retirement, financial, and medical benefits to aged, disabled, widows, and orphans.

18. The amount withheld for federal income taxes is based on employee earnings, frequency of pay, marital status, and the number of _____ _____ claimed.

19. A formal name for the Form W-2 is the _____ _____ _____ _____.

20. The tax imposed by Federal and state governments to financially assist unemployed workers is the _____ _____.

MULTIPLE CHOICE QUESTIONS

Circle the appropriate response.

1. Typical current liabilities include:

    a. Prepayments by customers.
    b. Travel advances to employees.
    c. The principal portion of a mortgage note that is due beyond year or the operating cycle, whichever is longer.
    d. Accumulated depreciation.

2. Contingent liabilities should be recorded in the accounts when:

    a. It is probable that the future event will occur.
    b. The amount of the liability can be reasonably estimated.
    c. Both (a) and (b).
    d. Either (a) or (b).

3. On June 1, Whit Corporation purchased a truck for $30,000. To pay for the truck, Whit issued and recorded a six-month note payable for $31,500. No other entry was recorded for the note until payment on December 1. The journal entry to record payment of the note would include:

    a. A debit to Interest Expense for $1,500.
    b. A debit to Discount on Notes Payable for $1,500.
    c. A debit to Notes Payable for $30,000.
    d. A debit to Cash for $31,500.

4. The Discount on Notes Payable:

    a. Is a contra liability account.
    b. Is a contingent liability account.
    c. Should be reported as an asset because of its debit balance.
    d. Is amortized to reduce interest expense over the life of the note payable.

5. If the journal entry to record an accrued liability were accidentally recorded twice, it would:

    a. Understate income for the year.
    b. Overstate income for the year.
    c. Have no effect on income for the year.
    d. Understate accrued liabilities at the end of the year.

6. Landry paid $5,000 cash for warranty service work. If a Warranty Liability account had been previously established, the proper journal entry to record the service work would be:

   a. Sales   5,000
         Cash   5,000
   b. Warranty Expense   5,000
         Warranty Liability   5,000
   c. Warranty Expense   5,000
         Cash   5,000
   d. Warranty Liability   5,000
         Cash   5,000

7. Golden Chemical Company anticipates that temporary differences will result in taxable income exceeding pretax accounting income by $1,000 per year for each of the next five years. Golden further anticipates that tax rates in future years will average 30%. How much deferred tax liability should Golden report?

   a. $0
   b. $1,500
   c. $3,500
   d. $5,000

8. The employee's withholding allowance certificate is popularly referred to as a:

   a. W-2.
   b. W-4.
   c. Form 1040.
   d. Payroll register.

9. The Social Security/Medicare taxes are levied on:

   a. Employees only.
   b. Employers only.
   c. Both employees and employers.
   d. Earnings in excess of base amounts.

10. The gross payroll for Zurich Corporation was $100,000. Federal income tax withheld from employee paychecks amounted to $24,000, state income tax withheld amounted to $3,000, and Social Security/Medicare taxes totaled $12,000 (both the employee and employer portion). Furthermore, employees elected to have $1,000 of insurance and charitable contributions withheld from their paychecks. How much was net pay?

    a. $34,000
    b. $60,000
    c. $66,000
    d. $72,000

DEMONSTRATION PROBLEMS

DP-1　Real Town Realtors conducts classes in real estate management. There are three levels of courses which are offered. Students must prepay the full cost of the course in advance of attendance. Information about registrations during 19X1 is as follows:

Course	1	2	3
Number of students	20	30	10
Selling price per course	$20	$30	$40

Forty percent of the classes had been conducted during 19X1. The remainder will be provided early in 19X2.

a. Prepare journal entries for 19X1 to record (1) the sale of the classes, and (2) the classes provided during the year.
b. Present proper disclosure for the unused classes on Real Town's December 31, 19X1, balance sheet.

DP-2   Lipton Feed & Seed purchased a new truck from Benjamin Motosh on July 1, 19X4, for $35,000. Lipton signed a one-year note for $39,200; interest is included in the note's face value. Prepare Lipton's journal entries:

   a.   To record the July 1, 19X4, purchase.
   b.   To record interest expense through December 31, 19X4.
   c.   To record the payment and complete the accounting for the note on June 30, 19X5.

DP-3 The payroll register of Circuit Manufacturing Company for the month of April contained the following information:

Office salaries	$20,000
Sales salaries	30,000

Payroll deductions were made for Social Security/Medicare taxes at the rate of 7% of total gross earnings, federal income taxes of $6,320, state income taxes at 6% of gross earnings, and dental insurance of $150.

a. Prepare the necessary entry to record the April payroll.
b. Record payroll tax expense, assuming that unemployment taxes are 6.0% on the first $7,000 paid to each employee (5.4% for state unemployment and 0.6% for federal unemployment). All employees have earned less than $7,000 for the year.

SOLUTIONS TO SELF TESTS

FULFILLMENT OF LEARNING OBJECTIVES

1(a)	Salaries payable
1(b)	True
1(c)	Prepayments (advances) to suppliers
2(a)	Same
2(b)	Correct
2(c)	True
3(a)	Estimated
3(b)	False
4(a)	Correct
4(b)	Period of sale
4(c)	Liability
5(a)	Principal
5(b)	False
6(a)	Lessee
6(b)	Operating lease
6(c)	Mortgage note
7(a)	Service
7(b)	Correct
8(a)	Taxable income
8(b)	A temporary difference
8(c)	False
9(a)	Unemployment taxes
9(b)	Gross earnings
9(c)	W-4
9(d)	Liability

FILL IN THE BLANKS

1. Current liabilities
2. Third party
3. Accrued expense
4. Accrued salaries, estimated liability for vacation pay
5. Contra liability
6. Discount amortization
7. Contingent liabilities
8. Probable, reasonably estimatible
9. Sale
10. Mortgage notes
11. Lessee, lessor
12. Capital leases
13. Pension plan
14. Pension fund
15. Temporary differences
16. Deferred income tax liabilities
17. Federal Insurance Contributions Act

18. Withholding allowances
19. Wage and tax statement
20. Unemployment tax

MULTIPLE CHOICE QUESTIONS

1. a. Prepayments by customers should be reported as a current liability entitled Unearned Revenue. Travel advances to employees is a current asset. The principal portion of a mortgage note which will be paid within (not beyond!) one year or the operating cycle, whichever is longer, is reported as a current liability. Accumulated depreciation is a contra asset.

2. c. To be recorded in the accounts, a contingent liability should be both probable and subject to reasonable estimation.

3. a. The appropriate journal entry is:

Notes Payable	31,500	
Interest Expense	1,500	
Discount on Notes Payable		1,500
Cash		31,500

4. a. Discount on Notes Payable is subtracted from the related Notes Payable, and is therefore a contra liability. The discount is not "contingent." Amortization of a discount increases interest expense.

5. a. The error would cause an expense to be overstated (via the extra debit), as well as overstating the related payable (via the extra credit). Therefore, income would be understated and liabilities would be overstated.

6. d. At the time warranty service is performed, the previously recorded liability should be reduced by the amount of the expenditure. The expense should have already been recorded in an earlier period.

7. b. $1,500. The deferred tax amount equals the anticipated income difference times the expected tax rate ($5,000 X 30%).

8. b. The W-4 is the withholding allowance certificate prepared at the time an employee is hired. The W-2 is the annual wage and tax statement furnished to an employee, the form 1040 is an individual's federal income tax return, and the payroll register is basically a special journal maintained by an employer for recording payroll related transactions.

9. c. Both the employee and the employer must pay equal amounts of the FICA tax. The tax is levied on income only up to a base amount.

10. c. $66,000. Net pay equals gross pay ($100,000) minus various withholdings attributable to the employees ($24,000 + $3,000 + ($12,000/2) + $1,000). The $12,000 is divided by 2 because the cost is borne equally by both the employee and employer.

DEMONSTRATION PROBLEMS

DP-1

(a) 1. Cash   1,700
        Unearned Revenue   1,700
    To record classes sold in advance
    1:   20 at $20 = $ 400
    2:   30 at $30 =   900
    3:   10 at $40 =   400
                            $1,700

     2. Unearned Revenue   680
         Revenue   680
     To record revenue for 19X1 ($1,700 X 40%)

(b) Current liabilities
     Unearned revenue $1,020

DP-2

(a) Truck   35,000
    Discount on Notes Payable   4,200
        Notes Payable   39,200
    To record truck purchase via note payable

(b) Interest Expense   2,100
        Discount on Notes Payable   2,100
    To accrue interest for 6 months and amortize the discount

(c) Notes Payable   39,200
    Interest Expense   2,100
        Discount on Notes Payable   2,100
        Cash   39,200
    To record payment of the note and amortize the discount

DP-3

(a)
Office Salaries Expense		20,000	
Sales Salaries Expense		30,000	
Social Security/Medicare Taxes Payable			3,500
Employees' Federal Income Tax Payable			6,320
Employees' State Income Tax Payable			3,000
Insurance Program Payable			150
Salaries Payable			37,030

To record payroll and withholdings
(Social Security/Medicare, 7% X $50,000 = $3,500; state income tax payable, 6% X $50,000 = $3,000)

(b)
Payroll Tax Expense	6,500	
FICA Taxes Payable		3,500
Federal Unemployment Taxes Payable		300
State Unemployment Taxes Payable		2,700

To record employer's payroll taxes
(Federal unemployment tax, 0.6% X $50,000 = $300; state unemployment tax, 5.4% X $50,000 = $2,700)

CHAPTER 12

BONDS PAYABLE AND THE TIME VALUE OF MONEY

LEARNING OBJECTIVES

After studying this chapter, you should be able to:

1. Recognize the basic differences between bondholders and stockholders.

2. Identify the different types of bonds that may be issued.

3. Account for bond issues, including those issued between interest dates.

4. Distinguish between contract and effective interest rates, and premiums and discounts.

5. Explain the concept of present value.

6. Calculate amortization under both the straight-line and effective-interest methods.

7. Account for bond retirements and convertible bonds.

CHAPTER HIGHLIGHTS

I. **BONDS** enable a borrower to split a large loan into many small units. Each of these units (or bonds) is essentially a note payable. The terms of a bond issue are specified in the bond indenture, and compliance with the terms is monitored by an independent trustee.

II. There are many **TYPES OF BONDS** that may be issued by corporations and government units.

   A. Specifically, there are **SECURED AND DEBENTURE BONDS**. Secured bonds have specific assets pledged as collateral, whereas debenture bonds are unsecured.

   B. Differences are also noted between **REGISTERED AND COUPON BONDS**. Most bonds issued in recent years are registered bonds; the issuing company maintains a record of the owner's name and address, and automatically mails interest payments. In contrast, the issuing company does not maintain ownership records for coupon bonds. Coupon bonds are accompanied by small, detachable coupons which must be turned in by the holder of the bond in exchange for each periodic cash interest payment.

C. **OTHER BOND CLASSIFICATIONS** include serial bonds (which mature on a staggered basis over the life of the bond), sinking fund bonds (which require the company to set aside money periodically for the retirement of the bonds at maturity), convertible bonds (which can be exchanged for shares of capital stock at the option of the bondholder), and callable bonds (which give the issuing company the right to retire the bonds prior to scheduled maturity).

III. **ACCOUNTING FOR BOND ISSUES** begins when a company receives cash (a debit) in exchange for bonds payable (a credit). As interest is paid, bond interest expense is recorded. At maturity, cash is given (a credit) to retire the bonds payable (a debit).

A. If **BONDS** are **ISSUED BETWEEN INTEREST PAYMENT DATES**, the issuing company is entitled to the face amount of the bonds plus any accrued interest (attributable to the time period from the printed or last interest date up to the issue date). On the next interest payment date, the issuing company must pay a full period's interest (typically six months), even though the bonds have been outstanding a shorter period of time. In essence, the accrued interest received on the date of issue is returned. The reason for this complication is to allow the company to pay a full period's interest on each payment date, regardless of the amount of time the bonds have been held by their owner. The appropriate journal entry for bonds issued at face value between interest payment dates is to debit Cash for the total proceeds, credit Bonds Payable for the face amount, and credit Bond Interest Payable for the accrued interest. On the next interest payment date, Cash is credited for a full period's interest, and Bond Interest Payable (which arose at the time of issue) and Bond Interest Expense (accruing since the date of issue) are debited.

IV. There are several **FACTORS THAT AFFECT ISSUE PRICES** of bonds; perhaps the most important is the relationship between the contract interest rate (the interest rate stated on the face of the bond) and the market (or effective) interest rate at the time of issue. For example, if a 10% stated rate bond is issued at a time when the market rate of interest is 11%, the bond would sell at less than its face amount (because the contract interest rate is inferior to the going market rate). Bonds that sell at less than face amount are said to sell at a discount. Alternatively, if the market rate of interest is 11%, but a particular bond has a 13% stated rate, then the bond would sell at a premium.

A. To determine the amount an investor would pay for a bond requires **PRESENT VALUE** computations. A bond is a contract to pay a regular cash interest payment plus a fixed amount of cash at maturity (the face value). The "value" of this cash flow can be determined by finding its present worth at the market rate of interest. The appendix of this chapter includes a detailed introduction to present value computations.

B. **BONDS ISSUED AT A DISCOUNT** are entered into the accounting records by debiting Cash for the proceeds, debiting Discount on Bonds Payable (a contra liability account) for the amount of the discount, and crediting Bonds Payable for the face amount of the bonds. This technique results in the balance sheet revealing (on the issue date) bond carrying value (bonds payable minus the discount) equal to the cash received.

1. At the maturity date of a bond, the issuer will have to repay the face value. The difference between the face value and the lesser amount of cash received at the time of issue is the discount. Therefore, the **MEANING OF A BOND DISCOUNT** is that additional interest cost (beyond the periodic cash interest payments) is associated with

the bond issue. The discount must be recognized as interest expense through a process known as discount amortization.

2. **DISCOUNT AMORTIZATION:** The **STRAIGHT-LINE METHOD** divides the original discount by the number of months the bonds will be outstanding, resulting in a constant monthly amortization amount. Periodically (based on the number of months that have elapsed), Bond Interest Expense is debited and Discount on Bonds Payable is credited. This amount of expense is combined with the cash interest payments to determine total interest expense. Discount amortization causes the carrying value of the bonds on the balance sheet to increase (i.e., bonds payable less unamortized discount). By maturity, the balance of the discount is reduced to zero, and the carrying value of the bonds is equal to their face value -- which is the amount that must be repaid at that time.

   a. Recording the amortization of bond discount and the related cash payment can occur via two separate journal entries, or via **A COMPOUND ENTRY APPROACH**. With the latter approach, Bond Interest Expense is simply debited for the total of the credits that are made to Discount on Bonds Payable and Cash.

3. **DISCOUNT AMORTIZATION:** The **EFFECTIVE-INTEREST METHOD** is a theoretically preferable approach to recording discount amortization; it recognizes interest expense as a constant percentage of the bond's carrying value (rather than as an equal amount each year). The amount of discount amortization is the difference between the cash paid for interest and the amount of bond interest expense, with interest expense being calculated as the effective interest rate times the bond's carrying value for the period.

   a. The textbook provides **AN EXAMPLE** of the detailed computations that pertain to the effective-interest amortization method.

C. When bonds are issued at a premium, the journal entry to record the issue debits Cash for the amount received, credits Bonds Payable for the face amount, and credits Premium on Bonds Payable for the difference. The carrying value of **BONDS ISSUED AT A PREMIUM** is determined by adding the unamortized premium to the face amount of the bonds.

   1. The **MEANING OF A BOND PREMIUM** is just the opposite of a discount. Over the life of the bond issue, interest expense is reduced by premium amortization. This reduction is logical because the face value repaid at maturity is less than the original issue price.

   2. **PREMIUM AMORTIZATION** is recorded by debiting the Premium on Bonds Payable account and crediting Bond Interest Expense for the amortization amount. Amortization can be calculated by the straight-line method (an equal amount each period) or by the effective-interest method (the effective interest rate times the bond's carrying value for the period, less the cash paid for interest).

      a. The textbook provides an example of the detailed computations that pertain to the **EFFECTIVE-INTEREST AMORTIZATION** method.

D. When an accounting period ends on other than an interest payment date, the **YEAR-END INTEREST ACCRUALS** must be recorded. The cash portion of interest which has accumulated is recorded by debiting Interest Expense and crediting Interest Payable. In addition, any premium or discount must be amortized (for the amount attributable to the period from the last amortization date through the end of the accounting period). The journal entry for the next interest payment date must reflect that interest was accrued and amortization recorded at the end of the prior period.

E. Accounting for a **BOND RETIREMENT** (or a bond refunding -- replacing one bond issue with another) necessitates a credit to Cash for the amount paid to reacquire the bonds, a debit to Bonds Payable (and a debit to any unamortized premium or a credit to any unamortized discount), and a debit (or credit) to Loss (or Gain) on Bond Retirement. The loss or gain equals the difference between the amount paid and the bond's carrying value.

1. Companies might issue **CONVERTIBLE BONDS** which can be exchanged for a fixed number of shares of the company's capital stock. If the stock appreciates and the exchange occurs, then the bonds and any unamortized premium or discount must be removed from the books; the capital stock is recorded at the carrying value of the debt. No gain or loss is recognized on this transaction.

F. In an effort to protect bondholders, companies are sometimes required to make periodic deposits to **BOND SINKING FUNDS**. Such funds are invested and eventually used to repay bonds.

V. **APPENDIX: THE TIME VALUE OF MONEY**

A. As **AN INTRODUCTORY EXAMPLE**, consider that a person would rather have cash sooner than later; the cash can be invested to generate additional returns. Simply stated, money has a time value.

B. To appreciate the time value concept, one must understand both **SIMPLE INTEREST AND COMPOUND INTEREST**. Simple interest is computed as "Principal times Rate times Time." For example, $100 invested at 10% for two years would generate interest of $20 ($100 X 10% X 2). In contrast, compound interest allows for the earning of interest on previous interest. For example, $100 invested at 10% for two years (compounded annually) would generate interest of $21; the $100 investment would earn $10 and grow to $110 by the end of the first year, then the $110 would earn an additional $11 ($110 X 10%).

C. The compound interest computations just introduced give rise to the concept of **FUTURE VALUE**. Simply stated, $100 invested today at 10% annually compounded interest has a future value of $121 in two years. Table I in the textbook contains future value factors. To understand this table, observe, for example, that the factor located in the 8% column and 3-period row is 1.25971. Hence, $1 invested for three years at 8% annually compounded interest will grow to $1.25971; an investment of $100 would grow to $125.971, and so on for other investment amounts.

D. The inverse of future value is known as **PRESENT VALUE**. Present value is the amount a future sum is worth today. It is the reciprocal of future value. Referring to the previous example, $121 to be received in two years is worth $100 today (assuming a 10% interest rate). Table III in the textbook reveals various present value factors. For example, the 10% column, 2-period row, reveals a factor of 0.82645 (notice that $121 X 0.82645 = $100).

E. Many cash flows occur in level streams rather than as lump-sum amounts. Such payment streams are called annuities, and tables are available for calculations pertaining to **PRESENT VALUE AND ANNUITIES**. Referring to Table IV in the textbook, note that the 10% column, 5-period row, reveals a factor of 3.79079. This means that the present value of an investment of $1 per year (at the end of each year) for five years is $3.79079.

   1. Information about **FUTURE VALUE AND ANNUITIES** is available in Table II. For example, an annual investment of $1 per year for five years (at 10% interest) will grow to $6.10510.

F. When considering present value computations for **PERIODS OF LESS THAN ONE YEAR**, an adjustment is needed. By way of example, the present value of $1 invested for five years at 10% compounded semiannually can be determined by referring to the 5% column and ten-period row of the present value table. In other words, there are ten semiannual interest periods in five years, and a 10% annual rate equates to a 5% semiannual rate.

G. **PRESENT VALUE AND BOND PRICES** are related. Recall that a bond is a stream of future cash flows (an annuity for the periodic interest payment and a lump-sum at maturity). To determine the price of a bond, one need merely find the present value (using the market rate of interest) of the bond's cash flow.

   1. There are many **OTHER APPLICATIONS OF PRESENT VALUE**. Examples include lease accounting, pension accounting, and goodwill computations.

CLASS NOTES

CLASS NOTES

CLASS NOTES

CLASS NOTES

CLASS NOTES

SELF TESTS

FULFILLMENT OF LEARNING OBJECTIVES

Circle the appropriate response.

L.O. 1(a) Which of the following interests would have a prior claim on assets in the event of bankruptcy?

bondholders or stockholders

L.O. 1(b) Stockholders are said to have a residual claim on business assets.

true or false

L.O. 2(a) Secured bonds are often known as debentures.

true or false

L.O. 2(b) Most bonds issued in recent years have been:

registered or coupon

L.O. 3(a) When bonds are issued between interest payment dates, the first interest payment will involve cash flow for:

a full period's interest
or
a partial period's interest

L.O. 3(b) At the time a bond is issued, the Bonds Payable account is established for the face amount of the bond.

correct or incorrect

L.O. 4(a) When a bond's contract interest rate is higher than the market (effective) rate of interest at the time of issue, the bonds will be issued at a:

premium or discount

L.O. 4(b) The interest rate stated on the face of a bond is the:

contract rate or effective rate

L.O. 4(c) If a bond is issued at a premium, what relation will interest expense bear to the amount of cash paid for interest each period over the life of the bond?

greater than or less than

L.O. 5(a)   The stream of level cash flows is known as a(n):

lump sum   or   annuity

L.O. 5(b)   To determine the issue price of a bond, one would need to discount the future cash flow of the bond using factors related to:

present value   or   future value

L.O. 5(c)   As the effective interest rate increases, the issue price of a bond (as determined by its discounted cash flow) will:

increase   or   decrease

L.O. 6(a)   Which amortization technique is theoretically superior?

straight-line   or   effective-interest

L.O. 6(b)   The amortization of a premium will cause interest expense to:

increase   or   decrease

L.O. 6(c)   Which of the following amortization techniques result in a level amount of interest expense over the life of a bond issue?

straight-line   or   effective-interest

L.O. 6(d)   Bond interest expense for a period is equal to the cash paid for interest plus the premium amortized.

true   or   false

L.O. 7(a)   Gains and losses result on:

bond retirements   or   bond conversions

L.O. 7(b)   When a bond is retired, any unamortized premium or discount should continue to be amortized over the remaining periods the bond would have been outstanding.

true   or   false

FILL IN THE BLANKS

1. The provisions of a bond issue are normally stipulated in an accompanying document called a _____ _____.

2. In contrast to secured bonds, _____ _____ have no assets pledged as security.

3. _____ bonds permit the issuer to repay bondholders prior to the stipulated maturity date.

4. The set amount to be repaid on a bond's maturity date is known as _____ _____, whereas, the bond payable amount less any unamortized discount or plus any unamortized premium is known as _____ _____.

5. The interest rate printed on the face of a bond certificate is called the _____ _____ _____, whereas the actual interest rate is the _____ _____ _____.

6. When bonds are sold at more than face value, the difference between the issue price and the face value is commonly referred to as a _____.

7. Under _____-_____ _____, an equal amount of discount is allocated to each interest period, whereas, under the _____-_____ method of amortization, interest expense is calculated as a constant percentage of the bond carrying value.

8. Premium amortization causes interest expense to _____.

9. Bonds may be called and replaced by an issue that carries a lower interest rate under a technique known as bond _____, or may be retired and canceled under a technique known as bond _____.

10. A fund that is set aside to provide for the eventual repayment of bonds at maturity is known as a _____ _____ _____.

11. A method of calculating interest which allows for interest on the interest is called _____ _____.

12. _____ _____ is the amount to which an outlay will grow by the end of a designated time period, while _____ _____ is the inverse or reciprocal technique.

13. An _____ is a series of equal cash flows.

MULTIPLE CHOICE QUESTIONS

Circle the appropriate response.

1. Bonds payable should be disclosed on the balance sheet.

    a. At their face value minus any unamortized premiums.
    b. At their face value plus any unamortized premiums.
    c. At their maturity value.
    d. At their face value.

2. When the contract interest rate for a bond exceeds the effective interest rate of the bond, then:

   a. The price of the bond will be equal to the future cash flow associated with the bond.
   b. The bond will be issued at a premium.
   c. The bond will be issued at a discount.
   d. The face value of the bond will fluctuate over its life.

3. When interest payment dates on a bond are June 1 and December 1, and the bond is sold on July 1, the amount of cash received at issuance will be:

   a. Decreased by accrued interest from July 1 to December 1.
   b. Decreased by accrued interest from June 1 to July 1.
   c. Increased by accrued interest from July 1 to December 1.
   d. Increased by accrued interest from June 1 to July 1.

4. Which of the following statements is false?

   a. Convertible bonds typically have a higher interest rate than similar bonds which are not convertible.
   b. On the balance sheet, bond sinking funds should typically be disclosed as a long-term investment.
   c. Gains and losses on retirement of debt are reported on the income statement.
   d. Most bonds issued in recent years have been registered bonds.

5. On April 1, 19X1, Carl Corporation issued $100,000 of 12%, 10-year bonds. The bonds were issued at par plus accrued interest, are dated January 1, 19X1, and pay interest on July 1 and January 1. Carl's year-end is December 31. The entry to record payment of bond interest on July 1, 19X1, is:

   a. Bond Interest Expense   3,000
         Cash   3,000
   b. Bond Interest Expense   6,000
         Cash   6,000
   c. Bond Interest Expense   3,000
      Bond Interest Payable   3,000
         Cash   6,000
   d. Bond Interest Expense   3,000
         Bond Interest Payable   3,000

6. On June 1, Surge Corporation issued $100,000 of 9%, 5-year bonds. The bonds are dated June 1, 19X1. The bonds were issued at 96, and pay interest on December 1 and June 1. The entry to record issuance of the bonds is:

    a.   Cash   100,000
            Bonds Payable   100,000

    b.   Cash   96,000
            Discount on Bonds Payable   4,000
            Bonds Payable   100,000

    c.   Cash   104,000
            Bond Interest Payable   4,000
            Bonds Payable   100,000

    d.   Cash   96,000
            Bond Interest Expense   4,000
            Bonds Payable   100,000

7. On June 1, 19X1, German Corporation issued $100,000 of 7%, 5-year bonds dated April 1, 19X1, at 101 plus accrued interest. Interest is paid on April 1 and October 1. The proper entries to record bond interest expense for the year ended 19X1 would include a decrease in interest expense for premium amortization in the amount of (round to the nearest dollar and assume straight-line amortization):

    a. $0
    b. $117
    c. $121
    d. $200

8. Jeske Company issued $1,000,000 of 8% bonds at a time when the market rate of interest was 10%. If the bonds were issued at a $250,000 discount and interest was paid annually, how much was interest expense for the first full year of the bond issue (utilize the effective-interest amortization technique)?

    a. $25,000
    b. $75,000
    c. $80,000
    d. $100,000

9. The present value factor at 8% for one period is 0.92593, for two periods is 0.85734, for three periods is 0.79383, for four periods is 0.73503, and for five periods is 0.68058. Given these factors, what amount should an individual have today to be able to withdraw $1,000 each year for three years, with the first withdrawal to be made one year from today?

    a. $1,000/0.79383
    b. $1,000 X 0.92593 X 3
    c. $1,000 X (0.92593 + 0.85734 + 0.79383)
    d. $1,000 X 0.79383

10. The present value factor at 8% for one period is 0.92593, for two periods is 0.85734, for three periods is 0.79383, for four periods is 0.73503, and for five periods is 0.68058. Given these factors, what amount should be deposited in a bank today to grow to $100 three years from now?

   a. $100/0.79383
   b. $100/(0.92593/3)
   c. ($100/0.92593 + $100/0.85734 + $100/0.79383)
   d. $100 X 0.79383

DEMONSTRATION PROBLEMS

DP-1   Pinto Corporation issued $100,000 of 10% bonds on April 1, 19X1, at 103 plus accrued interest. The bonds are dated January 1, 19X1, and pay interest each June 30 and December 31. They mature on January 1, 19X7. Pinto Corporation uses the straight-line amortization technique (round total amortization to the nearest dollar).

    a.   Prepare journal entries to record (1) the bond issue on April 1, (2) the first interest payment and premium amortization on June 30, 19X1, and (3) the second interest payment and premium amortization on December 31, 19X1.

    b.   Compute Pinto's 19X1 bond interest expense.

DP-2　Emerald Corporation issued $100,000 of 8% bonds for $92,278 on January 1, 19X6. The bonds pay interest on June 30 and December 31, and were priced to yield an effective interest rate of 10%.

    a.   Prepare the required journal entry to record the bond issue on January 1.
    b.   Prepare entries to record the interest payment and discount amortization on June 30 and December 31. Emerald uses the effective-interest method of amortization. Round computations to the nearest dollar.
    c.   Compute 19X6 bond interest expense.
    d.   Present the proper disclosure of the bond issue on December 31, 19X6.

DP-3   Rounding to the nearest dollar, determine the price of a 10%, $1,000 bond which is issued at a time when the market rate of interest is 8%. The bond pays interest semiannually and has a five-year period to maturity (refer to the present value tables included in your textbook).

SOLUTIONS TO SELF TESTS

FULFILLMENT OF LEARNING OBJECTIVES

1(a)	Bondholders
1(b)	True
2(a)	False
2(b)	Registered
3(a)	A full period's interest
3(b)	Correct
4(a)	Premium
4(b)	Contract rate
4(c)	Less than
5(a)	Annuity
5(b)	Present value
5(c)	Decrease
6(a)	Effective-interest
6(b)	Decrease
6(c)	Straight-line
6(d)	False
7(a)	Bond retirements
7(b)	False

FILL IN THE BLANKS

1. Bond indenture
2. Debenture bonds
3. Callable
4. Face value, carrying value
5. Contract interest rate, effective interest rate
6. Premium
7. Straight-line amortization, effective-interest
8. Decrease
9. Refunding, retirement
10. Bond sinking fund
11. Compound interest
12. Future value, present value
13. Annuity

MULTIPLE CHOICE QUESTIONS

1. b. Bonds are disclosed on the balance at their face amount, minus any unamortized discount or plus any unamortized premium.

2. b.   The bond would be issued at a premium because the contract yield is superior to the going rate of interest for similar bonds. The price of the bond will be less than the future cash flow (it will be equal to the present value of the future cash flow). The face value of a bond does not change over time.

3. d.   At the time of issue, the issuer receives the price of the bond plus accrued interest since the last interest date. In the example, interest would have accrued from June 1 to July 1.

4. a.   Convertible bonds generally have a lower interest rate than similar bonds which are not convertible. The reason is that the conversion feature adds value to the bonds, and allows the issuer to offer a lower interest rate and still attract investors. The other statements are factual.

5. c.   The entry reflects that the $6,000 paid is one-half for interest expense (from April 1 to July 1) and one-half for the accrued interest which was received on April 1 when the bonds were issued.

6. b.   The bonds were issued at a $4,000 discount. Choice "b" is the only choice which reflects this fact.

7. c. $121. The monthly amortization is $17.24 ($1,000/58 months from issue date to maturity). The total amortization is $121 ($17.24 X 7 = $121).

8. b. $75,000. The bonds' carrying value ($1,000,000 - $250,000) times the effective interest rate (10%) yields the total interest expense.

9. c.   The present value of the $1,000 due in one year is $925.93 ($1,000 X 0.92593), the present value of $1,000 due in two years is $857.34 ($1,000 X 0.85734), and the present value of the amount due in three years is $793.83 ($1,000 X 0.79383). Answer "c" is the choice that will produce this result.

10. d.   The amount to invest today is the present value of $100, or $100 times the present value factor of 0.79383.

DEMONSTRATION PROBLEMS

DP-1

(a) 1. Cash   105,500

Cash	105,500	
Bonds Payable		100,000
Premium on Bonds Payable		3,000
Bond Interest Payable		2,500

To record issuance of bonds at 103 plus accrued interest ($100,000 X 10% X 3/12 = $2,500)

2.

Bond Interest Payable	2,500	
Bond Interest Expense	2,500	
Cash		5,000

To record semiannual interest payment

Premium on Bonds Payable	130	
Bond Interest Expense		130

To record premium amortization for 6 months ($3,000/69 months from issue date to maturity = $43.48 per month; $43.48 X 3 months = $130)

3.

Bond Interest Expense	5,000	
Cash		5,000

To record semiannual interest payment

Premium on Bonds Payable	261	
Bond Interest Expense		261

To record premium amortization for 3 months ($3,000/69 months from issue date to maturity = $43.48 per month; $43.48 X 6 months = $261)

(b) Bond interest expense for 19X1 is $7,109 ($2,500 - $130 + $5,000 - $261 = $7,109).

DP-2

(a) Jan. 1 Cash   92,278
            Discount on Bonds Payable   7,722
                Bonds Payable   100,000
            To record sale of bond issue

(b) June 30 Bond Interest Expense   4,000
                Cash   4,000
            To record semiannual interest payment
            ($100,000 X 8% X 6/12 = $4,000)

       30   Bond Interest Expense   614
                Discount on Bonds Payable*   614
            To record semiannual discount
            amortization

    Dec. 31 Bond Interest Expense   4,000
                Cash   4,000
            To record semiannual interest payment
            ($100,000 X 8% X 6/12 = $4,000)

       31   Bond Interest Expense   645
                Discount on Bonds Payable*   645
            To record semiannual discount
            amortization

*DISCOUNT AMORTIZATION TABLE

Semi-Annual Interest Period	Effective Semiannual Interest Expense (5% X Carrying Value)	Semi-annual Interest Payment (4.0% X Face Value)	Discount Amortization	Bond Discount Balance	End-of-Period Bond Carrying Value
Issuance				$7,722	$92,278
1	$4,614	$4,000	$614	7,108	92,892
2	4,645	4,000	645	6,463	93,537

(c) Bond interest expense is $9,259 ($4,614 + $4,645).

(d) Long-term liabilities
    Bonds payable $100,000
    Less: Discount on bonds payable   6,463 $93,537

DP-3

The present value of the bond is $1,081.11.

Six-Month Period	Cash Flow		Present Value Factor, 4%		Present Value
1-10	$ 50*	X	8.11090	=	$ 405.55
10	1,000	X	0.67556	=	675.56
					$1,081.11

* $1,000 X 10% X 6/12 = $50

CHAPTER 13

ENTITY ALTERNATIVES AND OWNERS' EQUITY

LEARNING OBJECTIVES

After studying this chapter, you should be able to:

1. Identify the distinctive features of a sole proprietorship and account for related equity transactions and events.

2. Explain the unique characteristics of a partnership.

3. Account for partnership formation and income distribution, including situations that give rise to an earnings deficiency.

4. State the features, advantages, and disadvantages of a corporate entity.

5. Summarize the distinctions between common and preferred stock.

6. Calculate the dividends associated with preferred stock.

7. Explain the concepts of and demonstrate the accounting treatments for par, no-par, and stated-value stock, and stock subscriptions.

8. Prepare and interpret the stockholders' equity section of a corporate balance sheet.

CHAPTER HIGHLIGHTS

I. **SOLE PROPRIETORSHIPS** are businesses owned by one person. The proprietorship is viewed as a separate, distinct accounting entity, even though the economic affairs of the business are commingled with the personal financial affairs of the owner.

   A. The **OWNER'S EQUITY IN THE SOLE PROPRIETORSHIP** is much simpler than that of a corporation. Corporate equity includes separate components for capital stock, retained earnings, and so forth. The equity of a sole proprietorship will consist of a single Capital account. The account reflects not only investments by the owner, but also accumulated earnings. A Drawing account may be used to accumulate information about owner withdrawals, but this account is closed to the Capital account at the end of an accounting period.

      1. **OWNER INVESTMENTS AND WITHDRAWALS** are recorded by crediting Capital (as investments are received) and debiting Drawing (as withdrawals are made). Importantly, drawings are not expenses.

2. **THE CLOSING PROCESS** for a sole proprietorship is similar to that demonstrated earlier in the text for a corporation; revenues and expenses are closed to Income Summary, and the balance of Income Summary is then closed to Capital. Likewise, the Drawing account is closed to Capital.

3. A unique financial statement for the sole proprietorship is the **STATEMENT OF OWNER'S EQUITY**. This statement reveals the beginning capital balance, increases due to owner investments and net income, and decreases due to withdrawals. This statement is prepared in lieu of a statement of retained earnings.

II. **PARTNERSHIPS** are an association of two or more persons to carry on as co-owners of a business for profit.

   A. Partnerships have a number of unique characteristics. The **CHARACTERISTICS OF A PARTNERSHIP** are as follows:

   1. **UNLIMITED LIABILITY OF OWNERS** is a partnership feature that means partners are each individually responsible for all partnership debts. This characteristic is directly attributable to the fact that a partnership is not a separate legal entity.

   2. Legal requirements for formation of a partnership are few; the **EASE OF FORMATION** of a partnership is demonstrated by the fact that one can be created without any written agreements. Preferably, however, a written agreement (known as the Articles of Partnership) should be drafted.

   3. **MUTUAL AGENCY** is another partnership feature, meaning that any individual partner can commit or obligate the entire partnership.

   4. **CO-OWNERSHIP OF PROPERTY AND INCOME** is another unique feature, meaning that property is jointly owned and earnings are shared among the partners (equally or in some other agreed manner).

   5. A partnership is said to be dissolved whenever a partner leaves the partnership or a new partner is admitted. Dissolution does not mean that operations cease; it simply means that a new partnership is formed. This unique feature demonstrates the **LIMITED LIFE** of a partnership.

   6. **AN OVERVIEW:** The **ADVANTAGES AND DISADVANTAGES OF PARTNERSHIPS** consist of ease of formation, operating flexibility, and an informal decision process -- versus the problems associated with mutual agency, limited life, and unlimited liability.

   B. **PARTNERSHIP ACCOUNTING** is similar to accounting for a sole proprietorship. Owner investments and net income continue to be recorded directly to Capital accounts, and withdrawals are entered in Drawing accounts. The distinction is that a separate Capital account and a separate Drawing account must be maintained for each partner.

   1. The accounting for **PARTNERSHIP FORMATION AND OWNER INVESTMENTS** is accomplished by debiting Cash (and other assets) for amounts contributed by partners, crediting any liabilities assumed by the partnership, and crediting the partner's Capital accounts for the net value of the partner's investment. Assets and liabilities should be recorded at their fair value.

2. To begin to appreciate partnership accounting, one must first develop an understanding of partnership earnings and its nature and distribution. Partnership income is the "traditional" excess of revenues over expenses, except that special care must be given to the evaluation of compensation to a partner for services rendered and to interest on invested capital. These items are considered when dividing profits -- not as an expense in computing profit. The **INCOME DISTRIBUTION** of a partnership can occur in a number of different ways; in the absence of a specific agreement, profits and losses are divided equally.

   a. Profit and loss distribution agreements frequently include salary allowances in **RECOGNITION OF** the value of **SERVICES** which individual partners provide to the partnership. These salary allowances are not expenses, they are merely a mathematical tool to divide the income among the individual partners.

   b. In addition to recognizing time contributed (via salary allowances), **RECOGNITION OF INVESTED CAPITAL** is also common. For example, interest allowances (i.e., a percentage of invested capital) may be computed on the beginning or average capital balances. Again, the interest amount is not an expense, merely an income division tool. After satisfying salary, interest, and other profit/loss division agreements, the remaining amount of income is divided equally or according to some agreed ratio. The amount of income attributed to each partner would be closed to that partner's Capital account as part of the closing process.

   c. An **EARNINGS DEFICIENCY** arises when income is negative or insufficient to cover salary and interest allowances. It is customary to fully satisfy the salary and interest provisions, and then distribute the resulting negative amount according to the agreed ratio.

3. In accounting for partnerships, **OTHER EQUITY ISSUES** frequently arise. Examples include the admission of a new partner by the purchase of an interest from an existing partner, and the direct receipt of an investment from a new partner (at more or less than book value). These issues are reserved for advanced accounting courses.

III. The nature of **CORPORATIONS** is such that they are regarded as legal entities having existence separate and distinct from their owners (i.e., stockholders).

   A. **CORPORATE FORM OF ORGANIZATION: ADVANTAGES**

      1. **TRANSFERABILITY OF OWNERSHIP** is easily accomplished through the purchase and sale of shares of stock. Stock is a transferable unit of ownership.

      2. **PERPETUAL EXISTENCE** means that corporations continue to operate indefinitely (or until the business can no longer operate or the shareholders elect not to operate). Changes in stock ownership do not cause operations to cease.

      3. **LIMITED LIABILITY OF STOCKHOLDERS** means that the owners of a corporation are not liable for debts and losses of the company beyond the amount of their investment in the entity's stock.

4. **EASE OF RAISING CAPITAL** is facilitated because the ownership interest is easily divided into units. This allows capital to be attracted from many different investors.

B. **CORPORATE FORM OF ORGANIZATION: DISADVANTAGES**

1. **DOUBLE TAXATION** means that corporate earnings are taxed twice; once when the corporation earns money, and again when dividends are paid to shareholders who must pay tax on dividends received.

2. **HEAVY REGULATION** is a common problem for larger corporations. These entities must report to regulatory agencies like the Securities and Exchange Commission.

C. The **ORGANIZATION OF A CORPORATION** begins with the granting of a charter by the state in which the corporation is established. The charter is the state's recognition of the existence of the "legal entity." Once the charter is obtained, an initial stockholders' meeting is held to allow shareholders to elect their board of directors, who in turn hire the various officers of the corporation. The officers then manage day-to-day affairs of the business. The directors function to protect the basic interests of the stockholders.

1. Forming a corporation can become quite costly, and the related **ORGANIZATION COSTS** should be reported as a separate intangible or other asset. This asset will be charged to expense over the future -- typically five years.

D. The most typical type of stock is **COMMON STOCK**.

1. The **RIGHTS OF COMMON STOCKHOLDERS** usually consist of the following features: (1) the right to share in dividend distributions; (2) the preemptive right, which allows existing shareholders the first option (or right of refusal) on new shares which may be issued; (3) the right to share in proceeds of liquidation (after all creditors and other priority claims are settled); and (4) the right to vote on the election of directors and other important matters.

E. Another type of stock is **PREFERRED STOCK:** The **NATURE AND CHARACTERISTICS** demonstrate preferential rights over those of common shareholders.

1. **NO VOTING RIGHTS** is one feature associated with preferred stock, and is one of its limitations.

2. **DIVIDEND PREFERENCE** is the most commonly cited special feature of preferred stock. Dividend preference means that preferred shareholders are entitled to a normal annual dividend requirement (usually stated as a percentage of par value) before any distributions can be made to common shareholders. Furthermore, preferred stock is frequently cumulative; if the annual dividend requirement cannot be satisfied, it will become a dividend in arrears, and all dividends in arrears must be paid before any dividends can be paid to common shareholders.

    a. **AN EXAMPLE** of the computations for preferred dividends is provided in the textbook.

3. The **PARTICIPATION FEATURE** means that the preferred shareholders may be entitled to more than the "normal" annual dividend, provided common shareholders have also received a reasonable dividend payout.

4. **ASSET PREFERENCE UPON LIQUIDATION** is a typical feature of preferred stock, meaning that liquidation will result in the payment of set amounts to preferred shareholders before common shareholders will receive any distributions.

5. Preferred stock is sometimes **CALLABLE** at the option of the corporation, which reserves the right to buy back preferred shares at a set price.

6. Preferred stock is sometimes **CONVERTIBLE**, meaning that its holder can exchange the shares for a fixed number of common shares.

F. Most stock is **PAR-VALUE STOCK**. Par value represents the legal capital per share (i.e., the minimum amount of capital that must be maintained in the business for protection of the creditors). Par value is generally a small number and is unrelated to the market value or issue price of the stock.

1. When **ISSUING PAR-VALUE STOCK** to the general public, necessary first steps are to advertise the issuance and prepare a document that contains information about the corporation. This document is the formal offering document and is called a prospectus.

2. The **ISSUE PRICE** of a stock depends on the corporation's financial record and potential.

3. In **ACCOUNTING FOR** the issuance of common and preferred **PAR-VALUE STOCK**, the initial entry is to debit Cash for the amount received, credit Stock (Common or Preferred) for the par value of the shares issued, and credit (typically) the difference to Paid-in Capital in Excess of Par Value. Importantly, these entries are made only when the corporation issues stock; as shares of stock are subsequently bought and sold between individual shareholders, the corporation is not directly affected.

4. The **BALANCE SHEET PRESENTATION** of a corporation's stockholders' equity includes rather detailed descriptions of the type of stock outstanding and its basic features (e.g., for preferred stock, cumulative 7% preferred stock, $100 par value, 10,000 shares authorized, 5,000 issued and outstanding). In addition, the paid-in capital in excess of par on common and preferred are disclosed, and retained earnings is separately presented. Within stockholders' equity, an important subtotal is total paid-in capital, which represents the sum of the par value and amounts of paid-in capital in excess of par value.

G. Occasionally, a corporation may issue **NO-PAR STOCK**, which is recorded by debiting Cash and crediting Common Stock for the issue price. A separate Paid-in Capital in Excess of Par Value account is not needed.

1. Some states authorize **STATED-VALUE STOCK** (instead of par-value stock). Stated-value stock is accounted for like par-value stock; the entry to record the issuance involves a debit to Cash, a credit to Common Stock (for its stated value), and a credit

to Paid-in Capital in Excess of Stated Value (for amounts received in excess of stated value).

H. Corporations may engage in **ISSUING STOCK FOR ASSETS OTHER THAN CASH**. The general rule is to record the asset and stock at the fair value of the asset or stock, whichever is more clearly determinable.

I. Smaller corporations may utilize **STOCK SUBSCRIPTIONS** to facilitate the issuance of stock. With stock subscriptions, the corporation exchanges a promise to issue stock in the future for a given amount of money. This promise is established in the accounts by debiting Subscriptions Receivable, crediting Common Stock Subscribed (for par value), and crediting Paid-in Capital in Excess of Par Value for the difference. When the receivable is collected, the corporation debits Cash and credits Subscriptions Receivable. The stock is then issued and recorded by debiting Common Stock Subscribed and crediting Common Stock.

J. An exhibit in the text presents **CORPORATE EQUITY: A COMPREHENSIVE ILLUSTRATION**. You should review this exhibit, carefully considering all of the features discussed for common and preferred stock.

CLASS NOTES

CLASS NOTES

CLASS NOTES

CLASS NOTES

SELF TESTS

FULFILLMENT OF LEARNING OBJECTIVES

Circle the appropriate response.

L.O. 1(a)   A sole proprietorship is viewed as a separate legal and taxable entity.

true   or   false

L.O. 1(b)   The owner's equity section of the balance sheet for a sole proprietorship would be described as:

simple   or   complex

L.O. 1(c)   The closing entries for a sole proprietorship would involve which type of entry to the owner's Drawing account?

debit   or   credit

L.O. 2(a)   Which of the following characteristics of a partnership means that each partner can act to commit the entire partnership?

mutual agency   or   co-ownership of income

L.O. 2(b)   The articles of partnership detail the rights, responsibilities, and duties of partners.

correct   or   incorrect

L.O. 3(a)   The contribution of assets to a partnership by individual partners should be recorded on the partnership's books at:

book value   or   fair value

L.O. 3(b)   Which of the following income distribution techniques should be used to recognize the amount of a partner's invested capital?

interest allowance   or   salary allowance

L.O. 3(c)   If an earnings deficiency arises while distributing partnership income, no additional salary and interest provisions should be satisfied.

true   or   false

L.O. 4   The feature of limited liability means that a stockholder can never lose more than the par value of the stock in which they have invested.

true   or   false

L.O. 5(a) Which of the following features would typically be associated with common stock?

preemptive rights   or   cumulative

L.O. 5(b) In the event dividends are paid to only one class of stock, which class is ordinarily paid?

preferred stock   or   common stock

L.O. 6(a) Dividends that have not been paid on cumulative preferred stock are said to be:

in arrears   or   forgiven

L.O. 6(b) If a corporation has dividends in arrears on preferred stock for two years ($5,000 per year), and declares $20,000 of dividends during the current (third) year, how much will be paid to the common shareholders?

$5,000   or $10,000

L.O. 7(a) Organization costs should be:

expensed as incurred
or
recorded as a separate asset

L.O. 7(b) Which of the following types of stock is accounted for similar to par-value stock?

no-par   or   stated-value

L.O. 7(c) When common stock is issued on a subscription basis, the collection of amounts due on the subscription usually involves a debit to which of the following accounts?

Stock Subscriptions Receivable
or
Common Stock Subscribed

L.O. 8(a) Total paid-in capital equals the par value of capital stock plus:

paid-in capital in excess of par value
or
retained earnings

L.O. 8(b) In preparing the stockholders' equity section (and related notes), how much detail is required?

limited   or   significant

FILL IN THE BLANKS

1. The _____ _____ is a business enterprise owned by one person.

2. Individual proprietors have _____ _____ with regard to debts of their businesses.

3. The statement of owner's equity for a sole proprietorship reveals not only net income and owner withdrawals, but also increases caused by _____ _____.

4. An association of two or more persons to carry on as co-owners of a business for profit describes a _____.

5. When a partnership's life is ended, the business is said to be _____.

6. In the absence of an agreement to the contrary, the income of a partnership should be divided on an _____ basis.

7. _____ _____ and _____ _____ are not business expenses; rather, these amounts are considered only in the division of net income of a partnership.

8. An _____ _____ arises whenever the amount of income earned by the partnership is insufficient to cover allowances for income distributions.

9. A _____ is an artificial being, invisible and intangible, and existing only in contemplation of law.

10. A _____ _____ _____ is a corporation which has shares of stock owned by relatively few persons.

11. The taxing of income to the corporation, and the subsequent taxing of dividends to the stockholders is commonly termed _____ _____.

12. A corporation is created by obtaining a _____ from one of the states.

13. The _____ _____ allows existing shareholders the opportunity to maintain their respective interests in a corporate entity by acquiring additional shares on a pro rata basis.

14. For a preferred stock to have dividends in arrears, it must be _____.

15. The feature that allows a corporation to reacquire stock, at the corporation's option, is commonly known as the _____ feature; the feature that allows the shareholder to exchange preferred shares for common shares is called the _____ feature.

16. The significance of par value is that it represents _____ _____ per share of stock.

17. The number of shares that a corporation is permitted to issue is termed the _____ shares, whereas the number of shares actually issued and held by stockholders is termed _____ shares.

18. When stock is sold on an installment basis, it is termed a stock _____.

MULTIPLE CHOICE QUESTIONS

Circle the appropriate response.

1. Which of the following is not a distinctive feature of a partnership?

    a. Ease of formation
    b. Unlimited liability
    c. Perpetual existence
    d. Mutual agency

2. Harris and Benson formed a partnership, but did not prepare a formal partnership agreement. During the year, Harris worked 2,000 hours and represented 20 clients. Benson represented 5 clients and worked 1,000 hours. How much of the partnership profit of $120,000 should be credited to Harris?

    a. $0
    b. $60,000
    c. $80,000
    d. $96,000

3. Winston invested $100,000 and Peterson invested $200,000 in a partnership. The following terms regarding division of income were agreed on: Winston is to receive a salary of $15,000, Winston and Peterson are each entitled to an allowance equal to 10% of original capital investment, and the balance is to be divided equally. How should a net income of $40,000 be divided?

    a. Winston, $20,000; Peterson, $20,000
    b. Winston, $15,000; Peterson, $25,000
    c. Winston, $22,500; Peterson, $17,500
    d. Winston, $25,000; Peterson, $15,000

4. Of the following characteristics, which is not generally regarded as a right of common shareholders?

    a. Preemptive right
    b. Voting rights
    c. Preference in liquidation
    d. Transferability of shares

5. The appropriate journal entry to record the issue of 1,000 shares of $1 par-value common stock at $4 per share would be:

a.	Cash	4,000	
	Common Stock		4,000
b.	Cash	4,000	
	Common Stock		1,000
	Paid-in Capital in Excess of Par		3,000
c.	Cash	4,000	
	Common Stock		1,000
	Retained Earnings		3,000
d.	Cash	1,000	
	Paid-in Capital in Excess of Par	3,000	
	Common Stock		4,000

6. A corporation arranged to issue 5,000 shares of $2 par-value common stock. The subscription agreement called for the first payment of $10 per share to be made two months after the initial subscription date. The second and final payment of $5 per share is to be made four months after the initial subscription date. The correct entry to record the initial subscription is:

a.	Stock Subscriptions Receivable	75,000	
	Common Stock Subscribed		10,000
	Paid-in Capital in Excess of Par		65,000
b.	Stock Subscriptions Receivable	10,000	
	Common Stock Subscribed		10,000
c.	Stock Subscriptions Receivable	75,000	
	Common Stock Subscribed		75,000
d.	Common Stock Subscribed	10,000	
	Common Stock		10,000

7. A corporation arranged to issue 5,000 shares of $2 par-value common stock. The subscription agreement called for the first payment of $10 per share to be made two months after the initial subscription date. The second and final payment of $5 per share is to be made four months after the initial subscription date. The correct entry to record the issuance of stock after collection of the final payment is:

a.	Stock Subscriptions Receivable	75,000	
	Common Stock Subscribed		10,000
	Paid-in Capital in Excess of Par		65,000
b.	Stock Subscriptions Receivable	10,000	
	Common Stock Subscribed		10,000
c.	Stock Subscriptions Receivable	75,000	
	Common Stock Subscribed		75,000
d.	Common Stock Subscribed	10,000	
	Common Stock		10,000

8. Magic Corporation paid $100,000 in dividends. The corporation had 10,000 shares of common stock outstanding and 5,000 shares of $100 par value 5% preferred stock. The preferred stock was two years in arrears prior to the current year. How much per share was paid to the common stockholders?

    a. $0
    b. $25,000
    c. $50,000
    d. $75,000

9. If 1,000 shares of $10 par-value common stock are issued in exchange for land with a fair market value of $25,000, the land and common stock (along with any additional paid-in capital) should be recorded at:

    a. $0
    b. $1,000
    c. $10,000
    d. $25,000

10. In reviewing corporate equity on a balance sheet, what would be included in the description "Total Capital Stock"?

    a. Par value of preferred
    b. Par value of common
    c. Paid-in capital in excess of par value
    d. Both (a) and (b)

DEMONSTRATION PROBLEMS

DP-1   Smiley, Smithers, and Smithem invested $10,000, $20,000, and $30,000, respectively in the SS&S Partnership. The articles of partnership contain the following stipulations: (1) the partners are allowed 10% interest allowances on investments; (2) Smiley and Smithers each have salary allowances of $8,000; (3) remaining profits and losses are shared equally among the partners. Prepare the appropriate distribution of net income or net loss among Smiley, Smithers, and Smithem for the following independent cases:

a. Net income of $52,000.
b. Net income of $19,000.
c. Net loss of $2,000.

DP-2 Edison Corporation began operations in Year 1. The following information was extracted from the balance sheet of Edison Corporation: Preferred stock, 10% non-participating, cumulative, $50 par value, 3,000 shares authorized, 2,000 shares issued and outstanding; common stock, $2 par value, 300,000 shares authorized, 100,000 shares issued and outstanding. Dividends declared for the past four years were as follows:

Year 1	none
Year 2	$10,000
Year 3	$28,000
Year 4	$ 5,000

a. Calculate the dividends paid to preferred stockholders and common stockholders in each of the four years.
b. Repeat requirement (a), assuming the preferred stock is not cumulative.

DP-3   The Lazlo Corporation was incorporated in May. The firm's charter authorized the sale of 100,000 shares of $1 par-value common stock. The following transactions occurred during the year:

(a) Received subscriptions for 10,000 shares at $5 per share; half the amount due was collected on that date.

(b) Received the balance due on subscriptions and issued the shares as agreed.

(c) Issued 1,000 shares of common stock for $7 per share; cash was collected and the shares were issued.

(d) Issued 1,000 shares to Axton Realty Company for land valued at $50,000.

Prepare journal entries for the preceding transactions.

SOLUTIONS TO SELF TESTS

FULFILLMENT OF LEARNING OBJECTIVES

1(a)　　False
1(b)　　Simple
1(c)　　Credit
2(a)　　Mutual agency
2(b)　　Correct
3(a)　　Fair value
3(b)　　Interest allowance
3(c)　　False
4　　　 False
5(a)　　Preemptive rights
5(b)　　Preferred stock
6(a)　　In arrears
6(b)　　$5,000
7(a)　　Recorded as a separate asset
7(b)　　Stated-value
7(c)　　Common Stock Subscribed
8(a)　　Paid-in capital in excess of par value
8(b)　　Significant

FILL IN THE BLANKS

1. Sole proprietorship
2. Unlimited liability
3. Owner investments
4. Partnership
5. Dissolved
6. Equal
7. Salary allowances, interest allowances
8. Earnings deficiency
9. Corporation
10. Closely held corporation
11. Double taxation
12. Charter
13. Preemptive right
14. Cumulative
15. Callable, convertible
16. Legal capital
17. Authorized, outstanding
18. Subscription

MULTIPLE CHOICE QUESTIONS

1. c. A partnership has a limited life, terminating with the admission or withdrawal of a partner. Partnerships are easily formed, each partner is responsible for all partnership debts (unlimited liability), and one partner's acts bind all the partners (mutual agency).

2. b. $60,000. Harris is entitled to half of the $120,000 profit. This result is dictated by the absence of a formal agreement.

3. c.

	Winston	Peterson	Total
Salary provision	$15,000	$ -	$15,000
Interest provision	10,000	20,000	30,000
Deficiency split equally			
(($40,000 - $15,000 - $30,000)/2)	(2,500)	(2,500)	(5,000)
Income Distribution	$22,500	$17,500	$40,000

4. c. Common shareholders are entitled only to the residual interest in a liquidation; creditors and preferred shareholders have the preference. In the absence of modification, common shares hold a preemptive right, have voting privileges, and are readily transferable.

5. b. The journal entry to record the issue of $1 par value common stock for $4 per share is:

Cash	4,000	
Common Stock		1,000
Paid-in Capital in Excess of Par		3,000

6. a. The journal entry to record the initial subscription is:

Stock Subscriptions Receivable	75,000	
Common Stock Subscribed		10,000
Paid-in Capital in Excess of Par		65,000

The receivable is based on the $15 per share total price ($15 X 5,000), and the stock subscribed amount is based on the $2 par value.

7. d. The journal entry to record the issuance of subscribed shares is:

Common Stock Subscribed	10,000	
Common Stock		10,000

The common stock is recorded and the common stock subscribed is removed, based on the $2 par value.

8. b. $25,000. Of the $100,000 total dividend distribution, $75,000 is for preferred stockholders. The $75,000 consists of $25,000 for the current year ($100 X 0.05 X 5,000 shares), and $50,000 for the two years of dividends in arrears.

9. d. $25,000. Stock issued for assets should be recorded at the fair value of the stock or assets, whichever is more clearly determinable.

10. d. Total capital stock consists of the par value of common and preferred shares. Total paid-in capital would include total capital stock and paid-in capital in excess of par value.

DEMONSTRATION PROBLEMS

DP-1

(a)	Smiley	Smithers	Smithem	Total
Interest on investment	$ 1,000	$ 2,000	$ 3,000	$ 6,000
Salary allowances	8,000	8,000		16,000
Remainder of $30,000 ($52,000 - $22,000) divided equally	10,000	10,000	10,000	30,000
	$ 19,000	$ 20,000	$ 13,000	$ 52,000

(b)	Smiley	Smithers	Smithem	Total
Interest on investment	$ 1,000	$ 2,000	$ 3,000	$ 6,000
Salary allowances	8,000	8,000		16,000
Deficiency of $3,000 ($19,000 - $22,000) divided equally	(1,000)	(1,000)	(1,000)	(3,000)
	$ 8,000	$ 9,000	$ 2,000	$ 19,000

(c)	Smiley	Smithers	Smithem	Total
Interest on investment	$ 1,000	$ 2,000	$ 3,000	$ 6,000
Salary allowances	8,000	8,000		16,000
Deficiency of $24,000 (net loss of $2,000 + $22,000) divided equally	(8,000)	(8,000)	(8,000)	(24,000)
	$ 1,000	$ 2,000	$ (5,000)	$ (2,000)

292 Entity Alternatives and Owners' Equity

DP-2

(a)

Year	Dividends Declared	Annual Preferred Requirement	Dividends in Arrears	Dividends Distributed Preferred	Dividends Distributed Common
1	$ 0	$10,000	$10,000	$ 0	$ 0
2	10,000	10,000	10,000	10,000	0
3	28,000	10,000	0	20,000*	8,000
4	5,000	10,000	5,000	5,000	0

Annual dividend requirement on preferred stock: $100,000 stock issued X 10% = $10,000.

* $20,000 owed ($10,000 in arrears + $10,000 for Year 3 dividend requirement); the $8,000 balance goes to common stockholders.

(b)

Year	Dividends Declared	Dividends Distributed Preferred	Dividends Distributed Common
1	$ 0	$ 0	$ 0
2	10,000	10,000	0
3	28,000	10,000	18,000
4	5,000	5,000	0

DP-3

(a)	Subscriptions Receivable: Common Stock	50,000	
	Common Stock Subscribed		10,000
	Paid-in Capital in Excess of Par		40,000
	To record subscriptions to 10,000 shares of		
	$1 par-value common at $5 per share		
	Cash	25,000	
	Subscriptions Receivable: Common Stock		25,000
	To record collection of half of the stock		
	subscriptions receivable		
(b)	Cash	25,000	
	Subscriptions Receivable: Common Stock		25,000
	To record collection of half of the stock		
	subscriptions receivable		
	Common Stock Subscribed	10,000	
	Common Stock		10,000
	To record issuance of subscribed shares		
(c)	Cash	7,000	
	Common Stock		1,000
	Paid-in Capital in Excess of Par		6,000
	To record issuance of 1,000 shares of $1		
	par-value common at $7 per share		
(d)	Land	50,000	
	Common Stock		1,000
	Paid-in Capital in Excess of Par		49,000
	To record issuing stock in exchange for land		
	valued at $50,000		

CHAPTER 14

CORPORATIONS: ADDITIONAL EQUITY ISSUES AND INCOME REPORTING

LEARNING OBJECTIVES

After studying this chapter, you should be able to:

1   Describe treasury stock and account for its acquisition and reissuance.

2   Handle cash dividends, stock dividends, and stock splits in the accounting records.

3   Explain the proper treatment of prior period adjustments and restrictions that may be imposed on retained earnings.

4   Apply the disclosure rules for discontinued operations, extraordinary items, accounting changes, and intraperiod tax allocation.

5   Explain the meaning of and compute earnings per share.

6   Define and calculate book value per share.

CHAPTER HIGHLIGHTS

I. **TREASURY STOCK** is the term used to describe shares of a company's own stock that have been reacquired.

   A. **ACQUISITIONS OF TREASURY STOCK** are accounted for by debiting Treasury Stock and crediting Cash for the cost of the shares reacquired. Treasury Stock is not reported as an asset; rather, it is subtracted from stockholders' equity. Treasury shares reduce the number of shares outstanding.

   B. When the **REISSUANCE OF TREASURY STOCK** occurs, Cash is debited for the amount received, Treasury Stock is credited for the cost of the shares sold, and the amount received in excess of cost is credited to Paid-in Capital from Treasury Stock. The latter account is reported as part of additional paid-in capital within the stockholders' equity section of the balance sheet. Importantly, no gain or loss is reported on the income statement.

      1. If the **REISSUANCE** of treasury shares is at an amount **BELOW COST**, the accounting can become slightly more complicated; Cash is debited for the amount received, Treasury Stock is credited for the cost of the shares, and the difference is debited to

Paid-in Capital from Treasury Stock (to the extent any balance has been previously established in this account) or Retained Earnings.

II. **RETAINED EARNINGS** is the portion of stockholders' equity that has been generated by profitable operations and kept in the business. In the closing process, the Income Summary account is debited for the income that has been earned and Retained Earnings is credited. A company can develop a negative or debit balance in Retained Earnings (known as a deficit) by having large losses and/or distributing more money to owners than has been earned.

   A. **DIVIDENDS** represent a distribution of earnings to stockholders, and may be in the form of cash, property, or additional shares of stock.

      1. There are three important dates associated with dividend distributions. These **DIVIDEND DATES** are the date of declaration (when the board of directors takes action to formally approve the dividends), the date of record (when the corporate records are reviewed to determine the appropriate owners of stock who are entitled to receive the dividends), and the date of payment (when the dividends are actually distributed to the shareholders).

      2. Most dividends are **CASH DIVIDENDS**. A company must have adequate cash available and a Retained Earnings balance large enough to support the distribution.

         a. The **ACCOUNTING FOR CASH DIVIDENDS** commences on the date of declaration. Dividends is debited and Dividends Payable is credited. Dividends Payable is reported as a current liability, and the Dividends account is closed to Retained Earnings at the end of an accounting period. No journal entry is needed on the date of record. On the date of payment, Dividends Payable and Cash are both reduced.

      3. **STOCK DIVIDENDS** involve the issuance of additional shares of stock to existing shareholders on a proportional basis. For example, a shareholder who owns 100 shares of stock will own 110 shares after a 10% stock dividend. Importantly, all shareholders would have 10% more shares, so the percentage of the total outstanding stock owned by a specific shareholder is not increased.

         a. Several **REASONS FOR ISSUING STOCK DIVIDENDS** are suggested. First, stock dividends enable a corporation to engage in a distribution to shareholders without reducing cash. Second, stock dividends are not taxable. Third, by increasing the number of shares outstanding, it is likely that the per share market value will be decreased, making the stock more attractive to a greater number of investors.

         b. The **ACCOUNTING FOR STOCK DIVIDENDS** depends on the size of the distribution. A small stock dividend (generally less than 20-25% of the existing shares outstanding) is accounted for at market price on the date of declaration. Specifically, Retained Earnings is debited for the market value of the additional shares issued, an account called Stock Dividend Distributable is credited for the par value of the shares, and the difference (the excess of market over par) is credited to the Paid-in Capital in Excess of Par Value account. On the date of distribution, Stock Dividend Distributable is debited and Common Stock is credited.

c. When evaluating **STOCK DIVIDENDS AND CORPORATE EQUITY**, be aware that stock dividends do not change total stockholders' equity. Individual equity components do change, however.

d. When evaluating **STOCK DIVIDENDS AND MARKET VALUE**, note that stock dividends are generally accompanied by a decrease in market value per share. This results because more shares are outstanding, while the amount of equity is unchanged. Furthermore, the larger the stock dividend, the greater would be the decrease in market value per share. Because of this fact, large stock dividends (those In excess of 25%) are accounted for differently than small stock dividends. Specifically, the Retained Earnings account is debited for the par or stated value of the shares to be distributed.

4. **STOCK SPLITS** are events that increase the number of shares outstanding and reduce the par or stated value per share. For example, a two-for-one stock split would double the number of shares outstanding and halve the par value. Importantly, the total par value of shares outstanding is not affected by a stock split (number of shares times par value per share does not change). Therefore, no journal entry is needed to account for a stock split. A memorandum notation in the accounting records indicates the decreased par and increased number of shares.

B. There are **OTHER ITEMS THAT AFFECT RETAINED EARNINGS**.

1. **PRIOR PERIOD ADJUSTMENTS** result from the correction of errors in the financial statements of earlier accounting periods. For example, if depreciation expense were not recorded in an earlier period, the necessary correction would require an increase to the Accumulated Depreciation account (credit) and a reduction in Retained Earnings (debit).

2. **RESTRICTIONS ON RETAINED EARNINGS** may reduce or preclude the distribution of dividends. Such restrictions may arise out of borrowing agreements or other contractual requirements, or may be self-imposed (e.g., an action by the board of directors to indicate to shareholders that capital is being reserved for a particular use (such as future plant expansion)). Restrictions may be disclosed via notes to the financial statements. Such actions do not reduce total retained earnings or cash, they merely restrict a portion of retained earnings.

C. **REPORTING CHANGES IN RETAINED EARNINGS** may be in the familiar format of the statement of retained earnings. In the alternative, a corporation may use a statement of stockholders' equity (for a complete example refer to the textbook). The statement of stockholders' equity reveals changes in retained earnings as well as other equity accounts.

III. Proper **CORPORATE INCOME REPORTING** requires that the major components which comprise net income be segregated. Therefore, the income statement will reveal ordinary business income from continuing operations, and separate components for unusual and special events. The elaborate format for the income statement is helpful for income analysis and comparison.

A. One of the special categories within the corporate income statement is the **DISCONTINUED OPERATIONS** section. When a business discontinues a segment (a separate, major line of business activity), the income from operating the discontinued segment, along with any gain or loss on the final disposal of the segment, should be reported (net of related tax consequences) in a section called Discontinued Operations. Discontinued operations should be reported immediately after income from continuing operations.

B. The next separate category on the income statement is for **EXTRAORDINARY ITEMS**. Extraordinary items are gains and losses that result from events that are both unusual in nature and infrequent in occurrence.

   1. In **APPLYING THE GUIDELINES** for extraordinary items, one must be careful that both criteria (unusual and infrequent) are satisfied. Consideration must be given to the particular business, and its operating location and environment.

   2. **DISCLOSURE OF EXTRAORDINARY ITEMS** is accomplished via a separate section immediately following discontinued operations, and should be on a net-of-tax basis.

C. **CHANGES IN ACCOUNTING PRINCIPLE** are likely to result in separate income statement reporting of an amount known as the cumulative effect. When a company changes an accounting method (e.g., straight-line to double-declining balance depreciation), it must compute the cumulative effect of the change (i.e., the amount higher or lower that income would have been in all prior periods had the new method been in use during those periods). This cumulative amount is reported on the income statement of the period of change in a separate category immediately following any extraordinary items.

D. For proper income reporting, companies must show income from continuing operations and the special categories just introduced net of their related tax consequences. This **NET-OF-TAX REPORTING** approach is called intraperiod tax allocation. Intraperiod tax allocation recognizes that various factors contribute to a corporation's tax bill, and proper reporting dictates that events be reported along with their related tax costs or savings. Intraperiod tax allocation is also applicable to prior period adjustments in the statement of retained earnings.

IV. The assessment of the degree of profitability is enhanced by the reporting of **EARNINGS PER SHARE** information. In its simplest form, earnings per share is income divided by the number of shares. A related measure is the price-earnings ratio which compares the market price per share to the earnings per share.

A. A more detailed look at earnings per share reveals that the fundamental computation is based on **WEIGHTED-AVERAGE SHARES OUTSTANDING**. Because earnings are generated throughout the year, the computation should be based on average shares outstanding during the year (rather than shares at the end of the year). The related calculation of weighted-average shares is a layering process that (1) considers the number of shares outstanding during various periods throughout the year, and (2) weights those shares by the fraction of the year outstanding (e.g., if 1,000 shares are outstanding for three months and 2,000 shares are outstanding for nine months, then weighted-average shares = 1,750 ((1,000 X 3/12) + (2,000 X 9/12))).

B. The "earnings" amount to use in the earnings per share calculations is really **EARNINGS AVAILABLE TO COMMON STOCKHOLDERS**. It is important to recognize that some of a corporation's net income may not be available to common stockholders. Specifically, if there is preferred stock outstanding, net income is reduced by the amount of preferred stock dividends (to find the earnings available to common stockholders). In summary, earnings per share is earnings available to common stockholders divided by weighted-average common shares outstanding.

C. Earnings per share is further complicated by **PRIMARY VERSUS FULLY DILUTED EARNINGS PER SHARE** concepts. Primary earnings per share is income available to common stockholders divided by weighted-average shares. Fully diluted earnings per share, however, takes into account the potentially dilutive effect of convertible securities. Fully diluted earnings per share includes the assumption that convertible preferred stocks (and other convertible securities) are exchanged for common shares, thereby increasing the number of shares outstanding. The increased number of shares (assumed) is divided into an amount of income which is calculated based on the assumption that the convertible stock has been converted (i.e., that dividends on convertible preferred stock do not have to be paid).

D. **EPS DISCLOSURE** parallels the information shown on the income statement. That is, earnings per share information may be presented for income from continuing operations, discontinued operations, extraordinary items, the cumulative effect, and net income.

V. **BOOK VALUE PER SHARE** is the amount of stockholders' equity per share of stock. For a corporation with a simple capital structure, book value per share equals total stockholders' equity divided by common shares outstanding at the end of the accounting period.

A. Book value computations become slightly more complex when **AN EXAMPLE WITH TWO CLASSES OF STOCK** is examined. The book value for preferred shares equals the equity attributable to preferred stock divided by the number of preferred shares outstanding. The amount of equity attributable to preferred shares is generally considered as the call price (i.e., redemption or liquidation price), plus any dividends that are due. The remaining amount of equity (total equity minus equity attributable to preferred stock) is divided by the number of common shares outstanding to calculate book value per common share.

B. One should be careful in assessing the **MEANING OF BOOK VALUE**. Importantly, book value is not the same thing as market value or fair value; book value is based on historical-cost measures included in the balance sheet.

CLASS NOTES

CLASS NOTES

CLASS NOTES

CLASS NOTES

CLASS NOTES

SELF TESTS

FULFILLMENT OF LEARNING OBJECTIVES

Circle the appropriate response.

L.O. 1(a)   Treasury stock is stock of one corporation that is owned by another corporation.

correct or incorrect

L.O. 1(b)   Treasury stock should be reported as:

a reduction of stockholders' equity
or
an asset

L.O. 1(c)   The reissuance of treasury stock would never result in a credit to:

Gain on Sale or Paid-in Capital

L.O. 2(a)   For a cash dividend, stockholders' equity would be reduced on the:

date of declaration or date of payment

L.O. 2(b)   A small stock dividend (one that is less than 20-25%) should be accounted for based on:

par value or fair value

L.O. 2(c)   The accounting for a stock split requires the recording of a journal entry.

true or false

L.O. 3(a)   The utilization of a prior period adjustment is appropriate for:

correction of an error or an appropriation

L.O. 3(b)   Stock dividends are reported on the statement of retained earnings.

true or false

L.O. 4(a)   Which of the following would precede the other on a detailed corporate income statement?

discontinued operations or extraordinary items

L.O. 4(b)   To report an event as an extraordinary item, how many of the criteria (unusual in nature and infrequent in occurrence) must be satisfied?

at least one or both

L.O. 4(c) Continuing operations, discontinued operations, extraordinary items, changes in accounting principle, and prior period adjustments should all be reported net of their related tax effect.

true   or   false

L.O. 5(a) Earnings per share is a popular measure of corporate book value.

true   or   false

L.O. 5(b) The calculation of earnings per share is based on:

weighted-average common shares outstanding
or
shares outstanding at the end
of an accounting period

L.O. 5(c) Which of the following takes into account potential dilution from convertible securities?

primary earnings per share
or
fully diluted earnings per share

L.O. 6(a) Book value per share is the same as fair value per share.

true   or   false

L.O. 6(b) When two classes of stock are outstanding, the book value per share computation involves dividing total stockholders' equity by the sum of the number of common and preferred shares outstanding.

correct   or   incorrect

FILL IN THE BLANKS

1. Corporations frequently purchase shares of their own stock. These shares are termed _____ _____.

2. When a corporation reissues treasury stock at more than its cost, the _____-_____ _____ _____ _____ _____ account should be increased.

3. A debit balance in Retained Earnings is commonly referred to as a _____.

4. The _____ _____ _____ is the date that corporate records are reviewed to determine who will receive a previously declared dividend.

5. Accounting for a small stock dividend is based on _____ value, while a large stock dividend is based on _____ value.

6. A _____ _____ involves increasing the number of shares outstanding and reducing the stock's par or stated value per share.

7. Correction of an error that occurred in the computation of the net income of a previous period is accomplished by the use of a _____ _____ _____.

8. Providing a note to the financial statements indicating that part of the Retained Earnings balance is unavailable for distribution is known as a _____ of retained earnings.

9. A _____ is a major line of business or class of customer.

10. The accounting profession has stipulated that extraordinary items must be _____ _____ _____ and occur infrequently.

11. The _____ _____ is the difference in the total net income reported in prior years and the income that would have been reported had an alternative accounting principle been in use during those years.

12. In calculating earnings per share, the numerator should consist of _____ _____ _____ _____ _____ and the denominator should consist of _____ - _____ _____ _____ _____.

13. _____ earnings per share is calculated by ignoring the dilutive effect of convertible securities.

14. In calculating book value per share for a company with more than one class of stock, the amount allocated to preferred stock should be based on the preferred stock's call value, sometimes referred to as the _____ or _____ value.

MULTIPLE CHOICE QUESTIONS

Circle the appropriate response.

1. Which of the following statements about treasury stock is false?

   a. Gains are not recorded on treasury stock transactions, but losses are.
   b. Acquiring treasury stock causes stockholders' equity to decrease.
   c. Treasury stock is reported as a deduction from stockholders' equity.
   d. The excess of the sales price of treasury stock over its cost should be credited to Paid-in Capital from Treasury Stock.

2. Blair holds 1,000 shares of treasury stock that have a $5 per share par value, an original issue price of $15 per share, and a cost of $20 per share. Assume that Blair has a $3,000 credit balance in the Paid-in Capital from Treasury Stock account. If all of the treasury shares are reissued at $11 per share, the proper journal entry would be:

    a.   Cash   11,000
           Paid-in Capital from Treasury Stock   9,000
               Treasury Stock   20,000
    b.   Cash   11,000
           Treasury Stock   5,000
           Retained Earnings   6,000
    c.   Treasury Stock   20,000
           Cash   20,000
    d.   Cash   11,000
           Paid-In Capital from Treasury Stock   3,000
           Retained Earnings   6,000
               Treasury Stock   20,000

3. Jackson Corporation has 500,000 shares of common stock outstanding. On April 10, the board of directors declared a $0.60 per share cash dividend, to be paid to stockholders of record on April 25. The dividend was distributed on June 6. The proper journal entry to record on June 6 is:

    a.   Dividends Expense   300,000
           Cash   300,000
    b.   Dividends Payable   300,000
           Cash   300,000
    c.   Retained Earnings   300,000
           Cash   300,000
    d.   Dividends Payable   300,000
           Retained Earnings   300,000

4. Elmer Company has 500,000 shares of common stock authorized. The stock has a par value of $1.50 per share, and 150,000 shares are outstanding. The company declared a 5% stock dividend at a time when the market value was $7 per share. What entry, if any, should Elmer record for the declaration?

    a.   No entry
    b.   Retained Earnings   11,250
           Common Stock   11,250
    c.   Retained Earnings   52,500
           Stock Dividend Distributable   11,250
           Paid-in Capital in Excess of Par   41,250
    d.   Stock Dividends Payable   11,250
         Retained Earnings   41,250
           Common Stock   52,500

5. Which of the following is considered as extraordinary by the accounting profession?

    a. Write-down or write-off of receivables, inventory, and intangible assets.
    b. Gains and losses from the sale or abandonment of equipment used in a business.
    c. Effects of a strike, including those against competitors and major suppliers.
    d. Flood damage from unusually heavy rains in a normally dry environment.

6. Which of the following would not be reported as a separate component on the income statement?

    a. Cumulative effect of a change in accounting principle
    b. Discontinued operations
    c. Prior period adjustment
    d. Extraordinary item

7. Realwood Furniture Corporation had 100,000 shares of common stock outstanding on January 1. 50,000 additional shares were issued on July 1, and 25,000 shares were reacquired on September 1. What was the weighted-average number of share outstanding during the year?

    a. 140,000
    b. 125,000
    c. 118,750
    d. 116,667

8. The Phillips Corporation had 15,000 shares of common stock outstanding on January 1, and issued an additional 5,000 shares on June 1. There was no preferred stock outstanding. The corporation reports net income of $200,000. How much is earnings per share (to the nearest cent) for the calendar year?

    a. $10.00
    b. $11.16
    c. $11.43
    d. $13.33

9. The Phillips Corporation had 15,000 shares of common stock outstanding on January 1, and issued an additional 5,000 shares on June 1. There was preferred stock outstanding, and dividends on the preferred stock amounted to $20,000. The corporation reports net income of $200,000. The preferred stock is not convertible. How much is fully diluted earnings per share (to the nearest cent) for the calendar year?

    a. $9.00
    b. $10.00
    c. $10.05
    d. $10.29

10. If a corporation has total stockholders' equity of $1,000,000, 100,000 share of common stock outstanding, and 1,000 shares of $100 par value preferred stock outstanding, how much is book value per common share? Assume that the preferred stock is callable at $110 and dividends of $4,000 on preferred stock are due.

   a. $8.86
   b. $9.00
   c. $9.96
   d. $10.00

DEMONSTRATION PROBLEMS

DP-1   Business Systems Corporation began 19X1 with 100,000 shares of $5 par value common stock outstanding. The following stock-related transactions occurred during the year:

January 15 - The corporation declared a 10% stock dividend. On this date, the market value per share was $20.

January 30 - The previously declared stock dividend was distributed to shareholders.

May 7 - Acquired 6,000 treasury shares at $25 per share. This was the first treasury stock transaction in the company's history.

June 16 - Reissued half of the previously acquired treasury shares at $30 per share.

August 9 - Reissued the remaining treasury shares at $11 per share.

December 16 - Declared a three-for-one stock split.

Prepare all necessary journal entries for Business Systems.

DP-2 Consider the following facts and prepare the lower portion of Benson Corporation's income statement. Benson's year-end is December 31. Ignore the presentation of earnings-per-share amounts.

Benson's income from continuing operations before tax was $200,000.

A $50,000 loss was incurred from storm damage to a manufacturing plant. The plant was located in a region of the country where major storms are very rare.

Benson changed from straight-line to double-declining balance depreciation. Had the double-declining balance method been in use, prior years' income would have been $70,000 lower.

The company discontinued operations of a specialty manufacturing segment. A loss from operations of the segment amounted to $80,000, but the company realized a $100,000 gain on the sale of segment facilities.

Benson's tax rate is 40%, except for a special tax rate of 25% on the storm loss.

DP-3   Zenith, Inc. had the following stock outstanding during the year:

Common stock, $2 par value,
    1,000,000 shares outstanding $2,000,000

10% preferred stock, $50 par value,
    20,000 shares outstanding   1,000,000

Each share of preferred is convertible into 30 shares of common stock. Net income for the year totaled $400,000.

a. Compute primary earnings per share.
b. Compute fully diluted earnings per share.

SOLUTIONS TO SELF TESTS

FULFILLMENT OF LEARNING OBJECTIVES

1(a) Incorrect
1(b) A reduction of stockholders' equity
1(c) Gain on Sale
2(a) Date of declaration
2(b) Fair value
2(c) False
3(a) Correction of an error
3(b) True
4(a) Discontinued operations
4(b) Both
4(c) True
5(a) False
5(b) Weighted-average common shares outstanding
5(c) Fully diluted earnings per share
6(a) False
6(b) Incorrect

FILL IN THE BLANKS

1. Treasury stock
2. Paid-in Capital from Treasury Stock
3. Deficit
4. Date of record
5. Market, par
6. Stock split
7. Prior period adjustment
8. Restriction
9. Segment
10. Unusual in nature
11. Cumulative effect
12. Earnings available to common stockholders, weighted-average common shares outstanding
13. Primary
14. Redemption, liquidation

MULTIPLE CHOICE QUESTIONS

1. a. Treasury stock transactions are capital transactions, not income activities; therefore, neither gains nor losses are recognized. Acquiring treasury stock decreases stockholders' equity by the purchase price. Further, treasury stock is subtracted from stockholders' equity, and Paid-in Capital from Treasury Stock is credited for the sales price in excess of cost.

2. d. The proceeds received from the sale are debited to Cash ($11 X 1,000 shares = $11,000), Paid-in Capital from Treasury Stock is debited for the balance of the account ($3,000), and Retained Earnings is debited to balance ($6,000) the entry. The $20,000 credit to Treasury Stock is for the cost of the treasury shares sold.

3. b. Dividends Payable and Cash are reduced on the payment date. The Dividends Payable account would have been established on the date of declaration.

4. c. For small stock dividends (less than 20%), Retained Earnings is debited for the fair value of the declaration (150,000 shares X 5% = 7,500 shares; 7,500 shares X $7 = $52,500). Stock Dividend Distributable is credited for the par value of the shares to be issued (7,500 shares X $1.50 = $11,250). Paid-in Capital in Excess of Par Value is credited for the difference ($41,250).

5. d. Extraordinary items must be both unusual in nature and occur infrequently. The only choice that satisfies these conditions is "d."

6. c. Prior period adjustments are reported on the statement of retained earnings. The cumulative effect of a change in accounting principle, discontinued operations, and extraordinary items are all separately reported on the income statement.

7. d. 116,667.

100,000 X 6/12 =	50,000
150,000 X 2/12 =	25,000
125,000 X 4/12 =	41,667
Weighted Average	116,667

8. b. $11.16. The $200,000 net income is divided by the weighted-average shares outstanding ((15,000 X 5/12) + (20,000 X 7/12) = 17,916.67 shares).

9. c. $10.05. The income available to common shareholders ($200,000 - $20,000 preferred dividends = $180,000) is divided by the weighted-average shares outstanding ((15,000 X 5/12) + (20,000 X 7/12) = 17,916.67 shares).

10. a. $8.86. The equity attributable to common stockholders ($1,000,000 total equity - $110,000 call price of preferred stock - $4,000 dividends due on preferred stock = $886,000) is divided by the common shares outstanding (100,000).

DEMONSTRATION PROBLEMS

DP-1

Date		Account	Debit	Credit
Jan.	15	Retained Earnings	200,000	
		Stock Dividend Distributable		50,000
		Paid-in Capital in Excess of Par		150,000

To record declaration of 10% stock dividend (100,000 shares X 10% = 10,000 shares; 10,000 X $20 = $200,000)

	30	Stock Dividend Distributable	50,000	
		Common Stock		50,000

To record distribution of previously declared stock dividend

May	7	Treasury Stock	150,000	
		Cash		150,000

To record the purchase of 6,000 shares of treasury stock at $25 per share

June	16	Cash	90,000	
		Treasury Stock		75,000
		Paid-in Capital from Treasury Stock		15,000

To record the sale of 3,000 shares of treasury stock at $30 per share

Aug.	9	Cash	33,000	
		Paid-in Capital from Treasury Stock	15,000	
		Retained Earnings	27,000	
		Treasury Stock		75,000

To record the sale of 3,000 shares of treasury stock at $11 per share

Dec. 16   Memorandum note in the general journal should indicate that the company has authorized a three-for-one stock split. As a consequence, par value is reduced from $5 per share to $1.67 per share and the number of shares issued increases threefold.

DP-2

BENSON CORPORATION
INCOME STATEMENT
FOR THE YEAR ENDED DECEMBER 31, 19XX

. . . .

Income from continuing operations before tax		$200,000
Income tax on continuing operations		80,000
Income from continuing operations		$120,000
Discontinued operations		
Loss from discontinued segment operations, less applicable tax savings of $32,000	$(48,000)	
Gain on disposal of segment facilities, less applicable taxes of $40,000	60,000	12,000
Income before extraordinary item		$132,000
Extraordinary item		
Storm loss, less tax savings of $12,500		(37,500)
Cumulative effect on prior years of a change in accounting principle, less applicable tax savings of $28,000		(42,000)
Net income		$ 52,500

DP-3

(a) Primary earnings per share:

$$\frac{\text{net income } \$400{,}000 - \text{preferred dividends } \$100{,}000^*}{\text{common stock } 1{,}000{,}000 \text{ shares}}$$

$$= \frac{\$300{,}000}{1{,}000{,}000} = \underline{\$0.30} \text{ primary earnings per share}$$

* $1,000,000 X 10% = $100,000

(b) Fully diluted earnings per share:

$$\frac{\text{net income } \$400{,}000}{\text{common stock } 1{,}000{,}000 \text{ shares} + 600{,}000 \text{ shares from assumed conversion } (20{,}000 \text{ X } 30)}$$

$$= \frac{\$400{,}000}{1{,}600{,}000} = \underline{\$0.25} \text{ fully diluted earnings per share}$$

CHAPTER 15

LONG-TERM INVESTMENTS

LEARNING OBJECTIVES

After studying this chapter, you should be able to:

1. Account for investments in bonds.

2. Contrast the lower-of-cost-or-market and the equity methods of accounting for stock investments.

3. Identify parent/subsidiary relationships.

4. Explain the reason for consolidated financial statements and the related concepts of intercompany transactions and elimination entries.

5. Prepare consolidated financial statements immediately after acquisition.

6. Calculate and record a company's minority interest.

7. Account for subsidiaries acquired at a cost in excess of book value.

8. Distinguish between purchase and pooling-of-interests accounting.

CHAPTER HIGHLIGHTS

I. Accounting for **INVESTMENTS IN BONDS** is similar to accounting for bonds payable.

   A. **RECORDING THE INITIAL INVESTMENT** in bonds requires the establishment of an Investment in Bonds account (at the purchase price plus brokerage fees and other incidental acquisition costs). Importantly, premiums and discounts are not recorded in separate accounts. However, accrued interest on the date of purchase is separately debited to Bond Interest Receivable, and will be collected on the next interest date.

   B. The first bond interest payment received will be recorded by debiting Cash and crediting **BOND INTEREST REVENUE** (and Bond Interest Receivable if any accrued interest was recorded on the date the bonds were purchased -- or if any accrued interest was recorded at the end of a prior accounting period).

      1. If there are any **BOND DISCOUNTS**, they must be amortized over the life of the investment as an increase in interest revenue. This results because the bonds were purchased at less than their maturity value, but the maturity value will eventually be paid to the investor (plus regular interest payments). This extra amount (i.e., the

discount) represents a cash inflow in excess of the amount invested and should be recognized as income.

    a. The periodic amount of discount to amortize is best determined by the effective-interest method. Effective-interest **DISCOUNT AMORTIZATION** is calculated by multiplying a bond investment's carrying value by the effective interest rate (resulting in total interest revenue for the period), then subtracting the amount of cash received for interest during the same time period. The appropriate journal entry to record discount amortization is to debit Investment in Bonds and credit Bond Interest Revenue. The amortization process will continue over the life of the bonds. Note that the carrying amount of the investment will increase each time the discount is amortized. Also note that special attention must be paid to the number of months for which amortization is being computed (e.g., Assume that a $1,000, 8% bond was acquired at $960 on October 1, and has an effective yield of 10%. Interest revenue for the period from October 1 to December 31 would be $24 ($960 X 10% X 3/12), of which $20 ($1,000 X 8% X 3/12) would be receivable as cash interest, and the remaining $4 would be discount amortization).

  2. **PREMIUM AMORTIZATION** is calculated and recorded similar to discount amortization. However, when a premium exists, total interest revenue is less than the cash received. Therefore, premium amortization is recorded by debiting Bond Interest Revenue and crediting the Investment in Bonds account.

C. If a **SALE OF BONDS** occurs **BEFORE MATURITY**, then the accounting records must be brought up to date for any previously unrecorded amortization. The cash received from the sale is then recorded as Bond Interest Revenue (i.e., a credit for any accrued interest from the last interest payment date), a return of the investment in bonds (i.e., credit Investment in Bonds for their carrying value), and gain on the sale (if a credit is needed to balance the entry; or loss if a debit is needed to balance the entry). The gain or loss is the difference between the cash received for the bond (excluding any cash received for accrued interest) and the carrying amount of the bond.

II. The proper accounting for **INVESTMENTS IN STOCK** depends on the percentage of voting stock held by the investor. In general, less than 20% ownership requires use of the lower-of-cost-or-market method, 20% to 50% ownership requires use of the equity method, and greater than 50% ownership results in consolidated financial statements.

    A. The **LOWER-OF-COST-OR-MARKET METHOD** is used to account for long-term investments in stock when investors are unable to exercise significant influence over the investee corporation. Less than 20% ownership is presumed to indicate a lack of ability to exert significant influence (this presumption is set aside if evidence to the contrary demonstrates otherwise). When using the lower-of-cost-or-market method, the investment is initially entered in the accounts at acquisition cost. When the investee reports income, no journal entry is recorded by the investor. When the investee distributes dividends, the investor records them by debiting Cash and crediting Dividend Revenue. At the end of the accounting period, the market value of the investment is compared to cost; if the market value has declined below cost, the decline in value is recognized by debiting Unrealized Loss on Long-term Investments and crediting Allowance for Decline in Market Value of Long-term Investments. On the balance sheet, the long-term investment is reported at cost, less the balance of the related allowance.

1. The textbook provides **AN EXAMPLE** of the detailed journal entries associated with the lower-of-cost-or-market method.

B. The **EQUITY METHOD** is used to account for investments where the investor exercises significant influence over the investee (generally over 20% ownership). The initial accounting commences by recording the investment at cost. As the investee announces earnings, the investor records its share by debiting Investment and crediting Investment Revenue (e.g., for a 30% owned investment, the investor would record $300 of income if the investee reported net income of $1,000). When dividends are distributed by the investee, the investor debits Cash and credits the Investment account (dividends are treated as a return of the investment rather than income). Note that lower-of-cost-or-market adjustments are not utilized when the equity method is employed. Essentially, the Investment account tracks the equity of the investee, increasing as the investee reports income and decreasing as the investee distributes dividends.

1. The **RATIONALE FOR THE EQUITY METHOD** is based on the investor's ability to exercise significant influence. The investor can effectively regulate the operations and dividend policy of the investee. Hence, the welfare of the investor is tied to the performance of the investee, as are the accounting measurements (rather than being tied to divided policy which might be manipulated by the investor).

C. With **CONTROLLING INVESTMENTS** (generally demonstrated by greater than 50% ownership), alternative accounting procedures must be considered.

1. The majority owner of another corporation (the subsidiary) is termed the parent company. These definitions are significant in distinguishing between **LEGAL VERSUS ECONOMIC ENTITIES**. The parent and subsidiary are separate legal entities; however, they may be viewed as one economic (or operating) unit.

2. As a result, **CONSOLIDATED FINANCIAL STATEMENTS** should be prepared to present a combined picture of the parent and controlled subsidiaries. In preparing consolidated financial statements, accounts like Cash are merely summed together, resulting in a single total for cash owned by the two related entities.

3. However, some accounts may not be merely summed together. **INTERCOMPANY TRANSACTIONS** (such as a parent loaning money to a subsidiary) must be eliminated (otherwise, the consolidated statements would show both a receivable and a payable for the same amount).

4. The consolidation process is facilitated by the preparation of a **WORK SHEET** to accumulate information **AND** identify **ELIMINATIONS**. On the work sheet, the eliminating entry for an intercompany payable and receivable involves a debit to the Payable and a credit to the Receivable (thereby removing both of these accounts from consideration in the consolidation process). Importantly, such elimination entries are prepared on the work sheet only; they do not impact the general ledger of the parent or subsidiary.

5. If the **CONSOLIDATION** of financial statements occurs **UPON ACQUISITION**, note that the parent company would report an Investment in Subsidiary in its general ledger, while the subsidiary's general ledger would include various equity accounts.

a. Therefore, the first work sheet elimination entry is called **THE INVESTMENT ELIMINATION**. This elimination is executed by debiting the equity accounts of the subsidiary and crediting Investment in Subsidiary. The result of such action is that neither the Investment account nor the equity of the subsidiary appears on the consolidated statements. Instead, the consolidated statements will consist of the parent's assets (except for the investment in subsidiary), liabilities, and equity along with the assets and liabilities of the subsidiary.

6. Sometimes the parent may own less than 100% of the stock of the subsidiary, in which case a **MINORITY INTEREST** results. The minority interest is the ownership in the subsidiary by shareholders other than the parent. The Minority Interest account appears (as a credit) on the consolidated balance sheet, and is equal to the minority interest ownership percentage multiplied times the total stockholders' equity of the subsidiary. Procedurally, minority interest is established on the work sheet by debiting the equity accounts of the subsidiary and crediting Minority Interest. The remaining amount of subsidiary equity (not attributable to the minority interest) is eliminated against the Investment in Subsidiary account (as previously discussed).

7. Another complicating factor in the consolidation process arises if the **ACQUISITION OF a SUBSIDIARY** occurs **AT MORE OR LESS THAN BOOK VALUE**. A parent company may purchase the stock of a subsidiary by paying an amount which is different than the underlying equity of the subsidiary.

   a. As **AN EXAMPLE**, if a parent paid $100,000 for all of the stock of a subsidiary, and the subsidiary had total equity of $80,000, then the parent would have paid $20,000 in excess of book value. This excess might be traced to specifically undervalued assets owned by the subsidiary, or the parent may have paid the premium for an unidentifiable intangible value (goodwill). In consolidating, the parent's Investment in Subsidiary ($100,000) is credited and the equity accounts of the subsidiary ($80,000) are debited. The $20,000 difference is debited to any specifically undervalued assets and/or goodwill.

   b. On occasion, the **BOOK VALUE** of a subsidiary may be **IN EXCESS OF COST**. The accounting for such cases is appropriately reserved for more advanced courses.

8. In addition to the consolidated balance sheet, one must also consider the procedures for preparing a **CONSOLIDATED INCOME STATEMENT**. A consolidated income statement consists of summed amounts for sales of the parent and subsidiary (less any intercompany sales between the parent and subsidiary), along with summed amounts for various operating and other expenses (less any intercompany amounts like interest on intercompany loans).

D. **STOCK INVESTMENTS: A BRIEF OVERVIEW** reveals that the lower-of-cost-or-market method is used for less than 20% ownership (due to the lack of significant influence); dividends are reported as income and the balance sheet reveals the investment at cost (less any allowance for decline in market value). Where ownership is over 20% but less than 50%, the presumption of significant influence dictates use of the equity method. Investments are reported at cost, plus a share of net income, minus dividends received. Over 50% ownership indicates control and requires the presentation of consolidated financial statements.

E. **AN ADDENDUM: PURCHASE VERSUS POOLING OF INTERESTS.** In this chapter, purchase accounting was demonstrated. Purchase accounting results when one company (the parent) buys another. As an alternative, companies may carry out a business combination in such a way that neither company is buying the other; rather, the companies mutually combine ownership interests. Purchase accounting is based on fair market value of assets and liabilities acquired. Pooling-of-interests accounting is based on the book values of the assets and liabilities of the companies. Stated differently, the assets and liabilities of the companies are combined, with no change in valuation.

1. The **POOLING** of interests method **AND REPORTED EARNINGS** are intrinsically related. First, because assets are not revalued, future depreciation charges and goodwill amortization may be less than would result under purchase accounting. Hence, income is likely to be higher in future years under a pooling. Additionally, income statement accounts are combined retroactively with a pooling, but not under purchase accounting (where consolidated income statement accounts represent the parent's earnings for the entire period plus the subsidiary's earnings from the date of purchase only).

CLASS NOTES

CLASS NOTES

CLASS NOTES

CLASS NOTES

CLASS NOTES

SELF TESTS

FULFILLMENT OF LEARNING OBJECTIVES

Circle the appropriate response.

L.O. 1(a)   Bond investments are initially entered into the accounts at cost; that is, the purchase price plus brokerage fees and other related acquisition costs.

true   or   false

L.O. 1(b)   Accrued interest existing on the date of purchase of a bond investment is ultimately reported as bond interest revenue.

correct   or   incorrect

L.O. 1(c)   Which method of amortizing premiums and discounts on bond investments is conceptually superior?

straight-line   or   effective-interest

L.O. 1(d)   The amortization of a premium on a bond investment causes interest revenue to be:

reduced   or   increased

L.O. 2(a)   The lower-of-cost-or-market method is used to account for long-term stock investments when the investor is unable to exercise significant influence over the investee.

true   or   false

L.O. 2(b)   When using the lower-of-cost-or-market method, the amount of investee earnings has no effect on the investor's Investment account.

correct   or   incorrect

L.O. 2(c)   The equity method involves journal entries at the time the investee's earnings are announced, as well as when:

dividends are paid   or   market value declines

L.O. 3(a)   The preparation of consolidated financial statements for a parent and its majority-owned subsidiary is appropriate because of the concept of the:

legal entity   or   economic entity

L.O. 3(b)   Consolidated financial statements present a picture of the parent and its controlled subsidiaries as if only one company existed.

correct   or   incorrect

L.O. 4(a)   In preparing consolidated financial statements, intercompany transactions are eliminated via an entry that is recorded in the:

ledger   or   work sheet

L.O. 4(b)   In order to prepare consolidated financial statements, a required elimination entry would include a debit(s) to:

Investment in Subsidiary
or
the subsidiary's equity accounts

L.O. 5(a)   Consolidated financial statements prepared on the date of acquisition of a 100% owned subsidiary would include stockholders' equity equal to:

the parent's stockholders' equity
or
the sum of the parent and
subsidiary's stockholders' equity

L.O. 5(b)   The minority interest appears in the:

parent's general ledger
or
consolidated financial statements

L.O. 6(a)   The minority interest can be calculated as the percentage of ownership held by stockholders other than the parent, multiplied times the:

stockholders' equity of the subsidiary
or
parent's Investment in Subsidiary account

L.O. 6(b)   If a subsidiary is acquired at a cost in excess of book value, the difference should be adjusted to specific assets, liabilities, and unrecorded intangibles appearing in the consolidated financial statements.

true   or   false

L.O. 7(a)   The excess of the cost of an acquired company over the sum of the amounts assigned to identifiable assets acquired (less liabilities assumed) should be recorded as:

goodwill   or   minority interest

L.O. 7(b)   As a broad generalization, which consolidation technique tends to have a more favorable impact on reported earnings?

pooling of interests   or   purchase accounting

L.O. 7(c)　　As it relates to consolidated income, the purchase method generally results in the combining of income prospectively, while the pooling-of-interests method results in the combining of income retroactively.

true or false

FILL IN THE BLANKS

1. Bond investment _____ amortization causes investment income to be increased beyond the amount of cash received.

2. The amortization of the premium on an investment in bonds will cause the investment in bonds account to _____.

3. A _____ or _____ may result on the sale of a bond before maturity.

4. A company whose shares were acquired by an investor is known as the _____.

5. The ____-____-____-____-____ method is used to account for long-term stock acquisitions by investors who are unable to exercise significant influence over investees.

6. The equity method is appropriate for accounting for investments where the investor has acquired over _____ percent of the voting stock of another company.

7. The equity method focuses principally on changes in the investee's _____ _____, rather than on changes in the market value of the investee's stock.

8. A majority owner is termed the _____, and its majority-owned company is termed the _____.

9. _____ _____ _____ present a combined picture of the parent and its controlled subsidiary as if only one company existed.

10. _____ _____ are required for intercompany transactions included in the separate records of the parent and subsidiary.

11. Elimination entries are recorded only on a work sheet; they are _____ entered into the accounts of either the parent or subsidiary.

12. Owners of a subsidiary's stock other than the parent are known as _____ _____ shareholders.

13. If a subsidiary is acquired at a price in excess of the fair value of its identifiable assets and liabilities, an intangible asset called _____ will be recorded.

14. Two typical income statement transactions that require elimination are intercompany _____ and interest on loans between the parent and subsidiary.

15. Most business combinations are treated as if a _____ has occurred, but a limited number of transactions qualify for _____ - _____ - _____ accounting.

MULTIPLE CHOICE QUESTIONS

Circle the appropriate response.

1. Brooks Corporation purchased $100,000 of Madrid Company's 5-year bonds on April 1, 19X1. The bonds are dated January 1, 19X1, have a contract interest rate of 10%, and have semiannual interest payment dates of June 30 and December 31. Brooks paid $102,500 (including accrued interest) for the bonds. The journal entry to record the purchase is:

   a. Investment in Bonds   102,500
        Cash   102,500
   b. Investment in Bonds   100,000
        Bond Interest Receivable   2,500
        Cash   102,500
   c. Investment in Bonds   102,500
        Bond Interest Receivable   2,500
        Cash   105,000
   d. Investment in Bonds   100,000
        Premium on Bonds   2,500
        Cash   102,500

2. On January 1, 19X1, Corpus Corporation purchased $50,000 of Maxwell Corporation bonds at 96. The bonds are dated January 1, 19X1, and have a contract interest rate of 8%. The discount is amortized by the effective-interest method and the appropriate interest rate is 10%. Interest is paid annually on December 31 of each year. How much bond interest revenue should be reported for 19X1?

   a. $3,840
   b. $4,000
   c. $4,800
   d. $5,000

3. Select the correct journal entry to record the sale of $12,000 of bond investments. The bonds were purchased on January 1, 19X1, at face value, and were sold on August 1, 19X4, at 103, plus accrued interest. The bonds pay interest semiannually at a contract interest rate of 10%. Interest was last recorded and paid on June 30, 19X4.

a.	Cash	12,460	
	Bond Interest Revenue		100
	Gain on Sale of Bonds		360
	Investment in Bonds		12,000
b.	Cash	12,100	
	Gain on Sale of Bonds		100
	Investment in Bonds		12,000
c.	Cash	12,000	
	Investment in Bonds		12,000
d.	Cash	12,460	
	Bond Interest Revenue		460
	Investment in Bonds		12,000

4. Ace Corporation has a long-term investment in the common stock of another entity. This investment is accounted for by using the lower-of-cost-or-market method. A journal entry to record a $10,000 decline in market value below cost would necessarily involve:

   a. a debit to Unrealized Loss on Long-term Investments.
   b. a credit to Unrealized Loss on Long-term Investments.
   c. a debit to Allowance for Decline in Market Value of Long-term Investments.
   d. a debit to Investment Revenue.

5. Investor Corporation owns 30% of Investee Corporation. Investee had net earnings of $100,000 during the year and paid dividends of $30,000. Investor's Investment in Investee account contained a $70,000 balance at the beginning of the year. What would be the correct balance of this account at the end of the year?

   a. $70,000
   b. $91,000
   c. $100,000
   d. $140,000

6. If O'Donnell Corporation owns 90% of the stock of Perkins Company, and Perkins owes O'Donnell $25,000, the proper eliminating entry for the intercompany note would be:

a.	Notes Receivable (parent)	25,000	
	Notes Payable (sub)		25,000
b.	Notes Payable (sub)	25,000	
	Notes Receivable (parent)		25,000
c.	Notes Payable (sub)	22,500	
	Notes Receivable (parent)		22,500
d.	Notes Receivable (parent)	22,500	
	Notes Payable (sub)		22,500

7. Westcastle purchased 100% of the stock of Simpson Corporation on January 1, 19X1. On that date, Simpson had common stock of $100,000, additional paid-in capital of $50,000, and retained earnings of $200,000. Westcastle paid $350,000 for the investment. The work sheet elimination entry to consolidate the parent and subsidiary on January 1, 19X1, would include:

   a. A debit to Goodwill for $50,000.
   b. A credit to the Investment in Simpson account for $100,000.
   c. A debit to Common Stock for $100,000.
   d. A credit to Retained Earnings for $200,000.

8. Randall Corporation owns 90% of the stock of Folger Company. Folger Company has stockholders' equity of $300,000, which consists of common stock of $100,000, additional paid-in capital of $100,000, and retained earnings of $100,000. In the consolidated financial statements, the minority interest in Folger should be reported at:

   a. $0
   b. $10,000
   c. $20,000
   d. $30,000

9. Russell Enterprises purchased 100% of the outstanding stock of Jeremy Company for $400,000. Jeremy had cash of $100,000 and land valued at $200,000. Jeremy had no other assets or liabilities. Russell's entry to record the acquisition of Jeremy would be:

   a. Investment in Jeremy   300,000
      Goodwill   100,000
          Cash   400,000
   b. Investment in Jeremy   400,000
          Cash   400,000
   c. Cash   100,000
      Land   200,000
      Goodwill   100,000
          Cash   400,000
   d. No entry

10. Which of the following statements regarding consolidated financial statements is false?

   a. Intercompany transactions should be eliminated in preparing consolidated financial statements.
   b. If the purchase method of accounting is used, the assets of the subsidiary will be incorporated into a consolidated balance sheet (prepared on the date of purchase) at their fair market value.
   c. A company may elect either the purchase or pooling-of-interests accounting method for any business combination.
   d. The parent company's financial statements will include an account for investment in subsidiaries.

DEMONSTRATION PROBLEMS

DP-1 On January 1, 19X1, Woodbury Corporation purchased $200,000 of 8% bonds. The bonds are to be held as a long-term investment, and yield an effective-interest rate of 10%. Woodbury purchased the bonds for $175,076. Interest dates are June 30 and December 31. Woodbury uses the effective-interest method of amortization. Round computations to the nearest dollar.

a. Compute total interest received during 19X1.
b. Compute the amount of amortization to be recorded during 19X1. Woodbury records amortization on a semiannual basis.
c. Determine the amount of bond interest revenue to be reported on Woodbury's 19X1 income statement.

DP-2 On January 1, 19X1, White Rabbit Corporation acquired 20,000 shares of Aspen, Inc., and 60,000 shares of Winter Park Corporation. The acquisitions cost $115,000 and $480,000, respectively. Additional information about Aspen and Winter Park follows.

Aspen, Inc.
- Common shares outstanding — 80,000
- 19X1 net income — $144,000
- 19X1 dividends — $40,000
- 19X1 year-end market value per share — $10

Winter Park Corporation
- Common shares outstanding — 600,000
- 19X1 net income — $380,000
- 19X1 dividends — $120,000
- 19X1 year-end market value per share — $6

a. Determine whether the investments in Aspen and Winter Park should be accounted for by the lower-of-cost-or-market or equity method.
b. Present the proper disclosure for the long-term stock investments on White Rabbit's December 31, 19X1, balance sheet.
c. Compute the investment revenue and dividend revenue that White Rabbit should record on its 19X1 income statement.

DP-3 Wallace Corporation acquired 100% of the outstanding stock of Murphy Corporation for $109,000. On the date of acquisition, Murphy's balance sheet revealed the following information:

Cash and other current assets	$ 22,500
Property, plant, and equipment, net	135,000
Accounts payable	8,500
Notes payable	50,000
Common stock	25,000
Retained earnings	74,000

The fair market value of the property, plant, and equipment on the acquisition date totaled $137,500. Prepare the work sheet entry that is necessary to consolidate the balance sheets of Wallace and Murphy.

SOLUTIONS TO SELF TESTS

FULFILLMENT OF LEARNING OBJECTIVES

1(a)   True
1(b)   Incorrect
1(c)   Effective-interest
1(d)   Reduced
2(a)   True
2(b)   Correct
2(c)   Dividends are paid
3(a)   Economic entity
3(b)   Correct
4(a)   Work sheet
4(b)   The subsidiary's equity accounts
5(a)   The parent's stockholders' equity
5(b)   Consolidated financial statements
6(a)   Stockholders' equity of the subsidiary
6(b)   True
7(a)   Goodwill
7(b)   Pooling of interests
7(c)   True

FILL IN THE BLANKS

1. Discount
2. Decrease
3. Gain, loss
4. Investee
5. Lower-of-cost-or-market
6. Twenty
7. Retained earnings (or stockholders' equity)
8. Parent, subsidiary
9. Consolidated financial statements
10. Elimination entries
11. Not (or never)
12. Minority interest
13. Goodwill
14. Sales
15. Purchase, pooling-of-interests

MULTIPLE CHOICE QUESTIONS

1.   b.   The bonds were purchased for $102,500, representing $100,000 for the bond investment and $2,500 of accrued interest ($100,000 X 10% X 3/12). Choice "b" correctly reflects these amounts and accounts.

2.	c.	$4,800. Using the effective-interest amortization method, the amount of interest revenue equals the bond carrying value for the period ($50,000 X 96% = $48,000) times the interest rate (10%).
3.	a.	The bonds were sold for $12,360 ($12,000 X 103%), plus accrued interest ($12,000 X 10% X 1/12 = $100). The journal entry reflects the receipt of $12,460 cash, the removal of the $12,000 investment from the accounts, the $100 of interest revenue, and the gain of $360 ($12,360 - $12,000).
4.	a.	The journal entry to record the decline in market value below cost involves a debit to Unrealized Loss on Long-term Investments and a credit to Allowance for Decline in Market Value of Long-term Investments.
5.	b.	$91,000. The balance is determined by taking the beginning balance ($70,000), adding the share of income ($100,000 X 30% = $30,000), and subtracting the dividends received ($30,000 X 30% = $9,000).
6.	b.	Notes Payable is eliminated (debited) and Notes Receivable is eliminated (credited) for the full $25,000 amount. The percentage ownership has no impact on the intercompany debt.
7.	c.	The appropriate journal entry includes debits to Common Stock ($100,000), Paid-in Capital in Excess of Par ($50,000), and Retained Earnings ($200,000). The credit is to the Investment in Simpson account ($350,000).
8.	d.	$30,000. The minority interest simply equals the stockholders' equity ($100,000 + $100,000 + $100,000 = $300,000) times the percentage of stock not owned by the parent (10%).
9.	b.	The investment should be recorded by debiting Investment in Jeremy and crediting Cash for the $400,000 purchase price. When financial statements are consolidated, the Investment account will be eliminated against the equity accounts of Jeremy, and goodwill will be established.
10.	c.	The purchase and pooling-of-interests methods are not elective alternatives; if criteria are satisfied, the pooling technique will be used -- otherwise, the transaction is accounted for by the purchase method. The other choices are all true statements.

DEMONSTRATION PROBLEMS

DP-1

(a) Total interest received in 19X1 is $16,000 ($200,000 X 8%).

(b) Amortization to record -- 19X1:

($175,076 X 10% X 6/12) - ($200,000 X 8%
   X 6/12) = $ 754
(($175,076 + $754) X 10% X 6/12) -
   ($200,000 X 8% X 6/12) =   792
                                                                                                                                                                 $1,546

(c) Bond interest revenue -- 19X1:

$16,000 + $1,546 (discount amortization) = $17,546.

DP-2

(a) The equity method should be used for Aspen because 25% (20,000/80,000) of the outstanding common shares were acquired. The lower-of-cost-or-market method should be used for Winter Park because only 10% (60,000/600,000) of the common shares outstanding were acquired.

(b)
Long-term investments			
Investment in Aspen, Inc.*			$141,000
Investment in Winter Park Corp.		$480,000	
Less: Allowance for decline in market value of long-term investment		120,000	360,000
			$501,000

* $115,000 + ($144,000 X 25%) - ($40,000 X 25%) = $141,000

(c)
Investment revenue, equity method ($144,000 X 25%)	$36,000
Dividend revenue ($120,000 X 10%)	12,000
Total revenue	$48,000

DP-3

Common Stock: Murphy	25,000	
Retained Earnings: Murphy	74,000	
Property, Plant, & Equipment	2,500	
Goodwill	7,500	
Investment in Murphy		109,000

To eliminate Murphy's stockholders' equity accounts against the Investment account and to revalue the assets acquired

CHAPTER 16

STATEMENT OF CASH FLOWS

LEARNING OBJECTIVES

After studying this chapter, you should be able to:

1. Explain the purpose of the statement of cash flows.

2. Classify and analyze operating, investing, and financing activities.

3. Demonstrate the proper accounting treatment for significant noncash investing/financing transactions.

4. Use both the direct and indirect methods of computing cash flows from operating activities.

5. Prepare and interpret a statement of cash flows.

CHAPTER HIGHLIGHTS

I. The **STATEMENT** of cash flows has a specific **FORMAT, AND** includes three broad **CLASSIFICATIONS** that reveal information about operating activities, investing activities, and financing activities. In addition, businesses are required to reveal significant noncash investing/financing transactions.

   A. **OPERATING ACTIVITIES** are those transactions and events that enter into the determination of net income. Cash inflows from operating activities consist of items such as receipts from customers. Outflows consist of payments for inventory, employee salaries and wages, taxes, interest, and other normal business expenses.

   B. **INVESTING ACTIVITIES** are those that involve the investment of a firm's resources. Cash inflows would result from the sale of stocks and bonds, disposal of long-term productive resources, and receipt of principal repayments on loans made to others. Cash outflows from investing activities include payments made to acquire long-term assets or securities of other firms, loans made by the entity, and similar items.

   C. **FINANCING ACTIVITIES** provide a business with resources from owners or creditors. Typical inflows would be the proceeds received from stock and bond issues, borrowings under mortgage notes and loans, and so forth. Cash outflows for financing activities include repayments of loan principal, acquisitions of treasury stock, and dividend distributions.

D. **INVESTING AND FINANCING TRANSACTIONS THAT DO NOT AFFECT CASH** (such as exchanging common stock for a noncash asset like land) should be reported in a separate section of the statement of cash flows.

E. When preparing the statement of cash flows, companies broadly define "cash" to consist of both **CASH AND CASH EQUIVALENTS**. Cash equivalents are short-term, highly liquid investments that mature in 90 days or less.

II. **A FURTHER PROBE OF OPERATING ACTIVITIES** reveals that operating cash flow is not necessarily equal to net income. Recall that net income is computed on an accrual basis; that is, revenues are reported when earned and expenses when incurred. In contrast, cash from operations relates to the collection of sales proceeds and the actual payment of various operating expenses. Simply stated, cash basis revenues are reported when cash is received, and expenses are reported when paid.

A. One method for computing cash provided by operating activities is **THE DIRECT METHOD**. Under this technique, individual income statement items are translated from the accrual basis to the cash basis. The result of the translation produces amounts like cash received from customers, cash payments for merchandise, cash payments for selling and administrative expenses, and cash payments for interest and income taxes. The net of these amounts is net cash provided by operating activities (i.e., cash basis income).

1. **CASH RECEIVED FROM CUSTOMERS** is calculated by adding the decrease in accounts receivable (or subtracting the increase) to (from) accrual basis sales. For example, if accrual basis sales were $100 and accounts receivable decreased by $10, then cash collected from customers was $110.

2. Calculating **CASH PAYMENTS FOR MERCHANDISE** is slightly more involved. First, total purchases must be computed. Consider that beginning inventory plus purchases, minus ending inventory, equals cost of goods sold. If the amount of beginning inventory, ending inventory, and cost of goods sold are known, then purchases can be derived algebraically. Second, the amount of purchases paid in cash must be calculated. If accounts payable relate to merchandise purchases, then the amount of purchases plus the amount of the decrease (or minus the increase) in accounts payable would equal cash payments for merchandise purchases.

3. **CASH PAYMENTS FOR SELLING AND ADMINISTRATIVE EXPENSES** may be computed as the accrual basis selling and administrative expenses plus the increase in prepaid expenses (or minus the decrease).

4. **CASH PAYMENTS FOR INTEREST AND INCOME TAXES** are computed as the accrual basis expense amount plus the amount of decrease (or minus the increase) in any related interest or income tax payable.

5. In evaluating cash flows, one must recognize **THE NEED FOR FLEXIBILITY**, as the techniques just introduced will not work in all cases. For example, a company may have prepaid interest, which must be logically considered when calculating cash payments for interest.

6. The text includes **AN OVERVIEW** of the calculation of the net cash provided by operating activities under the direct method.

7. When computing cash flows from operating activities, certain income statement items were ignored. Specific **INCOME STATEMENT ITEMS THAT WERE DISREGARDED** include noncash expenses. Depreciation is an excellent example. Depreciation is an expense that reduces net income but does not consume cash. Therefore, noncash expenses like depreciation are not subtracted when calculating cash basis income. In addition, a company may generate nonoperating gains and losses that enter into the determination of net income. However, the cash flow from such events is reported as an investing or financing activity. Importantly, the gains and losses are deleted when converting from the accrual basis to the cash basis.

B. **THE INDIRECT METHOD** is an alternative method to calculate net cash flow from operating activities. While the methodology differs from the direct approach, the "bottom-line" amount for cash provided by operating activities is the same.

1. With the indirect method, amounts are added and subtracted from accrual basis income to calculate cash from operating activities. To begin, **NONCASH EXPENSES** must be added to accrual basis income because they reduce income without consuming cash. Similarly, **NONOPERATING GAINS AND LOSSES** must be subtracted (gains) or added (losses) because they increase and decrease accrual basis income but do not result from operating activities.

2. After adjusting for noncash expenses and nonoperating gains and losses, the change in certain **CURRENT ASSETS AND CURRENT LIABILITIES** must be evaluated. In general, increases in current assets are deducted from accrual basis income, while decreases are added. Conversely, increases in current liabilities are added and decreases are subtracted. The reason for these adjustments is that the changes in these accounts indicate a difference between accrual and cash basis income. For example, increases in accounts receivable represent sales not yet collected, and are therefore deducted in the conversion process. Do not include changes in nonoperating current assets and current liabilities (e.g., notes payable generated by financing activities) in this adjustment process.

III. The **PREPARATION OF A STATEMENT OF CASH FLOWS** requires reference to the income statement, statement of retained earnings, comparative balance sheets, and the ledger accounts.

A. **STEP 1: ANALYZE THE CASH ACCOUNT** to determine the change in cash (which is the bottom-line amount on the statement of cash flows).

B. **STEP 2: DETERMINE NET CASH FLOW FROM OPERATING ACTIVITIES** by utilizing either the direct or indirect method (as presented earlier in the chapter).

C. **STEP 3: ANALYZE REMAINING BALANCE SHEET ACCOUNTS** to determine the company's investing and financing activities.

1. If **LAND** increased during the year, the preliminary indication is that cash was exchanged for land in an investing activity. The statement of cash flows would reveal an investing cash outflow for the purchase of land.

2. Likewise, **BUILDINGS** may increase via a cash purchase; again a cash outflow from an investing activity. In the alternative, assets like land and buildings may be acquired in exchange for stock or notes payable. Such transactions are regarded as noncash

investing/financing activities and are listed in a separate schedule on the statement of cash flows.

3. In reviewing **ACCUMULATED DEPRECIATION: BUILDINGS**, one is likely to note an increase from depreciation during the year. The amount of depreciation is a noncash item, the treatment of which was covered in the discussion of operating activities.

4. **EQUIPMENT AND ACCUMULATED DEPRECIATION: EQUIPMENT** are two additional accounts that provide information about investing activities and depreciation expense. In reviewing these (and similar) accounts, the disposal of assets may also be revealed. When disposals occur, the cash generated from the sale (regardless of the amount of gain or loss) is reported as a cash inflow from investing activities.

5. Increases and decreases in **LONG-TERM INVESTMENTS** may also reveal cash flows related to investing activities.

6. **NOTES PAYABLE** accounts increase and decrease as cash inflows and outflows related to financing activities occur.

7. Likewise, the issuance of **BONDS PAYABLE** results in a financing cash inflow, and the retirement of bonds is accomplished via a financing cash outflow.

8. Increases in **COMMON STOCK AND PAID-IN CAPITAL IN EXCESS OF PAR** are indicative of additional cash inflows from financing activities via the issuance of stock.

9. Changes in **RETAINED EARNINGS** must be evaluated to determine the amount of net income (which is considered in calculating cash flows from operating activities) and dividends. Cash dividends paid represent a cash outflow from a financing activity.

D. **STEP 4: FINANCIAL STATEMENT PREPARATION** requires the compilation of cash flow information in an acceptable statement format. The appropriate formats are the direct and indirect approaches. With the direct approach, the first portion of the statement reveals cash flows from operating activities (cash receipts from customers less the cash payments for various expenses). This is followed with sections that provide information about cash flows from investing activities and cash flows from financing activities. Finally, a schedule of noncash investing/financing activities is revealed. An example follows.

SAMPLE COMPANY
STATEMENT OF CASH FLOWS
FOR THE YEAR ENDED DECEMBER 31, 19X2

Cash flows from operating activities		
Cash received from customers		$157,000
Less cash payments for:		
Purchases of merchandise	$124,000	
Selling & administrative expenses	10,000	
Interest	18,000	
Income taxes	10,000	162,000
Net cash used by operating activities		$ (5,000)
Cash flows from investing activities		
Purchase of land		(8,000)
Cash flows from financing activities		
Payment on mortgage		(2,000)
Net increase (decrease) in cash		$(15,000)
Cash balance, January 1, 19X2		25,000
Cash balance, December 31, 19X2		$ 10,000
Schedule of noncash investing/financing activities		
Common stock issued for machinery		$ 30,000

As an alternative, a company may use the indirect approach. The first section of the statement presents net cash flows from operating activities (beginning with net income and reconciling to the net cash provided by operating activities). Separate sections for cash flows from investing activities and cash flows from financing activities follow, and the additional information on noncash investing/financing activities is presented.

SAMPLE COMPANY
STATEMENT OF CASH FLOWS
FOR THE YEAR ENDED DECEMBER 31, 19X2

Cash flows from operating activities		
Net income		$ 15,000
Add (deduct) items to convert net income to a cash basis		
Machinery depreciation expense	$ 2,000	
Patent amortization expense	4,000	
Decrease in accounts receivable (net)	10,000	
Increase in inventory	(45,000)	
Increase in accounts payable	7,000	
Increase in income taxes payable	2,000	(20,000)
Net cash used by operating activities		$ (5,000)
Cash flows from investing activities		
Purchase of land		(8,000)
Cash flows from financing activities		
Payment on mortgage		(2,000)
Net increase (decrease) in cash		$(15,000)
Cash balance, January 1, 19X2		25,000
Cash balance, December 31, 19X2		$ 10,000
Schedule of noncash investing/financing activities		
Common stock issued for machinery		$ 30,000

E. Care should be used when evaluating the statement of cash flows. **SOME THOUGHTS ON INTERPRETATION** of the statement pertain to the ability to judge a firm's age and operating maturity based on its cash flows.

IV. **APPENDIX:** The appendix includes a **WORK SHEET FOR PREPARING A STATEMENT OF CASH FLOWS** using the **INDIRECT APPROACH**. Preparation of the work sheet includes five basic steps and the end result is a financial statement identical to those presented earlier. The work sheet is most useful in dealing with complex situations and helps ensure that no accounts or transactions are accidentally overlooked.

CLASS NOTES

CLASS NOTES

CLASS NOTES

CLASS NOTES

SELF TESTS

FULFILLMENT OF LEARNING OBJECTIVES

Circle the appropriate response.

L.O. 1(a) The statement of cash flows reveals the cash generated or consumed by a firm's operating, investing, and financing activities.

correct   or   incorrect

L.O. 1(b) The statement of cash flows is primarily designed to explain the changes in retained earnings.

true   or   false

L.O. 2(a) Which activities relate primarily to the production and sale of goods and services and enter into the determination of income?

operating activities   or   financing activities

L.O. 2(b) Which of the following would constitute a typical cash inflow from an investing activity?

sale of stocks of other firms
or
issuance of stock

L.O. 3(a) Only transactions that directly generate or consume cash are reported on a statement of cash flows.

true   or   false

L.O. 3(b) Which of the following would constitute a noncash investing/financing transaction?

exchanging land for stock
or
issuing a stock dividend

L.O. 3(c) Significant noncash investing/financing transactions are reported on a statement of cash flows prepared using either the direct method or:

the indirect method   or   investing method

L.O. 4(a) Which of the following approaches to preparing the statement of cash flows translates income from the accrual basis to the cash basis?

direct method   or   indirect method

L.O. 4(b)   Cash received from customers can be calculated by starting with accrual basis sales and adding:

> decreases in accounts receivable
> or
> increases in accounts receivable

L.O. 4(c)   To calculate cash flow from operating activities under the indirect method, nonoperating gains should be:

> added or subtracted

L.O. 4(d)   With the indirect approach to calculating cash flow from operating activities, increases in current assets related to operations should be subtracted from the accrual basis income figure.

> true or false

L.O. 5(a)   In preparing a statement of cash flows, the proceeds from a disposal of equipment should be reported as a cash inflow from investing activities.

> correct or incorrect

L.O. 5(b)   Cash dividends paid are reported as a financing cash:

> inflow or outflow

L.O. 5(c)   Both the direct and indirect methods are acceptable for external financial reporting.

> true or false

FILL IN THE BLANKS

1. _____ _____ are those which arise from transactions and events that enter into net income.

2. _____ _____ are those that involve investment of an entity's resources.

3. _____ _____ are those that supply a firm with funds from either the firm's owners or creditors.

4. Under both the direct and indirect approaches to preparing a statement of cash flows, a separate schedule of _____ investing/financing transactions should be presented.

5. Under the _____ _____, individual items on the income statement are translated from the accrual basis to the cash basis.

6. Under the _____ _____, operating cash flows are calculated by starting with accrual basis net income, then adding and subtracting amounts to convert to the cash basis.

7. If the indirect method is used, noncash expenses like depreciation should be _____ in calculating the cash provided by operating activities.

8. The purchase of land, disposal of equipment, and so forth are _____ activities.

9. The payment of dividends and receipt of proceeds from bond issues are examples of _____ activities.

10. The difference between the debit and credit column subtotals of the analysis columns of the cash flow work sheet represents the change in _____.

MULTIPLE CHOICE QUESTIONS

Circle the appropriate response.

1. On a statement of cash flows, which of the following types of activities would not be disclosed in a separate section?

    a. Operating activities
    b. Investing activities
    c. Financing activities
    d. Contractual activities

2. Which of the following activities would generally be regarded as a financing activity in preparing a statement of cash flows?

    a. Dividend distribution
    b. Proceeds from the sale of stocks of other firms
    c. Loans made by the entity to other businesses
    d. Employees' salaries and wages paid

3. In preparing the statement of cash flows, how should noncash investing/financing activities be reported?

    a. Not be reported
    b. Be reported in a separate schedule accompanying the statement of cash flows
    c. Be reported in the investing activities section of the statement of cash flows
    d. Be reported in the financing activities section of the statement of cash flows

4. For purposes of calculating cash receipts from customers, which of the following adjustments should be made to convert accrual basis sales to cash basis sales?

    a. Add an increase in accounts receivable to accrual basis sales
    b. Subtract an increase in accounts receivable from accrual basis sales
    c. Add cash in bank to accrual basis sales
    d. Add the change in cash to the accrual basis sales

5. If the indirect approach for the statement of cash flows is presented, which of the following items should be subtracted from accrual basis net income to derive cash flow from operating activities?

    a. Gains on the sale of investments
    b. Losses on the sale of investments
    c. Depreciation expense
    d. Amortization expense

6. As a generalization, the adjustment of accrual basis income to cash provided by operating activities requires which of the following to be added?

    a. Increases in current assets related to operating activities
    b. Increases in current liabilities related to operating activities
    c. Decreases in current liabilities related to operating activities
    d. Both (a) and (c) are correct.

7. When preparing a statement of cash flows under the indirect method, supplemental disclosure should be made for which of the following?

    a. Net cash consumed by operating activities
    b. Cash dividend distributions
    c. Noncash investing/financing activities
    d. All of the above

8. Wilkin Corporation reported accrual basis sales of $200,000, cost of goods sold of $80,000, and operating expenses, taxes, and interest summing to $30,000. In evaluating Wilkin's comparative balance sheets, it is determined that accounts receivable increased $10,000, inventory increased $5,000, and accounts payable decreased $7,000. There were no changes in prepaid expenses nor were there any interest or taxes payable at the beginning or end of the year. How much was cash basis income for Wilkin Corporation for the year?

    a. $68,000
    b. $82,000
    c. $105,000
    d. $112,000

9. Dixon Corporation reported 19X1 accrual basis net income of $50,000. Relevant information to adjust accrual basis income to cash basis income follows.

Depreciation expense	$12,000
Loss on the sale of land	16,000
Increase in accounts receivable	8,000
Decrease in merchandise inventory	4,000
Increase in accounts payable	3,000
Increase in taxes payable	2,000

How much is net cash provided by operating activities?

a. $47,000
b. $49,000
c. $51,000
d. $79,000

10. In preparing a work sheet for the statement of cash flows, the lower portion corresponds to a statement of cash flows prepared using the indirect method. Items in the debit column of this lower portion most closely correspond to items which:

a. Explain increases in cash.
b. Explain decreases in cash.
c. Relate to financing activities.
d. Relate to investing activities.

DEMONSTRATION PROBLEMS

DP-1 The Duke Company had the following transactions and events during the year:

Declared and paid a cash dividend of $1 per share on 10,000 common shares.

Borrowed $70,000 from a local bank on a long-term note.

Sold land having a book value of $40,000 for $200,000 cash.

Exchanged $30,000 of common stock for equipment to be used in the business.

Generated total cash sales to customers during the year of $140,000.

Consider each of these items independently. Determine whether the item arises from operating, investing, financing, or noncash investing/financing activities.

DP-2 Loveland Corporation provided the following information regarding its December 31, 19X1, and 19X2 balance sheets:

	19X2	19X1
Accounts receivable	$200,000	$240,000
Inventory	820,000	880,000
Accounts payable	900,000	950,000

Loveland makes all sales and purchases on account, and employs the accrual basis of accounting. The firm's 19X2 income statement reveals sales of $200,000 and cost of goods sold of $120,000. Determine the cash received from customers and the cash paid to suppliers during 19X2.

DP-3 The comparative December 31, 19X2, and 19X1 balance sheets of Proxmire Company included the following information:

	19X2	19X1
Cash	$14,000	$18,000
Accounts receivable, net	24,000	36,000
Merchandise inventory	66,000	52,000
Property, plant, & equipment	80,000	60,000
Accumulated depreciation	34,000	20,000
Accounts payable	39,000	31,000
Income taxes payable	19,000	13,000
Common stock	40,000	40,000
Retained earnings	52,000	62,000

The firm's accrual basis income statement revealed the following:

Sales	$250,000
Cost of goods sold	170,000
Selling and administrative expenses	50,000
Depreciation expense	14,000
Income taxes	6,000

Dividends declared and paid during 19X2 were $20,000, and no interest expense was incurred. Proxmire purchased $20,000 of equipment during the year.

a. Determine the increase or decrease in cash during 19X2.
b. Prepare a statement of cash flows using the direct method.
c. Prepare a statement of cash flows using the indirect method.

SOLUTIONS TO SELF TESTS

FULFILLMENT OF LEARNING OBJECTIVES

1(a)	Correct
1(b)	False
2(a)	Operating activities
2(b)	Sale of stocks of other firms
3(a)	False
3(b)	Exchanging land for stock
3(c)	The indirect method
4(a)	Indirect method
4(b)	Decreases in accounts receivable
4(c)	Subtracted
4(d)	True
5(a)	Correct
5(b)	Outflow
5(c)	True

FILL IN THE BLANKS

1. Operating activities
2. Investing activities
3. Financing activities
4. Noncash
5. Direct method
6. Indirect method
7. Added
8. Investing
9. Financing
10. Cash

MULTIPLE CHOICE QUESTIONS

1. d. The statement of cash flows includes separate sections for operating, investing, and financing activities. The statement is silent with regard to contractual activities.

2. a. Dividends are a return to the owners who provided financing for the company; hence, they are reported as a financing activity. Proceeds from the sale of the stock of other firms and loans made to others are investing activities. Salaries and wages relate to operations.

3. b. Noncash investing/financing activities must be reported in a separate schedule accompanying the statement of cash flows.

4. b. Increases in accounts receivable relate to accrual basis sales not yet collected. Therefore, the amount of the increase in accounts receivable must be subtracted from accrual basis sales in calculating cash basis sales. The total change in cash and cash in bank are unrelated to the conversion process.

5. a. Nonoperating gains must be subtracted from accrual basis income in working toward operating cash flows (i.e., accrual basis income was increased for this nonoperating amount); conversely, nonoperating losses would be added. The conversion process requires that depreciation and amortization be added to accrual basis income because they reduce accrual basis income without consuming cash.

6. b. Increases in current liabilities related to operations are indicative of expenses and purchases not yet paid. Therefore, such amounts must be added to accrual basis income when computing cash from operating activities; conversely, decreases would be subtracted. Increases in current assets related to operations are also subtracted.

7. c. Choices "a" and "b" are an integral part of the statement. Noncash investing/financing activities are supplemental.

8. a. $68,000. The accrual basis income ($200,000 - $80,000 - $30,000 = $90,000) is reduced by the increase in accounts receivable ($10,000), the increase in inventory ($5,000), and the decrease in accounts payable ($7,000).

9. d. $79,000. The $50,000 accrual basis income should be increased by depreciation expense ($12,000), loss on the sale of land ($16,000), decrease in merchandise inventory ($4,000), increase in accounts payable ($3,000), and increase in taxes payable ($2,000), and be decreased by the increase in accounts receivable ($8,000). ($50,000 + $12,000 + $16,000 + $4,000 + $3,000 + $2,000 - $8,000 = $79,000).

10. a. A close examination of the lower portion of a work sheet reveals that the debits generally relate to cash increases, whether related to operating, investing, or financing activities.

DEMONSTRATION PROBLEMS

DP-1

Dividends -- Financing activity

Long-term borrowing -- Financing activity

Land sale -- Investing activity

Stock for equipment -- Noncash investing/financing activity

Cash sales -- Operating activity

DP-2

Cash collections from customers:	
Sales on account	$200,000
Plus: Decrease in accounts receivable	
($240,000 - $200,000)	40,000
Collections from customers	$240,000
Merchandise purchases for the year:	
Cost of goods sold	$120,000
Less: Decrease in inventory	
($880,000 - $820,000)	60,000
Purchases for the year	$ 60,000
Cash paid to suppliers of merchandise:	
Purchases on account	$ 60,000
Plus: Decrease in accounts payable	
($950,000 - $900,000)	50,000
Cash paid to suppliers	$110,000

DP-3

(a) Cash decreased by $4,000 ($18,000 - $14,000).

(b)

PROXMIRE COMPANY
STATEMENT OF CASH FLOWS
FOR THE YEAR ENDED DECEMBER 31, 19X2

Cash flows from operating activities		
Cash received from customers*		$262,000
Less cash payments for:		
Purchases of merchandise**	$176,000	
Selling and administrative expenses	50,000	
Income taxes***	—	226,000
Net cash provided by operating activities		$ 36,000
Cash flows from investing activities		
Purchase of equipment		(20,000)
Cash flows from financing activities		
Dividends paid		(20,000)
Net increase (decrease) in cash		$ (4,000)
Cash balance, January 1, 19X2		18,000
Cash balance, December 31, 19X2		$ 14,000

*   Sales ($250,000) + decrease in accounts receivable ($12,000)
**   Cost of goods sold ($170,000) + increase in merchandise inventory ($14,000) - increase in accounts payable ($8,000)
*** Income tax expense ($6,000) - increase in income taxes payable ($6,000)

(c)

PROXMIRE COMPANY
STATEMENT OF CASH FLOWS
FOR THE YEAR ENDED DECEMBER 31, 19X2

Cash flows from operating activities		
Net income*		$ 10,000
Add (deduct) items to convert net income to a cash basis		
Depreciation expense	$ 14,000	
Decrease in accounts receivable	12,000	
Increase in merchandise inventory	(14,000)	
Increase in accounts payable	8,000	
Increase in income taxes payable	6,000	26,000
Net cash provided by operating activities		$ 36,000
Cash flows from investing activities		
Purchase of equipment		(20,000)
Cash flows from financing activities		
Dividends paid		(20,000)
Net increase (decrease) in cash		$ (4,000)
Cash balance, January 1, 19X2		18,000
Cash balance, December 31, 19X2		$ 14,000

* Sales ($250,000) - cost of goods sold ($170,000) - selling and administrative expenses ($50,000) - depreciation expense ($14,000) - income taxes ($6,000)

CHAPTER 17

THE FOUNDATION OF FINANCIAL ACCOUNTING AND REPORTING

LEARNING OBJECTIVES

After studying this chapter, you should be able to:

1. Summarize the objectives of financial reporting.

2. Identify and describe the desirable characteristics of accounting information: relevancy, reliability, comparability, and understandability.

3. Explain the need for generally accepted accounting principles and the roles of various groups in the development process.

4. Define the assumptions, concepts, and modifying conventions that underlie financial accounting and reporting.

5. Describe the revenue realization principle and apply the percentage-of-completion and installment methods.

6. Recognize the impact of inflation on financial statements.

CHAPTER HIGHLIGHTS

I. The **OBJECTIVES OF FINANCIAL REPORTING** relate to the information needs of financial statement users. User groups include creditors, stockholders, analysts, and others. Specifically, financial accounting should be helpful in decision making; be helpful in assessing the amounts, timing, and uncertainty of an organization's cash inflows and outflows; assist in the study of an enterprise's resources, claims against those resources, and changes in them; and, be helpful in examining an enterprise's financial performance (i.e., earnings and its components).

   A. To fulfill the objectives of financial reporting, certain **CHARACTERISTICS OF FINANCIAL INFORMATION** should be displayed. These characteristics include relevance, reliability, comparability, and understandability.

      1. **RELEVANCY** means that information bears on the actions and decision-making processes of the users of financial information.

2. **RELIABILITY** means that information accurately depicts the conditions it purports to represent. To be reliable, it is important that accounting information be free from bias (neutral).

3. **COMPARABILITY** means that accounting information for one entity is comparable with the accounting information of another entity. This does not necessarily mean that all companies use exactly the same accounting principles. Comparability also relates to the financial statements of a single firm over time. A company should generally use the same accounting principles consistently from period to period.

4. **UNDERSTANDABILITY** provides that accounting information should be comprehensible to those with a reasonable understanding of business and economic activities. Of course, these individuals must be willing to study the information with reasonable diligence.

II. The practices, principles, and procedures of financial accounting have evolved over time and are influenced by a number of standard-setting groups. **THE FOUNDATION OF ACCOUNTING** provides comprehensive guidance and controls the quality of accounting information.

   A. **GENERALLY ACCEPTED ACCOUNTING PRINCIPLES (GAAP)** are at the heart of accounting measurement and provide the underlying foundation for reporting and disclosure. Generally accepted accounting principles consist of assumptions, concepts, and procedures.

      1. **THE DEVELOPMENT OF GAAP** has been an orderly process evolving for over 60 years.

         a. **THE SECURITIES AND EXCHANGE COMMISSION** was established in the mid-1930s. The SEC is charged with the administration of laws that regulate the reporting practices of companies whose stock is publicly traded. The SEC has served principally in an advisory role in the development of major accounting standards.

         b. **THE AMERICAN INSTITUTE OF CERTIFIED PUBLIC ACCOUNTANTS AND THE ACCOUNTING PRINCIPLES BOARD** have been instrumental in establishing accounting principles. The American Institute of Certified Public Accountants is a national association of licensed CPAs. Through this association, the Committee on Accounting Procedure was created in the late 1930s. By the late 1950s, the Committee on Accounting Procedure gave way to a newly formed policy-making body called the Accounting Principles Board (APB). The APB issued several types of pronouncements. Most significant were the Opinions of the Accounting Principles Board, which suggested appropriate accounting practices for specific situations. Many Opinions are still in effect today.

         c. **THE FINANCIAL ACCOUNTING STANDARDS BOARD** (FASB) is the private sector organization that replaced the Accounting Principles Board. This organization is the dominant force in establishing accounting principles. The FASB is independent from the American Institute of Certified Public Accountants and other rule-making bodies.

d. **OTHER INFLUENTIAL BODIES** have played an advisory role in the evolution of accounting standards. Among these are the American Accounting Association, the Institute of Management Accountants, and the Internal Revenue Service.

B. Accounting is based on an underlying framework that consists of **SPECIFIC PRINCIPLES AND ASSUMPTIONS**. Included in this theoretical framework are the entity assumption, going-concern assumption, periodicity assumption, monetary unit assumption, historical-cost principle, objectivity principle, revenue realization principle, matching principle, consistency principle, disclosure principle, materiality, and conservatism. These assumptions and principles are introduced throughout the text, and are summarized as follows:

The **ENTITY ASSUMPTION** holds that accounting information should be presented for specific and distinct reporting units. In other words, the separate transactions of owners and others should not be commingled with the reporting of economic activity for a particular business.

In the absence of evidence to the contrary, accountants base their measurement and reporting on the **GOING-CONCERN ASSUMPTION**, presuming that the business will continue to operate and that assets will benefit future periods.

Accountants divide time into specific measurement intervals (i.e., monthly, quarterly, yearly) for reporting purposes. This **PERIODICITY ASSUMPTION** is necessitated by the regular and continuing information needs of financial statement users.

Accounting measures transactions and events in units of money. The **MONETARY UNIT ASSUMPTION** is believed to be essential to overcome the problems that would arise by mixing measures in the financial statements (e.g., imagine the confusion of combining acres of land, cash in bank, square feet of buildings, etc.).

The **HISTORICAL-COST PRINCIPLE** has been introduced earlier. Recall that accounting measures are based on exchange prices (cost) because of their objective and verifiable nature. This concept certainly has its critics who contend that fair value, however subjective, is sometimes significantly different than cost, and that the difference results in misleading financial statements.

The **OBJECTIVITY PRINCIPLE** requires that accounting information be free from bias and independently verifiable.

The **REVENUE REALIZATION PRINCIPLE** holds that revenues should normally be recognized when goods are sold or services are rendered.

The **MATCHING PRINCIPLE** is vital to proper income measurement. It holds that costs associated with the production of revenue be recognized when the revenue is recognized.

To assist in the comparison of financial statements over time, accountants strive to satisfy the **CONSISTENCY PRINCIPLE**. This principle maintains that the same accounting principle and practices should remain in use from period to period.

Financial statements should be accompanied by **FULL DISCLOSURE**. This **PRINCIPLE** requires that all information that is deemed to be significant enough to influence financial statement users be included in the financial statements or accompanying notes.

Obviously, many small transactions are more cumbersome to "properly" account for than the relative size of the transaction warrants. Accountants are allowed the discretion of taking accounting "shortcuts" when the **MATERIALITY** of the transaction does not warrant a technically correct accounting effort. Materiality is relative, and is a matter of judgement; it cannot be reduced to a single dollar value.

CONSERVATISM states that when alternative valuations and measurements are possible, the one selected should be that which is least likely to overstate assets and/or income.

1. At this point, **AN EXPANSION OF THE REVENUE REALIZATION PRINCIPLE** is in order. Normally, revenue is recognized when (1) the earnings process is complete, and (2) the amount of revenue can be objectively measured. The following exceptions to the general rule are occasionally made.

    a. **REVENUE RECOGNIZED DURING PRODUCTION** may occur for projects that take an extended period of time to complete (such as construction of a building). In such cases, the percentage-of-completion method may be utilized. Under this method, profit is recognized based on the percentage of work completed. For example, a project 30% completed during a particular year would result in recognition of 30% of the project's total estimated profit. In this manner, profit is recognized as work occurs rather than on a single completion date (which may be several years in the future). The percentage-of-completion method should not be used unless there is the ability to make reasonably dependable estimates of contract revenues, costs, and progress.

    b. **REVENUE RECOGNIZED UPON COMPLETION OF PRODUCTION** should occur for projects that take an extended period of time to complete but lack reasonably dependable estimates of contract revenues, costs, or progress.

    c. **REVENUE RECOGNIZED AT THE TIME OF RECEIPT** is the norm under cash basis accounting. However, the accrual basis provides for a similar recognition point if uncertainties surround the ultimate collectibility of a receivable. This recognition technique is called the installment method. As the receivable is collected, the amount of profit to recognize is determined by multiplying the cash collected by the profit rate (i.e., the percentage of total profit to total sales price).

III. A fundamental assumption underlying financial statement preparation is that of a stable monetary unit. However, inflation sometimes causes the value of the dollar to change over time. As a result, inaccuracies are injected into the historical-cost accounting model. Accountants have proposed different theoretical approaches for **ACCOUNTING FOR INFLATION**.

   A. One approach is **CONSTANT PURCHASING POWER ACCOUNTING**, under which historical-cost data are adjusted for changes in the value of the dollar by using a general price level index. For example, land that was acquired for $1,000 (at a time when the consumer price index was 100) would be reported on a constant purchasing power balance sheet at $2,500 (if the index had risen to 250).

1. Not all financial statement elements are adjusted in the same manner. Proper adjustment requires determination of **MONETARY AND NONMONETARY ITEMS**. Monetary items are fixed in amount and expressed in dollars. Examples include cash, accounts receivable, and many liabilities. These items can be expressed in the same number of dollars, no matter what the rate of inflation. For example, a one-dollar bill is always a one-dollar bill, even if the rate of inflation is 10% per year. Nonmonetary items, on the other hand, are not fixed in dollars. Examples include land, buildings, and so forth. These items do not represent a claim to a fixed amount of cash; they tend to command more dollars as inflation occurs.

2. The distinction between monetary and nonmonetary items is important because monetary items result in **PURCHASING POWER GAINS AND LOSSES**. For example, holding cash during a period of inflation results in a purchasing power loss because a fixed amount of cash will buy less and less over time. Likewise, liabilities that are fixed in dollars become easier to repay over time, as inflation reduces the purchasing power of the dollars necessary to extinguish the liability.

B. An alternative to constant purchasing power accounting is **CURRENT COST ACCOUNTING**. This approach has been proposed because the constant purchasing power approach presumes that all prices change at the same rate as the consumer price index. Of course, many assets change at a rate different from the rate of general inflation. To deal with this shortcoming, the current cost balance sheet discloses assets at their current cost (which may be defined and computed in any number of ways). As a result, the balance sheet shows assets and liabilities at their "worth," irrespective of when they were acquired (and irrespective of the general rate of inflation).

1. **HOLDING GAINS AND LOSSES** occur when an asset increases or decreases in value. Holding gains and losses may be divided into unrealized and realized. Unrealized gains and losses relate to assets still owned at the end of an accounting period. Realized gains and losses relate to assets that have been disposed. For example, land that cost $100,000 and has increased to $150,000 in value would be reported on a current cost balance sheet at $150,000; the $50,000 difference would be reported as an unrealized holding gain. Alternatively, if the land were sold for $150,000, the $50,000 amount would be characterized as a realized holding gain.

C. **THE FASB AND INFLATION** are not strangers. This standard-setting body has experimented with various reporting techniques to deal with the problems of inflation. To date, only a limited group of the nation's very largest companies have ever been required to report any supplemental information about the effects of inflation. At present, all inflation disclosures are voluntary.

CLASS NOTES

CLASS NOTES

CLASS NOTES

CLASS NOTES

CLASS NOTES

SELF TESTS

FULFILLMENT OF LEARNING OBJECTIVES

Circle the appropriate response.

L.O. 1(a)   An objective of accounting information is to provide information that is useful in the decision-making process of both investors and creditors.

                         true   or   false

L.O. 1(b)   One specific objective of financial accounting is to provide information useful in assessing the amounts, timing, and uncertainty of an organization's:

                         cash flows   or   sales projections

L.O. 1(c)   Financial statements are generally regarded as:

                         general purpose   or   special purpose

L.O. 2(a)   Which characteristic of financial accounting pertains to the degree to which information bears on the decision-making process?

                         relevancy   or   reliability

L.O. 2(b)   To be reliable, accounting information must display the characteristic of:

                         freedom from bias   or   understandability

L.O. 2(c)   To be understandable, accounting information must be comprehensible to those who (1) have a reasonable understanding of business and economic activities and (2) are willing to study the information with reasonable diligence.

                         correct   or   incorrect

L.O. 3(a)   The establishment of generally accepted accounting principles means that all organizations record and measure financial activity in the same manner.

                         true   or   false

L.O. 3(b)   The private sector group responsible for the establishment of financial accounting rules is the:

                         Securities and Exchange Commission
                         or
                         Financial Accounting Standards Board

L.O. 4(a)   A presumption that a business will continue to operate for an indefinite period of time unless there is substantial evidence to the contrary is the:

> going-concern assumption
> or
> periodicity assumption

L.O. 4(b)   The revenue realization principle holds that expenses should be recognized in the same period as the revenues that they helped to produce.

> true or false

L.O. 4(c)   The consistency principle is based on the idea that businesses should employ the same accounting practices in each reporting period to improve the:

> monetary unit of financial statements
> or
> comparability of financial statements

L.O. 4(d)   The idea that corporations should expense the cost of small items of equipment relates to the concept of:

> materiality or conservatism

L.O. 5(a)   The revenue realization principle holds that recognition should ordinarily occur at:

> the point of sale
> or
> the completion of production

L.O. 5(b)   The percentage-of-completion method is acceptable when dependable estimates of contract costs and revenues can be made, and:

> the extent of progress toward completion
> can be determined
> or
> there is considerable uncertainty about
> the eventual collection of the sales price

L.O. 5(c)   Under the installment method of revenue recognition, the amount of profit to recognize in any given period is the amount of the collection during the period:

> times the profit percentage
> applicable to the sale
> or
> times the profit percentage applicable to
> the sale, less profits previously recognized

L.O. 6(a)   Monetary items are those which are fixed in:

> dollars or historical cost

L.O. 6(b) Which financial statement elements are most apt to produce purchasing power gains and losses?

monetary or nonmonetary

L.O. 6(c) During inflationary periods, a purchasing power gain would result from a:

net monetary asset position
or
net monetary liability position

L.O. 6(d) Holding gains and losses related to assets unsold at the end of an accounting period are termed:

realized or unrealized

L.O. 6(e) The Financial Accounting Standards Board currently requires all companies to report supplemental information on the effects of inflation.

true or false

FILL IN THE BLANKS

1. An objective of financial accounting is to provide information useful in assessing the _____, _____, and _____ of an organization's cash inflows and outflows.

2. Information is deemed to be _____ if it influences the actions of a decision maker.

3. Usefulness of accounting information is enhanced if a company's financial statements are _____ with the statements of other enterprises.

4. Accounting information should be comprehensible to those who have a _____ understanding of business and economic activities.

5. _____ _____ _____ _____ are the assumptions, concepts, and procedures that collectively serve as the underlying foundation of accounting.

6. Congress established the _____ _____ _____ _____ to regulate business reporting practices for companies that issue publicly traded securities.

7. The _____ _____ _____ _____ _____ _____ is a national association of licensed CPAs, and, at one time, was the parent of the standard-setting _____ _____ _____.

8. The private sector organization currently in charge of formulating standards for financial reporting is the _____ _____ _____ _____.

9. The _____ assumption holds that an entity's life can be divided into discrete time periods.

10. The principle of recording goods, resources, and services at the exchange or transaction price is the _____-_____ principle.

11. The _____-_____-_____ method is an accounting technique that is appropriate for long-term contracts, resulting in income being recognized during construction.

12. The installment method of accounting does not conform to generally accepted accounting principles unless considerable _____ surrounds collectibility of the receivables.

13. A violated assumption of accounting during a period of inflation is the _____ _____ assumption.

14. With _____ _____ _____ accounting, historical-cost data are adjusted for changes in the value of the dollar by using a general price level index.

15. _____ items consist of cash and contractual claims that are fixed in amount, whereas _____ items are not fixed in dollars and include items like land and buildings.

16. A purchasing power _____ would result from holding monetary assets during a period of inflation.

17. _____ holding gains and losses relate to assets that are owned at the end of an accounting period, whereas _____ holding gains and losses are calculated on assets sold or consumed.

MULTIPLE CHOICE QUESTIONS

Circle the appropriate response.

1. Which of the following is a stated objective of financial reporting?

    a. To provide information useful in assessing the amounts, timing, and uncertainty of an organization's cash inflows and outflows.
    b. To provide information useful in preparing tax returns and other governmental reports.
    c. To provide information about the current cost of an enterprise's assets.
    d. To ensure that all companies use the same financial accounting principles.

2. The organization that has been given the authority by Congress to set accounting principles for public companies is the:

    a. Internal Revenue Service.
    b. Financial Accounting Standards Board.
    c. Securities and Exchange Commission.
    d. Institute of Management Accountants.

3. Relevance is a qualitative characteristic of accounting information. Which definition best applies to the concept of relevance?

   a. The quality of information that assures that information is reasonably free from error and bias.
   b. The capacity of information to make a difference in the decision process.
   c. The quality of information that enables users to comprehend the message being communicated.
   d. The quality of information that enables users to identify similarities and differences between two sets of economic phenomena.

4. Milby Corporation has recently experienced a significant decline in sales and income. The president of Milby has ordered a change from the accelerated depreciation method to the straight-line depreciation method, with the expectation of lower depreciation charges and increased income. If this suggestion is carried out, the company will be violating the principle of:

   a. Consistency.
   b. Entity.
   c. Periodicity.
   d. Historical cost.

5. An argument in support of reporting an asset at its current value amount (rather than historical cost) is related to the:

   a. Qualitative characteristic of relevance.
   b. Revenue realization principle, because the earnings process is not complete.
   c. Consistency principle, because assets have been recorded at historical cost in prior years.
   d. Objectivity principle.

6. The lower-of-cost-or-market accounting techniques for marketable securities and inventory are fundamentally attributable to which principle?

   a. Consistency
   b. Conservatism
   c. Realization
   d. Matching

7. McDaniel Bridge Construction contracted to build a concrete structure over Clear Lake. The contract price was $4,000,000, payable in equal annual installments. After two years, Carl McDaniel estimated the project to be 70% complete. McDaniel estimated total construction costs at $3,000,000, and had recognized $400,000 of profit by the end of year one. How much profit should be recorded for year two if McDaniel uses the percentage-of-completion method?

   a. $0
   b. $100,000
   c. $300,000
   d. $700,000

8. In preparing constant purchasing power financial statements, which of the following would generally be regarded as a nonmonetary item?

   a. Cash
   b. Accounts receivable
   c. Warranty liabilities
   d. Bonds payable

9. Lana Corporation purchased a building in 19X1 when the consumer price index was 120. The consumer price index was 180 by the end of 19X4 and 240 by the end of 19X5. Historical cost building depreciation expense is $100,000 per year. In Lana's supplementary constant purchasing power income statement for 19X5, how much should be reported for building depreciation expense?

   a. $100,000
   b. $150,000
   c. $175,000
   d. $200,000

10. At the beginning of the current year, Peacock Corporation purchased inventory for $4,000. On December 31, one-half of the inventory was sold for $7,000. The inventory that was sold would have cost $3,000 to replace on the date of sale. The remaining inventory also had a current cost of $3,000. How much is Peacock's realized holding gain under the current cost approach?

   a. $1,000
   b. $2,000
   c. $3,000
   d. $4,000

DEMONSTRATION PROBLEMS

DP-1   The following practices have been used for a number of years. Identify the assumption, principle, or concept that serves as the basis for each of these practices.

   a.   The cost of land is determined to be $200,000. This is the amount recorded in the accounting records.
   b.   Inventory and marketable securities are accounted for at lower of cost or market.
   c.   Notes are included in financial statements to summarize significant accounting policy choices.
   d.   Sales commission expense is recorded in the period of sale, irrespective of when paid.
   e.   Small purchases of office supplies are expensed as they occur.
   f.   A sale occurs and is recorded in 19X1, even though the related account receivable will not be collected until 19X2.
   g.   Once adopted, an accounting method should continue in use unless evidence indicates a need to change to an alternative method.

DP-2 MacIntosh Construction Corporation signed a $4,000,000 contract to build a new office building. The company estimated that total construction costs would amount to $3,500,000, and the project would require three years to complete. Actual costs incurred during 19X1 were $1,000,000; during 19X2, $1,500,000; and during 19X3, $1,000,000. Prepare a schedule that discloses the annual profit recognized. MacIntosh uses the percentage-of-completion method.

At completion of the construction project, MacIntosh sold a crane for $100,000. The crane had a recorded cost of $80,000. Of the $100,000 sales price, $50,000 was collected during 19X3, $40,000 was collected during 19X4, and $10,000 was collected during 19X5. Prepare a schedule that shows when the $20,000 profit should be recognized, assuming use of the installment method.

DP-3 Helms Corporation was formed in 19X1. During 19X1, 17,000 units of inventory were purchased at $3 per unit. By the end of the year, 10,000 units had been sold and 7,000 remained on hand. On the date of sale, and at the end of the year, the current cost of the inventory had changed to $3.20 per unit. If the company was to prepare supplemental current cost accounting information, determine the:

a. Realized holding gain.
b. Unrealized holding gain.
c. Cost of goods sold using current cost accounting.
d. Cost of goods sold using conventional accounting.

SOLUTIONS TO SELF TESTS

FULFILLMENT OF LEARNING OBJECTIVES

1(a)	True
1(b)	Cash flows
1(c)	General purpose
2(a)	Relevancy
2(b)	Freedom from bias
2(c)	Correct
3(a)	False
3(b)	Financial Accounting Standards Board
4(a)	Going-concern assumption
4(b)	False
4(c)	Comparability of financial statements
4(d)	Materiality
5(a)	The point of sale
5(b)	The extent of progress toward completion can be determined
5(c)	Times the profit percentage applicable to the sale
6(a)	Dollars
6(b)	Monetary
6(c)	Net monetary liability position
6(d)	Unrealized
6(e)	False

FILL IN THE BLANKS

1. Amounts, timing, uncertainty
2. Relevant
3. Comparable
4. Reasonable
5. Generally accepted accounting principles
6. Securities and Exchange Commission
7. American Institute of Certified Public Accountants, Accounting Principles Board
8. Financial Accounting Standards Board
9. Periodicity
10. Historical-cost
11. Percentage-of-completion
12. Uncertainty
13. Monetary unit
14. Constant purchasing power
15. Monetary, nonmonetary
16. Loss
17. Unrealized, realized

MULTIPLE CHOICE QUESTIONS

1. a. A stated objective of financial reporting is to provide information that is useful in assessing the amounts, timing, and uncertainty of an organization's cash inflows and outflows. Tax return preparation is not a primary financial accounting objective. Accounting is based on historical cost, not current cost. Different companies typically use different accounting methods.

2. c. Congress has given the ultimate authority for setting accounting principles to the Securities and Exchange Commission. The Internal Revenue Service deals with tax law implementation. The Financial Accounting Standards Board and the Institute of Management Accountants are both private sector groups.

3. b. Relevance means that information bears on the decision process. Choice "a" relates to reliability, choice "c" to understandability, and choice "d" to comparability.

4. a. Consistency pertains to the utilization of the same accounting principles from period to period (unless changes are made for justifiable reasons). The entity assumption defines the area of reporting interest, periodicity defines the division of a continuous process into discrete measurement intervals, and historical cost is a measurement method.

5. a. Current cost is sometimes argued to be more relevant than out-of-date historical-cost amounts. Arguments in support of historical cost relate to the fact that the increase in value has not been realized (converted to cash), consistency (historical cost has been in use for an extended period of time), and objectivity (historical cost is easily verified).

6. b. The selection of the lower asset value is clearly a conservative treatment. Consistency relates to using the same methods over time, realization defines the conversion to cash, and matching pertains to recognizing expense in the same periods as the related revenue.

7. c. $300,000. The total estimated profits are $1,000,000 ($4,000,000 - $3,000,000), of which 70% or $700,000 has been earned. Because $400,000 of the profit was previously recognized, an additional $300,000 should be recorded in year two. The pattern of payments has no bearing on the yearly profit recognition unless considerable uncertainty surrounds collectibility.

8. c. Monetary items are fixed in dollars: cash, accounts receivable, and bonds payable -- but not warranty liabilities, which are nonmonetary.

9. d. $200,000. The historical-cost depreciation expense ($100,000) should be multiplied by the ratio of the consumer price index at the end of 19X5 divided by the index on the date of the asset purchase (240/120).

10. a. $1,000. The realized holding gain relates to assets that have been sold. The realized holding gain is the difference between the historical cost ($4,000 X 50% = $2,000) and the current cost ($3,000) of the asset sold.

DEMONSTRATION PROBLEMS

DP-1

(a) Historical-cost principle

(b) Conservatism

(c) Full disclosure principle

(d) Matching principle

(e) Materiality

(f) Revenue realization principle

(g) Consistency principle

DP-2

Percentage-of-completion method profit

Year	(A) Actual Costs Incurred	(B) Percentage of Work Completed (A/$3,500,000)	(C) Profit Recognized ($500,000 X B)
19X1	$1,000,000	28.57%	$142,857
19X2	1,500,000	42.86%	214,286
19X3	1,000,000	Remainder	142,857
	$3,500,000		$500,000

Installment method profit

Year	Cash Collected		Profit Percentage		Profit Recognized
19X3	$50,000	X	20%	=	$10,000
19X4	40,000	X	20%	=	8,000
19X5	10,000	X	20%	=	2,000

DP-3

(a) 10,000 units sold X ($3.20 - $3.00) = $2,000

(b) 7,000 units in inventory X ($3.20 - $3.00) = $1,400

(c) 10,000 units X $3.20 = $32,000

(d) 10,000 units X $3.00 = $30,000

CHAPTER 18

FINANCIAL STATEMENTS: ANALYSIS AND FURTHER DISCLOSURES

LEARNING OBJECTIVES

After studying this chapter, you should be able to:

1. Recognize the advantages and problems of financial statement analysis.

2. Construct a horizontal analysis of comparative financial statements.

3. Prepare a vertical analysis and explain the associated benefits of common-size statements.

4. Compute and interpret liquidity, activity, profitability, and coverage ratios.

5. Use segment information to further analyze a company's operations.

6. Identify several of the basic issues of international accounting.

CHAPTER HIGHLIGHTS

I. This chapter provides insight into financial statement analysis.

    A. A few **WORDS OF CAUTION** reveal that financial statement analysis cannot be followed blindly. The various measures introduced in the chapter should be regarded as tools to facilitate analysis, not ends in themselves.

        1. An additional caution is that one must be careful when using **COMPARATIVE STANDARDS** to judge performance. Important and significant factors cause equally sound companies to have strikingly different measures.

II. The **TOOLS OF ANALYSIS** can be categorized as horizontal analysis, vertical analysis, and ratio analysis.

    A. The calculation of percentage changes for corresponding items in comparative financial statements is termed **HORIZONTAL ANALYSIS**. For example, if sales increased from $1,000,000 to $1,200,000, horizontal analysis would reveal a 20% increase. Likewise, horizontal analysis can be applied to each element in comparative income statements, statements of retained earnings, and balance sheets.

B. Another important analysis tool is **VERTICAL ANALYSIS**. With this technique, each element in a particular financial statement can be compared (in percentage terms) to some other benchmark within the same financial statement. For example, gross profit is often expressed as a percentage of sales (e.g., gross profit may be 30% of sales). This technique is useful to discern emerging trends and conditions.

    1. The key benefits of vertical analysis are that it provides insight into important relationships among financial statement components and results in the production of **COMMON-SIZE FINANCIAL STATEMENTS**. That is, the financial statements of Company A and Company B can be compared, even if the dollar magnitude of amounts reported in those financial statements is radically different.

C. The third financial statement evaluation technique is **RATIO ANALYSIS**. There are many types of ratios (i.e., mathematical expressions of relationships).

    1. One set of ratios are the **LIQUIDITY RATIOS**, which measure the ability of a business to meet current debts and obligations as they come due.

        a. The **CURRENT RATIO** is perhaps the most widely used measure of liquidity, and relates current assets to current liabilities. A current ratio of less than one would indicate that current assets are less than current liabilities. A current ratio of four would reveal that current assets are four times as much as current liabilities.

        b. The **QUICK RATIO** is another measure similar to the current ratio. However, the quick ratio excludes certain current assets. Specifically, cash, short-term investments, and accounts receivable are summed and divided by current liabilities.

    2. Another category of ratios are the **ACTIVITY RATIOS**, sometimes called turnover ratios.

        a. The **ACCOUNTS RECEIVABLE TURNOVER** ratio reveals the number of times each year a company's receivables are converted to cash, and is calculated as net credit sales divided by average accounts receivable.

        b. The **INVENTORY TURNOVER** ratio shows the number of times that a firm's inventory balance was sold, and is calculated as cost of goods sold divided by average inventory.

    3. The **PROFITABILITY RATIOS** are another major category of ratios used to examine the degree of operating success.

        a. One profitability ratio is **PROFIT MARGIN ON SALES**, which relates net income to sales, and is computed as net income divided by net sales. This ratio is also embodied in the vertical analysis introduced earlier in the chapter.

        b. **RETURN ON ASSETS**, often termed return on investment, measures profitability for a given level of asset investment. This ratio is computed as net income plus interest expense, divided by average assets.

- c. **RETURN ON COMMON STOCKHOLDERS' EQUITY** measures the profits generated on funds provided by investors. This ratio is calculated as net income minus preferred dividends, divided by average common stockholders' equity.

- d. **TRADING ON THE EQUITY** is sometimes called leverage. This concept describes the process of securing funds at fixed interest rates (and/or preferred dividend rates), and then investing the funds to earn a return greater than their cost. In general, a company that has a higher return on equity than on assets would be successfully trading on the equity. Such companies are generating more income on borrowed funds than those funds cost. Leverage is a two-edged sword because the cost of borrowed funds can rapidly consume income and equity if profit levels fail to meet expectations.

- e. **OTHER PROFITABILITY RATIOS** introduced earlier in the text include earnings per share, the price-earnings ratio, and the dividend payout ratio.

4. **COVERAGE RATIOS** are computed to judge the solvency of an entity.

- a. One coverage ratio is **DEBT TO TOTAL ASSETS**, which shows the percentage of total capital provided by the creditors of a business. This ratio is computed as total debt divided by total assets.

- b. Another ratio is the **TIMES INTEREST EARNED** ratio, and is computed as income (before income taxes and interest) divided by interest charges.

5. **RATIO ANALYSIS: A CONCLUDING COMMENT** is that ratios provide useful tools, but they are merely the starting point for further analysis. Ratios should not be used blindly.

III. In addition to the basic financial statements, users may gain additional insight by **ANALYSIS OF** supplemental information that pertains to **BUSINESS SEGMENTS**. Accounting standards require corporations that engage in operations in different major lines of business to satisfy special reporting requirements. Specifically, they must disclose sales, operating income, identifiable assets, and other items for each segment. This additional information allows financial statement users to discern trends and other details that might be obscured in the overall financial statements.

IV. As companies increasingly engage in operations on an international scale, the importance of **INTERNATIONAL ACCOUNTING** is increased. Areas of concern relate to the uniformity of international accounting standards, accounting for foreign currency transactions, translation of foreign currency financial statements, and the disclosure of international financial affairs.

- A. To address the need for **UNIFORMITY OF INTERNATIONAL ACCOUNTING STANDARDS**, several private sector and governmental standard-setting organizations have been established. Among these are the International Accounting Standards Committee and the International Federation of Accountants.

B. When a domestic corporation buys or sells goods in a foreign country and agrees to pay or receive payment in a foreign currency, then the value of the receivable or payable (expressed in U.S. dollars) will change if the exchange rate changes. The exchange rate between two currencies (at a given point in time) is termed the spot rate. Changes in the spot rate introduce unique problems in **ACCOUNTING FOR FOREIGN CURRENCY TRANSACTIONS**.

   1. **PURCHASE TRANSACTIONS** that will be settled in a foreign currency are initially recorded by debiting Purchases and crediting Accounts Payable. The amount to record equals the U.S. dollars it would take to settle that obligation (based on the spot rate) on the date of purchase. Subsequently, when the payable is satisfied, more or less U.S. dollars may be needed to buy the foreign currency needed to pay off the account payable (because of changes in the spot rate between the day the payable was recorded and the day it is settled). The difference between the recorded amount of the payable and the cash required to settle the payable is reported as a gain (if less cash is needed) or loss (if more cash is needed).

   2. **SALE TRANSACTIONS** introduce a similar problem. The receivable and sale are initially recorded at the amount of U.S. dollars it would take to settle the receivable on the date of sale. When settlement finally occurs, the amount of foreign currency collected may have a U.S. dollar value that is more or less than what was initially entered into the accounts. The difference is reported as an exchange gain (if more) or loss (if less).

   3. In addition to recording exchange gains and losses as just described, **END-OF-PERIOD ADJUSTMENTS** may be needed for foreign currency payables and receivables. Such adjustments relate to changes in the spot rate occurring between the day the payable or receivable was established and the balance sheet date. Essentially, foreign currency payables and receivables should be valued at market (based on the spot rate) on each financial statement date. The resulting change in the underlying U.S. dollar amount of the related payable or receivable is reported as an exchange gain or loss.

C. Another international accounting consideration pertains to the **TRANSLATION OF FOREIGN CURRENCY FINANCIAL STATEMENTS** of foreign affiliates. A domestic company may own a foreign subsidiary, and that subsidiary's financial statements may be denominated in a foreign currency. Before the parent company's financial statements can be consolidated with those of the subsidiary, the subsidiary financial statements must first be converted to U.S. dollars. The translation process is covered in advanced accounting courses.

D. As with segment reporting, there are also supplemental requirements pertaining to **DISCLOSURE OF INTERNATIONAL FINANCIAL AFFAIRS**. In general, sales, income, and assets of a company should be divided between domestic and foreign, with the foreign category further divided by major countries of origin.

CLASS NOTES

CLASS NOTES

CLASS NOTES

CLASS NOTES

SELF TESTS

FULFILLMENT OF LEARNING OBJECTIVES

Circle the appropriate response.

L.O. 1(a)   Financial statement analysis results in ratios and measures that provide definite conclusions about the financial condition of an entity.

         true   or   false

L.O. 1(b)   Comparative standards that allow for the examination of an entity's performance in comparison with the performance of similar companies are known as:

         industry norms   or   segment evaluations

L.O. 2(a)   Horizontal analysis allows comparison of the relative change in accounts from:

         year to year
         or
         within the same year

L.O. 2(b)   Horizontal analysis allows determination of ratios like gross profit as a percentage of sales.

         true   or   false

L.O. 3(a)   Vertical analysis provides ready determination of the percentage change from year to year for a specific account.

         correct   or   incorrect

L.O. 3(b)   Vertical analysis results in:

         common-size financial statements
         or
         activity measures

L.O. 3(c)   Common-size financial statements include certain:

         profitability ratios   or   activity ratios

L.O. 4(a)   Which of the following is excluded in calculating the quick ratio?

         merchandise inventory   or   short-term investments

L.O. 4(b)   Which type of ratio is useful for measuring the ability of a business to meet current debts as they come due?

         liquidity ratio   or   profitability ratio

L.O. 4(c)   Inventory turnover and accounts receivable turnover are examples of:

   activity ratios   or   coverage ratios

L.O. 4(d)   What is included in the numerator of the inventory turnover ratio?

   cost of goods sold   or   average inventory

L.O. 4(e)   The numerator for the return on assets ratio includes:

   net income and preferred dividends
   or
   interest expense

L.O. 4(f)   The times interest earned ratio consists of income before income taxes and interest divided by:

   interest charges   or   debt

L.O. 5   Segment disclosures make it more difficult for companies to hide segments that incur losses, produce substantial profits, or experience difficulty in generating sales.

   correct   or   incorrect

L.O. 6(a)   To date, no attempt has been made to establish uniformity for international accounting standards.

   true   or   false

L.O. 6(b)   If a foreign currency account payable is established in the accounts at $0.50 per unit, and the exchange rate subsequently changes to $0.60 per unit, then which of the following will result?

   exchange gain   or   exchange loss

L.O. 6(c)   Exchange gains and losses should be recognized on the date of settlement of the foreign currency payable or receivable, and also:

   at the end of each accounting period
   or
   on the day the transaction
   creating the payable or receivable occurs

L.O. 6(d)   The process of converting the financial statements of a foreign affiliate to U.S. dollars is known as:

   transaction   or   translation

L.O. 6(e)   Companies that meet certain guidelines must reveal specified segment information relative to their international operations.

   correct   or   incorrect

FILL IN THE BLANKS

1. Performance measures that represent the average of several companies in the same industry are known as _____ _____.

2. _____ _____ is the calculation of dollar and percentage changes for corresponding items in comparative financial statements.

3. _____ _____ is the process of comparing each figure on a financial statement to a related relevant amount. This technique results in _____-_____ financial statements.

4. _____ _____ measure the ability of a business to meet current debts and obligations as they come due.

5. One of the most widely used liquidity measures is the _____ _____, which compares current assets to current liabilities.

6. In calculating the quick ratio, the numerator would consist of _____, _____-_____ _____, and _____ _____.

7. Activity ratios are often termed _____ _____.

8. The _____ _____ ratio shows the number of times that a firm's inventory investment is turned into sales.

9. The ratio of net income to net sales is called the _____ _____ on sales.

10. The return on assets ratio is often known as the _____ _____ _____.

11. Another name for trading on the equity is _____.

12. The annual cash dividend per share divided by the current market price of stock is the _____ _____.

13. Insight into the amount of protection that is afforded the long-term creditors is provided by a ratio called _____ _____ _____ _____.

14. Key categories of information reported in segment information include _____, _____ _____, and _____ _____.

15. The exchange rate in effect at a particular point in time is known as the _____ _____.

16. Foreign currency payables and receivables will result in exchange gains and losses if exchange rates _____.

17. _____ is the process of converting the financial statements of a foreign affiliate to U.S. dollars.

MULTIPLE CHOICE QUESTIONS

Circle the appropriate response.

1. What is the term used to describe the calculation of dollar and percentage changes for corresponding items in comparative financial statements?

    a. Horizontal analysis
    b. Vertical analysis
    c. Ratio analysis
    d. Common-size financial statements

2. Vertical analysis:

    a. results in common-size financial statements.
    b. is helpful in evaluating the percentage increase or decrease in accounts from year to year.
    c. results in the presentation of liquidity ratios.
    d. All of these.

3. Financial statement ratio analysis may be undertaken to study liquidity, activity, profitability, and coverage of obligations. What does the current ratio measure?

    a. Liquidity
    b. Activity
    c. Profitability
    d. Coverage of obligations

4. Financial statement ratio analysis may be undertaken to study liquidity, activity, profitability, and coverage of obligations. What does the dividend payout ratio measure?

    a. Liquidity
    b. Activity
    c. Profitability
    d. Coverage of obligations

5. Taylor Corporation had net income of $100,000, paid income taxes of $30,000, and had interest expense of $8,000. What was Taylor's times interest earned ratio?

    a. 12.5
    b. 16.25
    c. 17.25
    d. 17.85

6. Selected information for 19X1 for the Russian Company is as follows: Cost of goods sold, $6,000,000; average inventory, $2,000,000; net sales, $8,000,000; average receivables, $3,000,000; and net income, $1,000,000. Assuming a business year consisting of 360 days, what was the inventory turnover ratio for Russian Company for 19X1?

    a. 3
    b. 4
    c. 5
    d. 6

7. Pyles Corporation wrote off a $200 uncollectible account receivable against the $2,400 balance in its Allowance for Bad Debts account. Compare the current ratio before the write-off (X) with the current ratio after the write-off (Y).

    a. X greater than Y
    b. X equals Y
    c. X less than Y
    d. Cannot be determined

8. Luby Corporation's net accounts receivable were $750,000 on December 31, 19X1, and $1,250,000 on December 31, 19X2. Net cash sales for 19X2 were $3,300,000. The accounts receivable turnover ratio for 19X2 was 16. What were the company's total net sales for 19X2?

    a. $12,800,000
    b. $16,000,000
    c. $16,100,000
    d. $19,300,000

9. Segment financial data:

    a. are disclosed in a separate required financial statement.
    b. pertain to disclosure of information about various balance sheet categories.
    c. are similar to interim financial data.
    d. provide information about different lines of business in which a company is engaged.

10. Darland Corporation (USA) purchased goods on account for 1,000 Swiss francs. On the date of purchase, the spot rate for the Swiss franc was $0.60. By the time the corporation settled its obligation, the spot rate had fallen to $0.55 per Swiss franc. How much was the foreign currency exchange gain or loss?

    a. $0
    b. $50 gain
    c. $50 loss
    d. $83 gain

DEMONSTRATION PROBLEMS

DP-1   Write the appropriate mathematical formula for each of the following ratios:

    a.   Current ratio
    b.   Quick ratio
    c.   Accounts receivable turnover ratio
    d.   Inventory turnover ratio
    e.   Profit margin on sales
    f.   Return on common stockholders' equity
    g.   Times interest earned

DP-2 Financial statements of Danner Corporation follow:

Danner Corporation
Comparative Balance Sheets
December 31, 19X2 and 19X1

	19X2	19X1
Current assets		
Cash and short-term investments	$ 600	$ 1,400
Accounts receivable (net)	4,600	6,000
Inventory	8,000	7,000
Land	9,400	4,000
Buildings and equipment (net)	2,400	1,400
Total assets	$25,000	$19,800
Liabilities & equity		
Accounts payable	$ 6,000	$ 3,600
Notes payable (short-term)	2,000	3,200
Bonds payable	6,000	4,200
Common stock	1,200	1,200
Retained earnings	9,800	7,600
Total liabilities & equity	$25,000	$19,800

Danner Corporation
Combined Statements of Income and Retained Earnings
For the Year Ended December 31, 19X2

Net sales		$70,000
Less:		
Cost of goods sold	$50,000	
Selling expenses	4,000	
Administrative expenses	7,000	
Interest expense	800	
Income taxes	2,000	63,800
Net income		$ 6,200
Retained earnings, January 1		7,600
		$13,800
Less: Cash dividends declared and paid		4,000
Retained earnings, December 31		$ 9,800

Compute the following items for the company for 19X2, rounding calculations to two decimal places where necessary.

a. Current ratio
b. Quick ratio
c. Accounts receivable turnover ratio
d. Inventory turnover ratio
e. Profit margin on sales
f. Return on assets
g. Return on common stockholders' equity
h. Debt to total assets
i. Dividend payout ratio
j. Number of times interest is earned

DP-3 Wilson Corporation is a U.S. company that engages in numerous transactions involving foreign currencies. Two of the firm's transactions follow.

Transaction #1 - Purchased merchandise on account from Bola Corporation of Switzerland, agreeing to pay 10,000 Swiss francs in 30 days. The spot rate was $0.70 per franc on the date of purchase, and increased to $0.72 by the settlement date.

Transaction #2 - Sold merchandise on account to Burns Corporation of London, agreeing to accept 1,000 British pounds in 90 days. The spot rate was $1.90 per pound at the time of settlement, up from $1.80 on the sale date.

Prepare journal entries for Wilson to record each of these transactions and their related settlement. Disregard any year-end financial statement adjustments.

SOLUTIONS TO SELF TESTS

FULFILLMENT OF LEARNING OBJECTIVES

1(a)	False
1(b)	Industry norms
2(a)	Year to year
2(b)	False
3(a)	Incorrect
3(b)	Common-size financial statements
3(c)	Profitability ratios
4(a)	Merchandise inventory
4(b)	Liquidity ratio
4(c)	Activity ratios
4(d)	Cost of goods sold
4(e)	Net income and preferred dividends
4(f)	Interest charges
5	Correct
6(a)	False
6(b)	Exchange loss
6(c)	At the end of each accounting period
6(d)	Translation
6(e)	Correct

FILL IN THE BLANKS

1. Industry norms
2. Horizontal analysis
3. Vertical analysis, common-size
4. Liquidity ratios
5. Current ratio
6. Cash, short-term investments, accounts receivable
7. Turnover ratios
8. Inventory turnover
9. Profit margin
10. Return on investment
11. Leverage
12. Dividend yield
13. Debt to total assets
14. Sales, operating income, identifiable assets
15. Spot rate
16. Change (fluctuate)
17. Translation

MULTIPLE CHOICE QUESTIONS

1. a. Horizontal analysis is the calculation of dollar and percentage changes for corresponding items in comparative financial statements. Vertical analysis (also termed common-size financial statements) is the comparison of each item in a financial statement to some other item within the same financial statement. Ratio analysis is the determination of mathematical relationships among various financial statement components.

2. a. Vertical analysis results in common-size financial statements. Horizontal analysis pertains to comparison of changes from year to year. Liquidity ratios are independently calculated.

3. a. The current ratio is a liquidity ratio.

4. c. The dividend payout ratio is a profitability ratio.

5. c. 17.25. Income before income taxes and interest ($100,000 + $30,000 + $8,000 = $138,000) is divided by interest charges ($8,000).

6. a. 3. Cost of goods sold ($6,000,000) is divided by average inventory ($2,000,000).

7. b. The write-off of an uncollectible account reduces Accounts Receivable and the corresponding contra account, Allowance for Bad Debts. Therefore, net accounts receivable, total current assets, and the current ratio are not changed by the write-off.

8. d. $19,300,000. Total net sales equals cash sales ($3,300,000) plus credit sales ($16,000,000). Credit sales are 16 times the amount of average accounts receivable (($750,000 + $1,250,000)/2 = $1,000,000).

9. d. Segment information is supplemental disclosure of information about operations in different industries. The information is presented in schedules accompanying financial statements.

10. b. $50 gain. The $0.05 decrease in the spot rate reduced the U.S. dollar equivalent by $50 ((1,000 X $0.60) - (1,000 X $0.55)). Because Darland had a payable, the reduction in the payable is a gain.

DEMONSTRATION PROBLEMS

DP-1

(a) Current ratio:

$$\frac{\text{current assets}}{\text{current liabilities}}$$

(b) Quick ratio:

$$\frac{\text{cash + short-term investments + accounts receivable}}{\text{current liabilities}}$$

(c) Accounts receivable turnover ratio:

$$\frac{\text{net credit sales}}{\text{average accounts receivable}}$$

(d) Inventory turnover ratio:

$$\frac{\text{cost of goods sold}}{\text{average inventory}}$$

(e) Profit margin on sales:

$$\frac{\text{net income}}{\text{net sales}}$$

(f) Return on common stockholders' equity:

$$\frac{\text{net income - preferred dividends}}{\text{average common stockholders' equity}}$$

(g) Times interest earned:

$$\frac{\text{income before income taxes and interest}}{\text{interest charges}}$$

DP-2

(a) Current ratio:

$$\frac{\text{current assets}}{\text{current liabilities}} = \frac{\$13,200}{\$8,000} = 1.65$$

(b) Quick ratio:

$$\frac{\text{cash + short-term investments + accounts receivable}}{\text{current liabilities}} =$$

$$\frac{\$600 + \$4,600}{\$8,000} = 0.65$$

(c) Accounts receivable turnover ratio:

$$\frac{\text{net credit sales}}{\text{average accounts receivable}} = \frac{\$70,000}{(\$6,000 + \$4,600)/2} =$$

$$\frac{\$70,000}{\$5,300} = 13.21 \text{ times}$$

(d) Inventory turnover ratio:

$$\frac{\text{cost of goods sold}}{\text{average inventory}} = \frac{\$50,000}{(\$7,000 + \$8,000)/2} =$$

$$\frac{\$50,000}{\$7,500} = 6.67 \text{ times}$$

(e) Profit margin on sales:

$$\frac{\text{net income}}{\text{net sales}} = \frac{\$6,200}{\$70,000} = 8.86\%$$

(f) Return on assets:

$$\frac{\text{net income + interest expense}}{\text{average assets}} =$$

$$\frac{\$6,200 + \$800}{(\$19,800 + \$25,000)/2} = \frac{\$7,000}{\$22,400} = 31.25\%$$

(g) Return on common stockholders' equity:

$$\frac{\text{net income - preferred dividends}}{\text{average common stockholders' equity}} =$$

$$\frac{\$6,200}{(\$8,800 + \$11,000)/2} = \frac{\$6,200}{\$9,900} = 62.63\%$$

(h) Debt to total assets:

$$\frac{\text{total debt}}{\text{total assets}} = \frac{\$14,000}{\$25,000} = 56.00\%$$

(i) Dividend payout ratio:

$$\frac{\text{cash dividends}}{\text{net income}} = \frac{\$4,000}{\$6,200} = 64.52\%$$

(j) Number of times interest is earned:

$$\frac{\text{income before income taxes and interest}}{\text{interest charges}} =$$

$$\frac{\$6,200 + \$2,000 + \$800}{\$800} = \frac{\$9,000}{\$800} = 11.25$$

DP-3

No. 1

Purchases	7,000	
Accounts Payable		7,000

Purchased merchandise on account
(10,000 francs X $0.70 = $7,000)

Accounts Payable	7,000	
Exchange Loss	200	
Cash		7,200

Acquired Swiss francs and paid related foreign currency payable
(10,000 francs X $0.72 = $7,200)

No. 2

Accounts Receivable	1,800	
Sales		1,800

Sold merchandise on account
(1,000 pounds X $1.80 = $1,800)

Cash	1,900	
Exchange Gain		100
Accounts Receivable		1,800

Collected British pounds on account and converted to U.S. dollars
(1,000 pounds X $1.90 = $1,900)

APPENDIX A

READING A CORPORATE ANNUAL REPORT

CHAPTER HIGHLIGHTS

I. **THE ANNUAL REPORT** is a corporate publication used to keep stockholders informed about the company's business affairs and economic well-being. Annual reports are the main source of communication between management and stockholders.

II. The appendix to the text includes complete **FINANCIAL STATEMENTS** for the K-mart Corporation.

    A. The purpose of the **INCOME STATEMENT** is to provide information concerning business profitability over time. In reviewing an income statement, notice that it may include special sections for income from continuing operations, discontinued operations, extraordinary items, and the like. Additionally, financial statement users should be careful to review the nature of revenues and expenses, watching for items that appear unusual.

        1. Careful evaluation of an income statement will provide information about the **QUALITY OF EARNINGS**. The quality of earnings refers to consistency of earnings and the accounting principles in use. Selection of accounting principles can sometimes significantly affect the short-term trend in reported earnings.

    B. The purpose of the **BALANCE SHEET** is to disclose the financial position of a company on a specific date. Careful review of a company's balance sheet will provide answers to questions about overall financial position, liquidity, and degree of stockholder versus creditor claims. Many of the fundamental financial statement ratios are calculated directly from the face of the balance sheet.

    C. The **STATEMENT OF CASH FLOWS** reveals the amount of cash generated or consumed by operating, investing, and financing activities. Cash is the life-blood of a business, and the statement of cash flows reveals trends and the ability of a company to continue to generate adequate cash flows to support on-going operations.

    D. The **STATEMENT OF STOCKHOLDERS' EQUITY** reveals information about changes in retained earnings, common stock, paid-in capital in excess of par, treasury stock, and so forth.

III. The **NOTES TO FINANCIAL STATEMENTS** are an important reporting component. Full disclosure of business and economic affairs requires detailed notes summarizing significant accounting policies, and providing supplemental and explanatory information.

    A. Companies are required to include a note that provides a **SUMMARY OF SIGNIFICANT ACCOUNTING POLICIES**. This note is typically the first note in the financial statements and covers major accounting policy choices (e.g., depreciation method, inventory method, and so on).

    B.   Specific accounting standards often require **SUPPLEMENTARY INFORMATION**. For example, an earlier chapter introduced segment reporting, which is required supplemental information. Another example of required supplemental information is interim financial statement data, which reports the results of the operations on a quarterly (one-forth of a year) basis.

    C.   Detailed **EXPLANATORY INFORMATION** is often the subject of a specific note. For example, the details of property, plant, and equipment are often set out in a separate note. Such notes merely summarize the measures reported on the face of the financial statements.

IV.   In addition to fundamental accounting data, **MANAGEMENT AND AUDIT REPORTS** are often included in annual reports. One such report is called Management's Discussion and Analysis, which provides an in-depth explanation of the differences between the current year's financial statements and those of preceding periods. Another report, entitled Report of Management's Responsibility for Financial Statements, informs users that management shoulders the burden for the estimates and accounting principles used in the financial statements. This report also notes the steps that have been taken to safeguard the company's resources, including the development of an internal audit department, review of the company's records by independent CPAs, and the presence of an audit committee (usually consisting of outside directors).

    A.   Financial statements of a major corporation are customarily accompanied by **THE AUDIT REPORT**. This report presents the opinion of the independent CPA who reviewed the fairness of the financial statements. Importantly, auditors do not guarantee financial statements, they merely express an opinion on the fairness of financial statements. The auditor's report may be unqualified or qualified. If an auditor is unable to express an unqualified opinion about the fairness of the financial statements, the auditor must note the reservations (e.g., qualified opinion due to lack of adequate company records).

V.   As **A FINAL THOUGHT ON ANNUAL REPORTS**, critics maintain that annual reports often contain "puff." Some claim that reports are worded and structured in a manner to downplay unfavorable events, while highlighting successes.

CLASS NOTES

CLASS NOTES

SELF TESTS

Two-Response Quiz

Circle the appropriate response.

1. The contents of an annual report are limited to the financial statements.

    true   or   false

2. A careful review of the nature of corporate earnings is referred to as an examination of the:

    quality of earnings   or   consistency of earnings

3. Which financial statement would be most useful in assessing the overall financial condition and liquidity of the firm?

    balance sheet   or   statement of cash flows

4. Notes to financial statements serve one of three basic functions; the summarization of significant accounting policies, disclosure of supplemental information, and providing explanatory information.

    true   or   false

5. Examples of supplementary information in notes to financial statements include segment reporting and:

    interim financial statements
    or
    income statements

6. Management of a company may prepare reports for inclusion in the annual report. Two such reports are management's discussion and analysis and:

    the audit report
    or
    the report of management's responsibility
    for financial statements

7. The audit report represents the auditor's:

    guarantee   or   opinion

8. When reading and evaluating an annual report, the users of financial statements should limit their evaluation exclusively to the financial statements, as the notes are generally unreliable.

true   or   false

9. In reviewing financial statements, one should make an assessment not only of the methods used to determine income, but also the sources from which the income arises.

correct   or   incorrect

FILL IN THE BLANKS

1. The _____ _____ is a corporate publication used to keep stockholders informed of the company's business affairs and economic welfare.

2. _____ of _____ refers to the nature of a company's income.

3. The purpose of the _____ _____ is to disclose the financial position of a company on a specific date.

4. To help users better understand financial statements, corporations include a series of _____ in their annual reports. These normally summarize significant accounting policies, disclose supplementary information, and provide _____ information.

5. Examples of supplementary reporting include segment information and _____ financial statements.

6. Many large corporations have established an _____ _____ that consists of outside directors. This group meets with management, the internal auditors, and the independent accountants to determine whether each group is carrying out its assigned responsibilities.

7. An _____ _____, prepared by an independent certified public accountant, provides the auditor's _____.

8. A(n) _____ opinion is issued when an auditor detects a problem or uncertainty related to a company's financial statements.

MULTIPLE CHOICE QUESTIONS

Circle the appropriate response.

1. Which of the following would likely be included in the annual report?

    a. Financial statements
    b. Pictures of products, operations, and selected personnel
    c. Information about the annual meeting
    d. All of the above

2. Which of the following is not one of the fundamental financial statements?

    a. Income statement
    b. Balance sheet
    c. Statement of cash flows
    d. Audit opinion

3. In evaluating a corporation's annual report, which of the following characteristics would indicate a better quality of earnings?

    a. Straight-line method instead of an accelerated depreciation method.
    b. Income arising from the sale of manufacturing facilities.
    c. FIFO instead of LIFO inventory method during a period of rising prices.
    d. The write-off of all questionable accounts receivable.

4. Which of the following statements about the balance sheet is false?

    a. The balance sheet reveals the current worth of a firm.
    b. Good management and favorable business location are not reported on the balance sheet.
    c. The balance sheet provides information concerning the stockholders' interest in the business, compared with that of creditors.
    d. The balance sheet reveals the overall financial condition of the enterprise.

5. The statement of cash flows provides information about cash generated from:

    a. operating activities.
    b. financing activities.
    c. investing activities.
    d. all of the above.

6. The statement of stockholders' equity would include information about changes in:

    a. common stock.
    b. retained earnings.
    c. treasury shares.
    d. all of the above.

7. Notes to financial statements will not include:

   a. a summarization of significant accounting policies.
   b. additional explanatory information.
   c. disclosure of supplemental information.
   d. a report of the audit committee.

8. Supplemental information contained in notes to annual financial statements would include:

   a. business segment information.
   b. an auditor's report.
   c. management reports.
   d. a report of the audit committee.

9. Many large corporations have established audit committees to assist in evaluating management, internal auditors, and the independent auditor. Which of the following individuals should comprise the audit committee?

   a. Outside directors (like executives from other businesses, university administrators, and so on).
   b. Officers of the corporation.
   c. The independent auditor.
   d. Outside directors who are not shareholders of the corporation.

10. The primary purpose of an audit report is to:

    a. reveal the auditor's opinion about the fairness of the financial statements.
    b. qualify the financial statements.
    c. guarantee the financial statements.
    d. determine and report on the the existence of fraud in the company.

DEMONSTRATION PROBLEMS

DP-1   In reviewing a complete set of financial statements for a large corporation, which four fundamental financial statements would likely be encountered?

DP-2   In evaluating a complete annual report, which two types of management reports would likely be encountered? Also, what is the nature of the report of the independent auditor?

DP-3 Comment in general as to the relative effect of the choice of depreciation and inventory methods on the quality of earnings of a particular company.

SOLUTIONS TO SELF TESTS

TWO-RESPONSE QUIZ

1. False
2. Quality of earnings
3. Balance sheet
4. True
5. Interim financial statements
6. The report of management's responsibility for financial statements
7. Opinion
8. False
9. Correct

FILL IN THE BLANKS

1. Annual report
2. Quality, earnings
3. Balance sheet
4. Notes, explanatory
5. Interim
6. Audit committee
7. Audit report, opinion
8. Qualified

MULTIPLE CHOICE QUESTIONS

1. d. Financial statements, pictures, information about the annual meeting, and so forth are all likely to be found in an annual report.

2. d. The fundamental financial statements are the income statement, balance sheet, statement of stockholders' equity (or retained earnings), and statement of cash flows. The audit opinion is not a financial statement.

3. d. The write-off of all questionable receivables is conservative and depresses income; hence, the quality of the reported earnings is improved. Straight-line depreciation and FIFO tend to produce higher short-term income than their alternatives, resulting in a lower quality of earnings. Income from the sale of facilities is not related to continuing operations, and must be discounted when considering the quality of earnings.

4. a. The balance sheet is based on historical cost, not current worth. Good management and favorable business location are not reported on the balance sheet. The balance sheet provides information concerning the stockholders' interest versus that of the creditors. The balance sheet portrays overall financial condition.

5. d. Operating, investing, and financing activities are all included on the statement of cash flows.

6. d. The statement of stockholders' equity would include information about changes in all equity components -- including common stock, retained earnings, and treasury stock.

7. d. Notes to the financial statements include a summary of significant accounting policies, explanatory information, and supplemental information. A report of the audit committee is not included as a note, but may be elsewhere in the annual report.

8. a. Business segment information is typical supplemental information included in the notes. The auditor's report, management reports, and reports of audit committees are included in the annual report, but not as a note to the financial statements.

9. a. The audit committee is comprised of outside directors, like executives of other firms and university administrators (these persons may also be shareholders, but are not officers of the corporation).

10. a. The audit report is merely an expression of opinion about the fairness of financial statements. Audits do not qualify (although an opinion may be qualified) or guarantee financial statements. Also, an audit does not ensure the absence of fraud.

DEMONSTRATION PROBLEMS

DP-1

The four fundamental financial statements are the balance sheet, income statement, statement of cash flows, and statement of stockholders' equity.

DP-2

A complete annual report would include management's discussion and analysis, which provides an in-depth explanation of the differences between the current year's financial statements and those of preceding years. The discussion is an overview of performance and special events. Another management report is the report on management's responsibility for financial statements, which informs users that management is primarily responsible for the content of the annual report and financial statements. The report will also note the steps taken to safeguard company resources and to ensure compliance with sound business practices. The report of the auditor is to provide information about the auditor's opinion regarding the fairness of financial statements.

DP-3

The quality of earnings is enhanced by the utilization of accelerated depreciation methods and the LIFO inventory technique (during periods of rising prices). These methods result in the lowest earnings from among acceptable alternatives, thereby producing the most conservative (hence, highest quality) income measures.

APPENDIX B

SPECIAL JOURNAL SYSTEMS

CHAPTER HIGHLIGHTS

I. The basic accounting system introduced earlier in the text can be enriched by the introduction of special journals. The **TYPES AND BENEFITS OF SPECIAL JOURNALS** depend on the specific processing environment, but are generally designed to simplify the recording and posting process by accumulating repetitive transactions. Special journals include the sales journal (for sales of merchandise on account), purchases journal (for purchases of merchandise on account), cash receipts journal (for receipts of cash), and cash payments journal (for payments of cash). In addition, a company would continue to use the general journal for all other transactions. Before proceeding you may find it helpful to review the portion of Chapter 6 entitled "Subsidiary Ledgers and Control Accounts."

   B. Perhaps the simplest special journal is the **SALES JOURNAL**. The sales journal is used to record sales on account.

      1. Maintaining and **POSTING THE SALES JOURNAL** is straightforward: at the time of sale, the date, customer's name, invoice number, and amount of sale are recorded in the journal. At the end of the month, the total of the sales journal is accumulated and a single posting to the general ledger is made: debit Accounts Receivable and credit Sales (representing total sales on account during the month). Additionally, subsidiary accounts receivable records are updated daily as each individual sale occurs (indicated by check marks in the sales journal). The sales journal eliminates the need for the formal recording and posting of each sale on account; rather a single monthly total for all sales on account is posted to the general ledger.

      2. The journals presented in the text are typical. However, many **JOURNAL VARIATIONS** are possible; a company would design whatever special journals are needed to handle repetitive transactions encountered by the firm.

   C. The **PURCHASES JOURNAL** parallels the sales journal. It is utilized for purchases of merchandise on account, with columns for the date, supplier's name, appropriate invoice information, and the amount of the purchase on account. The total of the amount column represents aggregate purchases on account and is debited to Purchases and credited to Accounts Payable. Additionally, individual amounts are credited to each supplier's individual subsidiary accounts payable ledger.

   D. The **CASH RECEIPTS JOURNAL** is used to record each transaction which involves the receipt of cash. Because cash can be received from numerous sources, multiple columns are included in this journal.

1. To understand the **OPERATION OF THE CASH RECEIPTS JOURNAL**, consider that every cash receipt necessarily involves a debit to Cash and a credit(s) to some other account (e.g., Accounts Receivable, Sales, or some other miscellaneous (sundry) account). Additionally, a cash receipt transaction could trigger the need for a debit to an account like Sales Discounts. For example, the collection of $980 on a $1,000 account receivable (subject to a $20 discount) is recorded as a debit to Cash ($980), a debit to Sales Discounts ($20), and a credit to Accounts Receivable ($1,000). Within a cash receipts journal, one would merely need record $980 in the Cash column, $20 in the Sales Discounts column, and $1,000 in the Accounts Receivable column. As another example, a cash sale would be reflected by recording the amount of the sale in the Cash column and the Sales column. Transactions that involve accounts other than those listed separately would necessitate utilization of the sundry column.

2. **POSTING THE CASH RECEIPTS JOURNAL** begins by totaling each of the columns in the Cash Receipts journal. Each column total is then posted to the appropriate ledger account: the total of the cash column is recorded as a debit in the Cash account, the total of the accounts receivable column is credited to Accounts Receivable, and so on. The sundry column represents numerous accounts; as a result, the column total cannot be posted to any specific account. Rather each of the items in the sundry column must be posted individually. Finally, notice that each item in the accounts receivable column provides the information needed to reduce (credit) a specific customer's subsidiary accounts receivable ledger.

E. The **CASH PAYMENTS JOURNAL** is used to record all cash disbursements. Procedurally, the operation of a cash payments journal is similar to that of a cash receipts journal. Of course, the specific columns are different: cash (credit), purchases discounts (credit), accounts payable (debit), and sundry (debit or credit). For example, a cash payment on account is recorded by noting the amount of the payment in the cash column, any discount taken in the discounts column, and the reduction in accounts payable in the accounts payable column.

1. **POSTING THE CASH PAYMENTS JOURNAL** involves totaling each column, and recording that total in the appropriate ledger account. As with the cash receipts journal, items in the sundry column must be posted individually. Also, note that individual items within the accounts payable column provide the basis for updating (debiting) subsidiary accounts payable accounts.

F. Special journals do not do away with the need for a **GENERAL JOURNAL**. Any transaction not recorded in a special journal must be recorded in the general journal. Examples include adjusting entries (e.g., depreciation), closing entries, and so forth.

G. **SEVERAL FINAL COMMENTS** are needed: (1) after posting all journals, preparation of the trial balance and financial statements is performed in a manner identical to that indicated earlier in the text, and (2) it is helpful to reconcile subsidiary ledger accounts with the corresponding control accounts.

CLASS NOTES

CLASS NOTES

SELF TESTS

Two-Response Quiz

Circle the appropriate response.

1. Special journals eliminate the need for a general journal.

    true   or   false

2. Cash disbursements should be recorded in the:

    cash receipts journal   or   cash payments journal

3. The total of a monthly sales journal would represent total sales on account for that month.

    correct   or   incorrect

4. The total of the purchases journal would be posted as a debit to Purchases and a credit to:

    Cash   or   Accounts Payable

5. Which column in the cash receipts journal involves postings to the general ledger and individual subsidiary accounts?

    cash column   or   accounts receivable column

6. The total amount of the sundry column in the cash payments journal would be posted to the general ledger.

    true   or   false

Fill In The Blanks

1. Sales on account would be recorded in the _____ _____.

2. The general ledger account for Accounts Receivable is called the _____ account, and is supported by information about individual customer's account balances in the _____ ledger.

3. The _____ column of the cash receipts journal is for the recording of amounts that do not fit into one of the separately designated columns.

4. Miscellaneous transactions that are not suited to a particular special journal, adjusting entries, and closing entries would ordinarily be recorded in the _____ _____.

MULTIPLE CHOICE QUESTIONS

Circle the appropriate response.

1. One of the major benefits of special journals is that they:

   a. do away with the need for a general ledger.
   b. reduce the amount of posting that is necessary to process transactions.
   c. do away with the need for a general journal.
   d. allow all journal entries to be recorded in chronological sequence in one centralized record.

2. The subsidiary accounts payable ledger accounts should be:

   a. debited for a number of individual amounts totaling the balance in the accounts payable column of the cash payments journal.
   b. credited for a number of individual amounts totaling the balance of the accounts payable column of the purchases journal.
   c. have an aggregate balance equal to the accounts payable balance in the general ledger.
   d. All of the above.

3. Stroder Company maintains a single column purchases journal. The total amount recorded in that journal for a period of time would represent that time period's:

   a. net increase in accounts payable.
   b. purchases of merchandise on credit, net of related purchase returns and allowances.
   c. purchases of merchandise for cash.
   d. purchases of merchandise on credit.

4. Russell Company maintains a system of special journals. Into which special journal would the cash purchase of an automobile best be recorded?

   a. General journal
   b. Purchases journal
   c. Cash receipts journal
   d. Cash payments journal

5. Russell Company maintains a system of special journals. Indicate the appropriate journal for the periodic recording of depreciation expense.

   a. Purchases journal
   b. Cash receipts journal
   c. Cash payments journal
   d. General journal

6. Russell Company maintains a system of special journals. Into which special journal would the receipt of a customer payment on account (net of related sales discount) be recorded?

    a. Sales journal
    b. Purchases journal
    c. Cash receipts journal
    d. Cash payments journal

7. Oakwood Corporation uses a single column sales journal. During February, all transactions were recorded correctly but the bookkeeper accidentally underadded total sales by $2,000. Therefore, the balance of the accounts receivable control account:

    a. equals the balance of related subsidiary ledger accounts.
    b. is greater than the balance of related subsidiary ledger accounts.
    c. is less than the balance of related subsidiary ledger accounts.
    d. is correct.

DEMONSTRATION PROBLEMS

DP-1   MZT Company employs the following special journals:

      Sales
      Purchases
      Cash Receipts
      Cash Payments
      General

All journals are similar in format to those illustrated in the text. The following transactions and events occurred during October.

a.   Sold merchandise on account to Jefferson Company.
b.   Acquired merchandise for cash for resale to customers.
c.   Recorded depreciation expense for the month.
d.   Acquired equipment to be used in the business on account.
e.   Collected $700 on account from a customer.
f.   Returned defective merchandise to the supplier for a cash refund.
g.   Paid a past due account payable by writing a check.
h.   Received payment from a customer net of the related sales discount.

Indicate the journal in which the preceding transactions and events would be recorded.

DP-2 The following errors were identified in the accounting records of Western Company:

(1) The total of the sales journal was overadded by $300.

(2) Individual amounts in the accounts receivable column of the cash receipts journal were not posted to the subsidiary ledger.

(3) The total of the sundry column in the cash payments journal was underadded by $600.

(4) A $1,000 collection on account from a customer was not recorded in the accounting records.

Indicate whether or not the trial balance will still be in balance after each of the four errors have been posted. Consider each case independently. Also, indicate whether the appropriate control account and subsidiary ledger will still be in agreement. If they will not be, indicate which of the two balances will be larger.

SOLUTIONS TO SELF TESTS

TWO-RESPONSE QUIZ

1. False
2. Cash payments journal
3. Correct
4. Accounts payable
5. Accounts receivable column
6. False

FILL IN THE BLANKS

1. Sales journal
2. Control, subsidiary
3. Sundry
4. General journal

MULTIPLE CHOICE QUESTIONS

1. b. Special journals greatly reduce the amount of posting, as periodic totals are posted instead of individual transactions. General ledgers and general journals remain an important feature of the accounting system, even if special journals are used. Because special journals result in recording different transactions in different journals, no centralized record reports all journal entries.

2. d. Each of the characteristics pertain to the subsidiary accounts payable ledger.

3. d. The purchases journal is for purchases of merchandise on credit. The total of the purchases journal is posted as a credit to accounts payable. The net change in accounts payable is influenced by numerous transactions in addition to purchases of merchandise on account (i.e., payments on account, purchases returns, etc.). Purchases returns and allowances are recorded in the general journal and cash purchases of merchandise are recorded in the cash payments journal.

4. d. Any transaction that involves the disbursement of cash is reported in the cash payments journal. The general journal is used for transactions that are not suited to a particular special journal. The purchases journal is for purchases of merchandise on account. The cash receipts journal is for all transactions that involve the receipt of cash.

5. d. Depreciation expense is an adjustment that would be recorded in the general journal. The purchases journal is for purchases of merchandise on account. Any transaction that involves the receipt of cash is reported in the cash receipts journal. The cash payments journal is for all transactions that involve the payment of cash.

6. c. Any transaction that involves the receipt of cash is recorded in the cash receipts journal. The sales discount is easily accommodated with a separate column within the cash receipts journal. The sales journal is for all sales of merchandise on account. The purchases journal is for all merchandise purchases on account. The cash payments journal is for all cash disbursements.

7. c. Because the column total is underadded, the posting to Sales and Accounts Receivable is understated. As a result, the general ledger Accounts Receivable account is less than the related subsidiary ledger accounts.

DEMONSTRATION PROBLEMS

DP-1

(a) Sales journal

(b) Cash payments journal

(c) General journal

(d) General journal

(e) Cash receipts journal

(f) Cash receipts journal

(g) Cash payments journal

(h) Cash receipts journal

DP-2

(1) The trial balance will still balance. Both sales and accounts receivable will be overstated. The control account and subsidiary ledger will not be in agreement; the subsidiary accounts are updated for each line item in the sales journal, but the general ledger accounts are posted for the "overadded" column total. Accordingly, the general ledger control account will be larger.

(2) The trial balance will still balance. The column total for accounts receivable (credit) from the cash receipts journal is correctly computed and posted. The control account and subsidiary ledger will not be in agreement; the subsidiary accounts are not reduced because of the error. As a result, the subsidiary account totals will be larger.

(3) The trial balance will balance. The sundry column total is not posted, rather each item in the sundry column is individually posted. This mistake will not cause the subsidiary and control accounts to differ.

(4) The trial balance will balance, even though cash and accounts receivable are both wrong. The total of the subsidiary ledger accounts agree with the general ledger totals (they are both overstated by $1,000, as accounts receivable would be reduced by the proper recording of the transaction).

APPENDIX C

CORPORATE INCOME TAXES

CHAPTER HIGHLIGHTS

I. **BUSINESSES AND THE TAX LAW** -- Because of constantly changing income tax legislation, businesses must devote substantial resources to monitor and comply with tax laws.

II. There are several facets to **COMPUTING CORPORATE TAXES**. A general formula is to calculate gross income and subtract deductions, to arrive at an amount called taxable income. This amount is then multiplied by the applicable tax rate to arrive at the tax obligation. From the tax obligation are subtracted prepayments and credits, to arrive at the tax owed or to be refunded.

   A. The basic philosophy for **GROSS INCOME, DEDUCTIONS,** and **TAXABLE INCOME** is simple; all receipts (unless specifically excluded by law) are included in the corporation's gross income, the only deductions permitted are those specifically allowed by the tax laws (i.e., salaries, wages, repairs, interest, advertising, depreciation, and so forth), and gross income minus allowable deductions equals taxable income. Corporate taxable income is generally taxed at a rate of 15 to 34%, depending on the specific amount of income generated.

   B. Once the income tax obligation is calculated, **PREPAYMENTS AND CREDITS,** and **TAXES OWED/REFUNDS** must be considered. Throughout the year, corporations should make periodic payments for their estimated amount of taxes. The exact tax liability, computed at the end of the year, is then compared to the prepayments to determine the amount that is owed (or the refund due). In addition to prepayments, tax credits (direct dollar-for-dollar reductions of a company's tax bill) are sometimes available. Credits are fairly limited, but are sometimes available to provide incentive for corporations to undertake specifically desirable tasks (such as rehabilitation of certified historic buildings).

   C. **SPECIAL TOPICS** relevant to corporate taxation are also introduced in the text.

   1. **DIVIDENDS RECEIVED** by one corporation from another are not fully included in taxable income of the recipient corporation. Tax laws allow a dividends-received deduction. This deduction (generally equal to 70% of the dividends received) reduces the degree of triple taxation; that is, the taxing of income when it is earned by the first corporation, then taxing the same income when it is received by a second corporation (in the form of a dividend), and then taxing it again when shareholders of the second corporation receive a dividend.

2. **CAPITAL GAINS AND LOSSES** may result when capital assets are sold. Capital assets include property owned by a corporation, except receivables, inventories, real and depreciable business property, and similar productive assets. Special calculations related to capital gains and losses begin with the netting of capital losses and gains. A net gain would be taxed as ordinary income at regular corporate tax rates. A net loss can be offset against net gains of the three prior years and the following five years.

3. When a company's deductions exceed gross income, **NET OPERATING LOSSES** occur. In the year of loss, no tax is owed. Furthermore, the loss may be carried back to offset income reported during the three prior years (thereby generating a claim for a refund), and forward for 15 years to reduce income subject to tax in those years.

D. A complete **CORPORATE TAX ILLUSTRATION** is provided in the text. In reviewing the text's exhibit, notice the inclusion of dividends and the dividends-received deduction, net capital gains, the computation of taxable income, the gross tax liability, and the taxes owed.

III. Careful **TAX PLANNING** can be utilized to reduce a tax liability. Such tax avoidance is accepted behavior. However, tax evasion is an unlawful attempt to understate income.

A. **TAX AVOIDANCE: AREAS TO CONSIDER** include the adoption of techniques that result in delayed recognition of revenue and accelerated recognition of expense. Examples include utilization of accelerated cost recovery methods and the LIFO inventory method. Also, corporations may alter their capital structure for more favorable tax consequences.

CLASS NOTES

CLASS NOTES

SELF TESTS

Two-Response Quiz

Circle the appropriate response.

1. Gross income includes all income that is received,

   unless specifically excluded by law
   or
   and is specifically listed in the law

2. Gross income is the firm's total income minus:

   allowable exclusions   or   allowable deductions

3. In general, nothing is deductible unless specifically stated in the tax laws.

   true   or   false

4. Gross income is the same thing as taxable income.

   true   or   false

5. Tax credits are direct dollar-for-dollar deductions from a company's:

   tax bill   or   taxable income

6. The dividends-received deduction is available to:

   individuals   or   corporations

7. Capital gains and losses result from the sale or disposal of capital assets like real depreciable business property.

   true   or   false

8. Net capital losses may be carried back three years and forward:

   five years   or   fifteen years

9. When a company's deductions exceed gross income, a net operating loss is said to occur. Net operating losses may be carried back three years and forward as many as fifteen years.

   correct   or   incorrect

10. Which of the following practices constitutes acceptable behavior?

    tax avoidance   or   tax evasion

FILL IN THE BLANKS

1. A corporation's _____ _____ is the firm's total income minus allowable exclusions.

2. Gross income minus the company's allowable deductions equals _____ _____.

3. Prepayments of taxes computed on the basis of estimated income are appropriately known as _____ _____.

4. _____ _____ are direct dollar-for-dollar reductions from the company's tax bill.

5. Capital gains and losses should be netted together to arrive at net _____ _____ or net _____ _____.

6. Net operating losses occur when a company's deductions exceed gross income, and can be carried back three years and forward _____ years.

7. _____ _____ represents a deliberate attempt to understate taxable income by unlawful manipulation of revenues and expenses.

MULTIPLE CHOICE QUESTIONS

Circle the appropriate response:

1. Gross income minus deductions from gross income equals:

    a. Taxable income.
    b. Tax obligation.
    c. Tax credit.
    d. Taxes owed or to be refunded.

2. The general rule of law relating to expenses is that:

    a. Expenses are not deductible unless specifically stated in the tax laws.
    b. Expenses are deductible unless specifically excluded by the tax laws.
    c. All expenses can be deducted to the extent of taxable income.
    d. Deductible expenses will not be permitted if tax prepayments have occurred.

3. All other things being equal, a corporation would prefer to:

    a. Have a tax credit instead of a tax deduction.
    b. Have a tax deduction rather than a tax credit.
    c. Have equal amounts of tax deductions and tax credits.
    d. Have estimated taxes equal prepaid taxes.

4. The dividends-received deduction was enacted by Congress for the purpose of:

   a. Avoiding triple taxation of corporate earnings.
   b. Assisting in the computation of capital gains and losses.
   c. Generating more revenue for the government.
   d. Replacing the three-year carryback for net operating losses.

5. Which of the following statements about capital gains and losses is true?

   a. Capital gains and losses result from the sale of any productive asset.
   b. Capital gains and losses are taxed at different rates.
   c. Capital gains and losses should be netted together before considering the impact on taxable income.
   d. Only 50% of a capital gain is subject to tax.

6. When a company's deductions exceed gross income, a net operating loss is said to occur. A special provision in the tax laws allow corporations to carry a net operating loss:

   a. Back three years.
   b. Forward fifteen years.
   c. Both (a) and (b).
   d. Neither (a) nor (b).

7. Cox Corporation reported sales and cost of goods sold of $100,000 and $60,000, respectively, for the year just ended. Other information follows:

Operating expenses	$10,000
Dividends received	8,000
Net capital gains	4,000
Estimated tax payments	7,000
Tax credits	1,000
Dividends-received deduction	70%

   How much is Cox Corporation's gross income?

   a. $52,000
   b. $60,000
   c. $92,000
   d. $100,000

Appendix C

8. Cox Corporation reported sales and cost of goods sold of $100,000 and $60,000, respectively, for the year just ended. Other information follows:

Operating expenses	$10,000
Dividends received	8,000
Net capital gains	4,000
Estimated tax payments	7,000
Tax credits	1,000
Dividends-received deduction	70%

How much is Cox Corporation's taxable income?

a. $26,000
b. $34,000
c. $36,400
d. $42,000

9. Cox Corporation reported sales and cost of goods sold of $100,000 and $60,000, respectively, for the year just ended. Other information follows:

Operating expenses	$10,000
Dividends received	8,000
Estimated tax payments	7,000
Tax credits	1,000
Dividends-received deduction	70%

Assuming a flat corporate tax rate of 20%, how much are the taxes owed or refund due to Cox Corporation?

a. $120 due
b. $7,120 due
c. $720 refund
d. $1,680 refund

10. Of the following, which is unacceptable behavior in attempting to reduce income taxes?

a. Evasion of taxes
b. Avoidance of taxes
c. Sheltering income
d. Advance tax planning

DEMONSTRATION PROBLEMS

DP-1 The following information was extracted from the records of Gaylord Corporation:

Gross profit	$450,000
Operating expenses	400,000
Dividends received during the year	10,000
Prepayments of income tax	5,000
Tax credit	2,000

Using the corporate tax rates presented in the text, compute the amount of tax the corporation owes the federal government or the refund due.

DP-2   American Corporation reported the following taxable income to the federal government:

        19X2 $100,000
        19X3   80,000
        19X4   30,000

In 19X5, the company had a $380,000 net operating loss. Assuming the corporation follows proper carryback procedures, compute the amount of loss that can be carried forward to 19X6 and subsequent years.

DP-3   Limestone Corporation reported capital gains and losses as follows:

19X1 gains of $100,000, losses of $50,000
19X2 gains of $80,000, losses of $30,000
19X3 gains of $80,000, losses of $40,000
19X4 gains of $100,000, losses of $90,000
19X5 gains of $80,000, losses of $300,000

Assuming proper tax accounting for the capital gains and losses, how much net capital loss carryforward is available for 19X6 and beyond? Show supporting computations.

SOLUTIONS TO SELF TESTS

TWO-RESPONSE QUIZ

1. Unless specifically excluded by law
2. Allowable exclusions
3. True
4. False
5. Tax bill
6. Corporations
7. False
8. Five years
9. Correct
10. Tax avoidance

FILL IN THE BLANKS

1. Gross income
2. Taxable income
3. Estimated taxes
4. Tax credits
5. Capital gain, capital loss
6. Fifteen
7. Tax evasion

MULTIPLE CHOICE QUESTIONS

1. a. Gross income minus deductions equals taxable income. The tax obligation is determined by applying the tax rates to the taxable income. Tax credits and tax payments are subtracted from the tax obligation to find the taxes owed or to be refunded.

2. a. Expenses are deductible only if specifically stated in the tax laws.

3. a. Tax credits are preferred to tax deductions. Tax credits reduce the tax liability on a dollar-for-dollar basis. Tax deductions reduce the amount of income that is subject to tax.

4. a. The dividends-received deduction is intended to reduce the degree of triple taxation. It has nothing to do with capital gains and net operating losses, and it reduces revenues to the government.

5. c. Capital gains and losses should be netted together to determine the appropriate tax consequences. Capital gains and losses relate to capital assets only. The gains and losses (while subject to various limitations) are subject to the same tax rate schedules as ordinary income.

6. c. Net operating losses may be carried back three years and forward 15 years.

7. a. $52,000. See below.

8. c. $36,400. See below.

9. c. $720 refund. See below.

Gross income		
Gross profit	$40,000	
Net capital gains	4,000	
Dividends received	8,000	
Total gross income		$52,000
Deductions		
Operating expenses	$10,000	
Dividends-received deduction		
($8,000 X 70%)	5,600	
Total deductions		15,600
Taxable income		$36,400
Tax on $36,400, at 20%		$ 7,280
Less: Tax prepayments	$7,000	
Tax credits	1,000	8,000
Taxes to be refunded		$ 720

10. a. Tax evasion is illegal. Tax avoidance, sheltering income, and tax planning are acceptable behavior.

DEMONSTRATION PROBLEMS

DP-1

Gross income		
Gross profit	$450,000	
Dividends received	10,000	
Total gross income		$460,000
Deductions		
Operating expenses	$400,000	
Dividends-received deduction		
($10,000 X 70%)	7,000	
Total deductions		407,000
Taxable income		$ 53,000
Tax on $50,000, per text	$ 7,500	
Tax on $3,000 excess ($53,000 - $50,000) at 25%	750	
Tax obligation		$ 8,250
Less: Tax prepayments	$ 5,000	
Tax credits	2,000	7,000
Taxes owed		$ 1,250

DP-2

Net operating loss, 19X5		$ 380,000
Less:	Operating loss carryback, 19X2	(100,000)
	Operating loss carryback, 19X3	(80,000)
	Operating loss carryback, 19X4	(30,000)
Available loss carryforward		$ 170,000

DP-3

19X1	$50,000 net capital gain
19X2	$50,000 net capital gain
19X3	$40,000 net capital gain
19X4	$10,000 net capital gain
19X5	$220,000 net capital loss

The 19X5 net capital loss can be carried back against the net capital gains of the three prior years. The net capital gains of the three prior years total $100,000. Therefore, $120,000 of net capital losses (after carryback) remain available for offset against capital gains resulting in the next five years.

APPENDIX: THE ELECTRONIC TUTORIAL

INTRODUCTION

These Computer-Assisted Accounting Tutorials are designed for use with Financial Accounting, 3rd edition by Solomon, Walther, and Vargo. The tutorials are written for students who are experiencing comprehension difficulties with classroom discussions or who desire a review upon completion of a chapter in the text.

A series of 10 lessons have been constructed that present essential accounting material on a step-by-step basis. As you proceed through each lesson, you will be queried on subject matter presentations via different types of questions (e.g., true/false, multiple choice, computational, and so forth). The various modules and their related chapter references follow.

MODULE NO.	TOPIC
0	Tutorial introduction
1	Debits and credits/journal entries (Ch. 2)
2	Adjusting entries (Ch. 3)
3	Accounting for uncollectible accounts (Ch. 8)
4	Inventory accounting methods (Ch. 9)
5	Depreciation accounting (Ch. 10)
6	Bond accounting (Ch. 12)
7	Present value (Ch. 12)
8	Corporate equity (Ch. 14)
9	Statement of cash flows (Ch. 16)

COMPUTER OPERATION

No previous computer knowledge is necessary. Simply arrive at your computer center for a tutorial session and be sure to bring along your textbook, a calculator, pencil and paper, and the study guide. (The study guide contains several exhibits that you will need.) The tutorials have been designed to run on an IBM-PC (or compatible) having two disk drives (or one disk drive and a hard disk), a DOS 2.1 operating system (or later version), and a minimum of 256K of memory.

To run the tutorials, first inset the DOS operating system into drive A. Then, while depressing the CTRL and ALT keys, press the DEL key. The computer will ask for date and time information; simply press the ENTER key in each instance. (Note: The ENTER key on many keyboards appears as: ←⏎) Upon completion of this routine your screen should contain the following: A>. Next, remove the DOS diskette and insert the tutorial disk in drive A. Type RUN and press the ENTER key. This action will access the program, which is totally self-explanatory in nature.

If desired, the diskette is easily installed on a hard disk by following the steps below.
1. Once the C prompt (C>) appears on the screen, type A: and press the ENTER key.
2. Next, place the tutorial diskette in drive A, type HINSTALL, and press the ENTER key.

To access the tutorials once they are stored on the hard disk:
1. Start up the system and get the C prompt (C>) to appear on the screen.
2. Type CD \Tutor and press the ENTER key.
3. Next, type RUN and press the ENTER key.

HOW TO USE THE TUTORIALS

The tutorials are meant to supplement and reinforce both the textbook and related classroom discussions. Thus, the authors strongly advise that no attempt be made to use the relevant tutorial until after the chapter has been read and the lecture has been attended.

We have written a computerized introduction to these tutorials (module #0) and we advise all users, whether you have computer expertise or not, to spend 10 valuable minutes learning how the tutorials function. This is an important investment of time on your part and helps to ensure a trouble-free program and learning experience. When the computer asks for the module number that you desire, simply type 0.

The length of each module varies, but should average approximately 45 minutes to complete. We suggest that only one module be worked in any given sitting to avoid problems with fatigue and a decrease in comprehension.

Good luck; we hope that you enjoy these computerized learning experiences. Comments and suggestions from users are welcomed and appreciated.

Exhibit 1
Sample Journal Page

DATE	ACCOUNTS	DEBIT	CREDIT
19X6			
Aug. 3	Cash	1,250	
	Fee Revenue		1,250
	To record fees received		
8	Electricity Expense	130	
	Accounts Payable		130
	Received electric bill		
12	Accounts Receivable	45	
	Fee Revenue		45
	Billed client for services		
17	Accounts Payable	130	
	Cash		130
	Paid electric bill		
20	Cash	25	
	Accounts Receivable		25
	Received cash on account		
24	Salaries Expense	200	
	Cash		200
	Paid office salaries		
29	Equipment	460	
	Cash		460
	Purchased equipment		

Exhibit 2
Adjusting Entries

The following facts pertain to the Whitfield Company as of December 31, the end of the firm's accounting period:

a. Prepaid Rent contains a debit balance of $4,800. This amount represents a payment for four months' rent, commencing on October 1.

b. Whitfield received a $2,500 advance payment from a customer on December 1. The firm credited Unearned Fee Revenue at that time. By year-end, 80% of the work necessary to earn the $2,500 had been performed.

c. The company's weekly payroll totals $5,000, with employees being paid each Friday for their work during the week. December 31, the end of the accounting period, falls on a Wednesday.

d. Whitfield has performed services valued at $4,500. The services have not as yet been entered in the accounting records.

The following adjusting entries are proposed for the above items:

a.	Rent Expense	1,200	
	Prepaid Rent		1,200
b.	Unearned Fee Revenue	2,000	
	Fee Revenue		2,000
c.	Salaries Expense	3,000	
	Salaries Payable		3,000
d.	Accounts Receivable	4,500	
	Fee Revenue		4,500

Exhibit 3
Aging of Accounts Receivable

The following data pertain to the Zip Company as of December 31, 19X1:

Zip Company
Aging Schedule of Accounts Receivable
December 31, 19X1

Length of Time Outstanding

Customer	Balance 12/31/X1	Under 61 days	61-90 days	91-120 days	121-180 days	Over 180 days
Berra Co.	$30,000	$10,000	$12,000		$8,000	
Cerney Inc.	4,000	4,000				
DMG Co.	10,000			$10,000		
Leach Co.	20,000			15,000		$5,000
Zero Ltd.	20,000	13,000	7,000			
Total	$84,000	$27,000	$19,000	$25,000	$8,000	$5,000

Estimated Uncollectibles

Age	Account Balances (from above)	X	Estimated % Uncollectible	=	Estimated Amount of Uncollectibles
Under 61 days	$27,000		1%		$ 270
61-90 days	19,000		3		570
91-120 days	25,000		6		1,500
121-180 days	8,000		25		2,000
Over 180 days	5,000		50		2,500
	$84,000				$6,840

Exhibit 4
Inventory Costing Methods

The following inventory data were obtained from the accounting records of Walton Company. The firm uses a periodic inventory system.

	Units	Cost per Unit	Total Cost
Beginning inventory	500	$8.00	$4,000
Purchases:			
January 16	500	8.20	4,100
March 8	1,200	8.50	10,200
June 17	700	9.00	6,300
August 3	900	10.00	9,000
October 23	2,000	11.50	23,000
December 5	800	11.75	9,400
Totals	6,600		$66,000

The ending inventory count on December 31 revealed that 1,100 units were still on hand.

Exhibit 5
Effective-Interest Bond Amortization

The Diablo Company issued $100,000 of 6%, 5-year bonds for $91,889. The bonds pay interest semiannually; at the time of issue the prevailing interest rate in the marketplace for similar obligations was 8%. Assume that the bonds were dated and issued on January 1, 19X1.

An abbreviated and partially completed effective-interest amortization table is presented below.

DISCOUNT AMORTIZATION TABLE

6-Month Period	Semiann. Interest Expense (4% X Carrying Value)	Semiann. Interest Payment (3% X $100,000)	Discount Amort.	Discount Balance	Carrying Value
Issue				$8,111	$ 91,889
1	$3,676	$3,000	$ A	7,435	92,565
2	3,703	3,000	703	6,732	93,268
3	B	3,000	731	6,001	93,999
4	3,760	C	760	5,241	94,759
5	3,790	3,000	D	4,451	95,549
6	3,822	3,000	822	E	96,371
7	3,855	3,000	855	2,774	F
8	3,889	3,000	889	1,885	98,115
9	G	H	I	J	K
Maturity	3,960*	3,000	960	---	100,000

* Difference due to rounding.

**Exhibit 6
Small Stock Dividends**

PART A

The following data pertain to the Crest Corporation:

STOCKHOLDERS' EQUITY

Common stock, $10 par value, 60,000 shares authorized, 50,000 shares issued and outstanding	$ 500,000
Paid-in capital in excess of par value	600,000
Retained earnings	400,000
Total stockholders' equity	$1,500,000

PART B

	Common Stock	Paid-in Capital in Excess	Retained Earnings
Beginning balance (from part A)	$500,000	$600,000	$400,000
July 1 entry		120,000	(160,000)
September 1 entry	40,000		
Ending balance	$540,000	$720,000	$240,000

Exhibit 7
Statement of Cash Flows

PART A

The comparative balance sheets of Lexington Company follow.

Lexington Company
Comparative Balance Sheets
December 31, 19X2 and 19X1

	Dec. 31, 19X2	Dec. 31, 19X1
Cash	$ 7,000	$ 9,000
Accounts receivable (net)	18,000	22,000
Merchandise inventory	52,000	35,000
Property, plant, & equipment	60,000	30,000
Less: Accumulated depreciation	(37,000)	(12,000)
Total assets	$100,000	$ 84,000
Accounts payable*	$ 37,000	$ 26,000
Income taxes payable	6,000	2,000
Common stock	36,000	36,000
Retained earnings	21,000	20,000
Total liabilities & stockholders' equity	$100,000	$ 84,000

* Relate to purchases of merchandise.

Other data:

Dividends declared and paid during 19X2 totaled $12,000. Lexington Company purchased $30,000 of equipment for cash on June 26, 19X2.

Exhibit 7 (cont.)
Statement of Cash Flows

PART B

Lexington Company's accrual-basis income statement revealed the following data:

Lexington Company
Income Statement
For the Year Ended December 31, 19X2

Sales*		$150,000
Less: Cost of goods sold		75,000
Gross profit		$ 75,000
Less: Selling & admin. expenses	$33,000	
Depreciation expense	25,000	
Income taxes	4,000	62,000
Net income		$ 13,000

* All sales are on credit.

Exhibit 7 (cont.)
Statement of Cash Flows

PART C

Below is a form for Lexington Company's statement of cash flows, prepared by using the direct method.

Lexington Company
Statement of Cash Flows
For the Year Ended December 31, 19X2

Cash flows from operating activities

    Cash received from customers $_____

    Less cash payments for:

        Purchases of merchandise $_____

        Selling & administrative expenses   _____

        Income taxes   _____ _____

    Net cash provided (used) by operating activities $_____

Cash flows from investing activities

    _____   _____

Cash flows from financing activities

    _____   _____

Net increase (decrease) in cash	$_____
Cash balance, January 1, 19X2	9,000
Cash balance, December 31, 19X2	$ 7,000

Exhibit 7 (cont.)
Statement of Cash Flows

PART D

Below is a form for Lexington Company's statement of cash flows, prepared by using the indirect method.

Lexington Company
Statement of Cash Flows
For the Year Ended December 31, 19X2

Cash flows from operating activities

    Net income $_____

    Add (deduct) items to convert net income to a cash basis

        Depreciation expense $_____

        _____ in accounts receivable   _____

        _____ in merchandise inventory   _____

        _____ in accounts payable   _____

        _____ in income taxes payable   _____

    Net cash provided (used) by operating activities $_____

Cash flows from investing activities

    _____   _____

Cash flows from financing activities

    _____   _____

Net increase (decrease) in cash $_____
Cash balance, January 1, 19X2   9,000
Cash balance, December 31, 19X2 $ 7,000

IMPORTANT: PLEASE READ BEFORE OPENING THIS PACKAGE
THIS PACKAGE IS NOT RETURNABLE IF SEAL IS BROKEN.

West Services, Inc.
58 West Kellogg Boulevard
St. Paul, Minnesota 55164

Accounting Tutorial
LIMITED USE LICENSE

Read the following terms and conditions carefully before opening this diskette package. Opening the diskette package indicates your agreement to the license terms. If you do not agree, promptly return this package unopened to West Services for a full refund.

By accepting this license, you have the right to use this Software and the accompanying documentation, but you do not become the owner of these materials.

This copy of the Software is licensed to you for use only under the following conditions:

1. PERMITTED USES
You are granted a non-exclusive limited license to use the Software under the terms and conditions stated in this license. You may:
  a. Use the Software on a single computer.
  b. Make a single copy of the Software in machine-readable form solely for backup purposes in support of your use of the Software on a single machine. You must reproduce and include the copyright notice on any copy you make.
  c. Transfer this copy of the Software and the license to another user if the other user agrees to accept the terms and conditions of this license. If you transfer this copy of the Software, you must also transfer or destroy the backup copy you made. Transfer of this copy of the Software, and the license automatically terminates this license as to you.

2. PROHIBITED USES
You may not use, copy, modify, distribute or transfer the Software or any copy, in whole or in part, except as expressly permitted in this license.

3. TERM
This license is effective when you open the diskette package and remains in effect until terminated. You may terminate this license at any time by ceasing all use of the Software and destroying this copy and any copy you have made. It will also terminate automatically if you fail to comply with the terms of this license. Upon termination, you agree to cease all use of the Software and destroy all copies.

4. DISCLAIMER OF WARRANTY
Except as stated herein, the Software is licensed "as is" without warranty of any kind, express or implied, including warranties of merchantability or fitness for a particular purpose. You assume the entire risk as to the quality and performance of the Software. You are responsible for the selection of the Software to achieve your intended results and for the installation, use and results obtained from it. West Services does not warrant the performance of nor results that may be obtained with the Software. West Services does warrant that the diskette(s) upon which the Software is provided will be free from defects in materials and workmanship under normal use for a period of 30 days from the date of delivery to you as evidenced by a receipt.

Some states do not allow the exclusion of implied warranties so the above exclusion may not apply to you. This warranty gives you specific legal rights. You may also have other rights which vary from state to state.

5. LIMITATION OF LIABILITY
Your exclusive remedy for breach by West Services of its limited warranty shall be replacement of any defective diskette upon its return to West at the above address, together with a copy of the receipt, within the warranty period. If West Services is unable to provide you with a replacement diskette which is free of defects in material and workmanship, you may terminate this license by returning the Software, and the license fee paid hereunder will be refunded to you. In no event will West be liable for any lost profits or other damages including direct, indirect, incidental, special, consequential or any other type of damages arising out of the use or inability to use the Software even if West Services has been advised of the possibility of such damages.

6. GOVERNING LAW
This agreement will be governed by the laws of the State of Minnesota.

You acknowledge that you have read this license and agree to its terms and conditions. You also agree that this license is the entire and exclusive agreement between you and West Services and supersedes any prior understanding or agreement, oral or written, relating to the subject matter of this agreement.

West Services, Inc.

THIS PACKAGE IS NOT RETURNABLE IF SEAL IS BROKEN